DATE DUE

TOMORROW'S PARENTS

A Study of Youth and Their Families

THE HOGG FOUNDATION RESEARCH SERIES
  Wayne H. Holtzman, Editor

ʊʊʊ

TOMORROW'S PARENTS

A Study of Youth and Their Families

By BERNICE MILBURN MOORE
and WAYNE H. HOLTZMAN

PUBLISHED FOR THE HOGG FOUNDATION FOR MENTAL HEALTH
BY THE UNIVERSITY OF TEXAS PRESS, AUSTIN

To 12,892 Texas High School Students,
Their Families, and Their Teachers

FOREWORD

Tomorrow's Parents is a book about families of the future, derived from a study of youth of the present. It is the culmination of a decade of field work, data analysis, and interpretation and writing.

The Texas Cooperative Youth Study took form at a meeting of chairmen of departments and teachers of home economics from colleges and universities, and the staff of the Division of Homemaking Education, Texas Education Agency, in Mineral Wells, Texas, in the mid-1950's. These educators felt there was need for a cooperative research project to determine the concerns and interests of youth in their own personal and family living. Information on these subjects was considered essential for the development of a new guide for the homemaking curriculum in public high schools. The curriculum up to that time had been based upon projected attitudes, interests, and needs of youth.

Consultation services and financial assistance for a statewide study were requested from The Hogg Foundation for Mental Health, The University of Texas. Dr. Robert L. Sutherland, director, agreed that the proposed investment of time, energy, and money by the various colleges and universities, by Agency personnel in home economics, and by The Hogg Foundation would pay lasting dividends to present and future families as well as to educational institutions in the state. Dr. J. W. Edgar, commissioner, and M. A. Browning, assistant commissioner of Vocational Education, Texas Education Agency, were cognizant of the development of the study from its beginning.

"Cooperation" may be defined as collective action for common benefit. This publication is a striking verification of this definition. A look at the future from the vantage point of information furnished by generous young people throughout the state was accomplished because they were willing to share of themselves and their ideas, attitudes, concerns, and interests for the benefit of others of their own age who would follow them into high school even before this study was completed. A staggering contribution in time and energy was made by professors of home economics education in colleges and universities, who took over the responsibility for the collection of data. The way for their successful work was paved by the state and area staff members of the Division of Homemaking, Texas Education Agency. Necessary funds for the study and the time of staff consultants for technical and coordinating assistance were furnished by The Hogg Foundation for Mental Health. Principals of high schools and teachers of homemaking in the 182 public schools involved, with other classroom teachers and counselors, set the local stages for accurate and careful data collection.

Out of all these efforts of the many, an attempt has been made to produce a book that is readable, and perhaps even enjoyable, for the youth who made it possible, for their teachers, for educational administrators of all levels, for their parents, and for anyone else interested in and concerned about families and their youth. Moreover, the research methodology employed in the study has been described so that this, too, will be of use to those primarily interested in research or desirous of learning more about making large-scale studies in action settings.

Last, it is hoped that *Tomorrow's Parents* will contribute to family life for a better tomorrow built on an already good today. At least Texas youth offer evidence that today does have much that is good and that tomorrow, no doubt, will be even better because of the parents they will become.

RUTH HUEY, *Director*
Division of Homemaking Education
Texas Education Agency

ACKNOWLEDGMENTS

The Texas Cooperative Youth Study was based upon the efforts of many people, and the authors of this report have written it for those who made it possible. Acknowledgments could be legion, and several are included in footnotes to the text. Others who shared in large or small measure are hereby thanked for their efforts. However, to some, special recognition must go because they have been a consistent part of the study team from its beginning, or because they have made outstanding contributions to its accomplishment. Beulah I. Coon, from the United States Office of Education, served as a special consultant from the day the study was presented for statewide consideration. Moreover, she was a critic-reader for the final manuscript version, as were Ruth Huey, Josephine Pazdral, and Margaret Scholl, of the Texas Education Agency; Gladys Short, of Southwest Texas State College; and Willa Vaughn Tinsley, of Texas Technological College. Much credit also goes to Edward Moseley, without whose major efforts the computations would never have reached their present state.

To Fred L. Strodtbeck, of the Departments of Sociology and Psychology, The University of Chicago, goes a special accolade for his assistance in placing the study within a theoretical framework and for his careful reading and editing of the manuscript. Reuben L. Hill, director of the Family Study Center and professor of sociology, The University of Minnesota, made many excellent suggestions in a meticulous and detailed criticism of this written report.

During 1962–1963, while the authors completed the manuscript, Wayne H. Holtzman served as a fellow at the Center for Advanced Study in the Behavioral Sciences, Stanford, California. Our thanks go to Dr. Ralph Tyler and the Center staff who made this possible.

Robert L. Sutherland gave his unfailing support from the time the research was only a partially formulated idea. He has offered helpful and thoughtful suggestions as efforts were made to bring the mass of collected data into manageable form. His reading of the manuscript in its various drafts and his editing have contributed much to the final version.

To Joan King Holtzman goes credit for the name of the book, as well as for her patience during the endless hours her husband worked on the study and the manuscript. To Harry Estill Moore is due appreciation for the concept of "conditioned participation" around which the writing of the findings was structured. To him, also, goes sincere gratitude for editorial assistance and for often needed encouragement given to his wife over the years of the study.

Margaret Warnken McQueen spent many hours getting tables, charts, and graphs into final form for production and added her editorial skills to provide a major contribution to this book.

Secretaries have come and gone, but to four go special thanks: Pearl Sandgarten Gardner, Helen Wooten Sanderson, Martha Gibbs, and Mary Beth Holmes Curtis. The latter two worked in the earlier years of the effort. The first two should probably be listed as co-authors since they put in time and skill far beyond that expected of secretaries as they brought the manuscript into final form for the press.

Ruth Huey, in her Foreword, has bowed to the youth of Texas, to their teachers, and to other educators. To us remains the privilege of listing by name those who, in truth, *were* the Texas Cooperative Youth Study during its ten years of development and accomplishment. With pride in recognizing them, we list the participants and offer them congratulations for a major job well done (Titles and residences are for the years of the study. Several persons listed have retired or changed positions, and some have moved.):

Special Consultants

ROBERT L. SUTHERLAND, director, The Hogg Foundation for Mental Health

BEULAH I. COON, specialist in research and special studies, Home Economics Education, United States Office of Education, Washington, D. C.

Central Work Committee

RUTH HUEY, director, Division of Homemaking Education, Texas Education Agency

LUCY RATHBONE, chairman, Department of Home Economics and administrator of the Collating Center for the study, The University of Texas

JOSEPHINE PAZDRAL, assistant director, Division of Homemaking Education, Texas Education Agency

GLADYS SHORT, area supervisor, Division of Homemaking Education, Texas Education Agency

GLADYS BABCOCK, associate professor, Home Economics Education, The University of Texas

ONAH JACKS, Department of Home Economics, Southwest Texas State College, San Marcos, Texas

WAYNE H. HOLTZMAN, associate director, The Hogg Foundation for Mental Health and director of statistical design and data analysis for the study

BERNICE MILBURN MOORE, assistant to the director, Community Programs and Professional Education, The Hogg Foundation for Mental Health and consultant, Division of Homemaking Education, Texas Education Agency, and state coordinator for the study

DAVID PROCTOR and EDWARD MOSELEY, research associates, The University of Texas

ANNE ARBUCKLE, WALTER HANAK, and ROZELLE BEZANT, research assistants, The University of Texas

Research Planning and Data Collection

Department of Home Economics and staff members from participating colleges and universities. Department chairmen are listed first.

WEATHY AIKEN and OPHELIA S. MANNING, Texas College of Arts and Industries, Kingsville, Texas

FAY ANTHIS and MINNIE AKKERMAN, The University of Houston

GLADYS ARMSTRONG, West Texas State College, Canyon, Texas

RUBY SEAL DENNIS, Mary Hardin-Baylor College, Belton, Texas

ELIZABETH M. GALLOWAY and LOIS B. WRIGHT, Prairie View Agricultural and Mechanical College, Prairie View, Texas

NEVA I. HENDERSON and BLANCHE PHILLIPS, Sam Houston State College, Huntsville, Texas

ONAH JACKS, Southwest Texas State College, San Marcos, Texas

CELIA S. LANE, JANIE COTTON, HORTENSE DIXON, ALLEE J. MITCHELL, JAYNE G. ROBINSON, and BURNADINE L. LEWIS, Texas Southern University, Houston, Texas

PAULINE BERRY MACK, JESSIE BATEMAN, DELTA DUNGAN, and VENETA YOUNG, Texas Woman's University, Denton, Texas

L. W. REESE MADLOCK, Texas College, Tyler, Texas

LUCY RATHBONE and GLADYS BABCOCK, The University of Texas, Austin, Texas

RETHA SANDERS, Baylor University, Waco, Texas

FLORENCE I. SCOULAR, NORMA PARTON, and FRANCES PENDER, North Texas State University, Denton, Texas

WATHENA TEMPLE and ORPHA DENNIS, East Texas State College, Commerce, Texas

WILLA VAUGHN TINSLEY, VIVIAN J. ADAMS, DORIS NESBITT, and GERALDINE CLEWELL, Texas Technological College, Lubbock, Texas

EDNA WILKIN and MARY WILL GREENWOOD, Stephen F. Austin State College, Nacogdoches, Texas

Special Field Staff

MABLE McBAIN, former supervisor of Homemaking Education, Houston Public Schools

GERTRUDE BARKLEY, former area supervisor, Division of Homemaking Education, Texas Education Agency

Area Supervisors, Division of Homemaking Education,
Texas Education Agency

HATTIE MARIE BAKER

HANNAH HOFF BROWN

ELIZABETH CHENOWETH

W. L. D. GLASS

MARIE W. HEALEY

MARY A. MOORE

RUTH PAYNE

ONEITA WILSON PIERCE

GLADYS SHORT

ELIZABETH SMITH

ESTHER SORENSEN

LENORA WALTERS

BERNICE MILBURN MOORE
WAYNE H. HOLTZMAN

INTRODUCTION

Stress and strain induced by middle-class pressures provide plot material for current novels and TV plays as well as ideas for articles addressed to parents and teachers. The book at hand does not gloss over these personal and family problems related to status seeking and mobility striving, but its major findings rescue the reader from the dismal premise that the more educated and affluent we become the sadder, the sicker, the more neurotic our society is. In fact, if one would like a refreshing breath of reassurance that neither families nor youth are on a crash course to doom, he might well pause to read the tersely, simply stated findings in this study.

The parent, the teacher, and the other workers with youth and with private and public community organizations will find the points of this book clearly applicable to their day-by-day problems and plans. The reader who wants to ease gently into the mysteries of modern research will find the going neither baffling nor boring. He will see how scientific methods illumine common problems around us. The research methodologist may marvel at the comprehensive sweep of this study (a stratified sample of 12,892 youth) and at the dispersed, yet integrated team of workers who gathered the data. He may also be fascinated by the statistical analyses which brought reliable meaning out of well over a million computations.

The study was made more in breadth than in depth. It is not psychoanalytical. It is not a probing analysis of role structure. Rather, it is a well-regulated comparison of many variables in the life situations of modern youth. The findings are valid nationally because from the large sample were drawn cells of data representative of youth in almost every economic and cultural situation.

The book is sociological and psychological in orientation. Also, it deals with the mental health of youth, if the reader agrees that the following have something to do with mental health: a person's feelings of self and social adequacy; his attitudes toward parents and teachers; his reaction toward authority and toward freedom; his degree of social isolation and of group integration; and his interest in his own family and his fellows, and his desire to learn to live well with them.

The authors find that the family is still society's principal means of transmitting cultural values to youth. The higher the educational and economic level of the family, the lower the degree of youth frustration, rebellion, and disorganization. While there are many qualified specific findings that apply differently to different subcategories of youth, the effectiveness of culture in reaching youth through families rises to a new importance, or, more accurately, regains its former status.

Families in our society have a way of using their bootstraps effectively even in one generation. The pay-off is readily visible in the lives of their children. Families who see to it that their boys and girls go farther than they did in school; parents who try to better themselves through learning about parenthood and homemaking, and who move upward a notch economically even if both have to work to do it, have a way of transmitting to youth this desire for an upward mobility in education and occupation which turns out to be generally more stabilizing than frustrating, more integrating than demoralizing. But these are too easy summaries of thirteen chapters. The reader can discover for himself just how large samples of youth respond to many different family and community situations.

If the book is not in line with the current tradition of popular literature about a sick society, then it is in keeping with the recent area studies which show how large numbers of youth respond to new opportunities when the culture which surrounds them is itself altered. Their response appears to be more behavioral if the opportunities are not merely talked about but are built into the cultural processes of family, school, employment, and neighborhood relationships.

The authors of the book know their business, and their work is dual. Dr. Moore has worked with and learned from youth, parents, and community institutions through two decades of consultation in action programs. In addition to this, she has brought to the study an administrative skill which guided it into a team project of rare proportions and success. (Not a single public school system of the 182 approached was afraid to cooperate—in a day when field studies are sometimes suspect.) She assembled the data, cooperated in the analysis of it, and wrote much of the text of the book.

Dr. Holtzman brought his intensive and extensive research-design experience to bear on the study. He refined the samples, led in designing the instruments, supervised the data processing, and wrote the sections of the book which deal with research methods.

Both authors have subjected their work to critical readers and to critical audiences. They have tested the usefulness of the findings through discussions with research peers, community workers (including teachers), and many parent and youth groups. At last, they are sufficiently satisfied with the manuscript to permit publication. For this reader such a reaction represents an overly cautious understatement. I am downright enthusiastic about the book.

ROBERT L. SUTHERLAND, *Director*
Hogg Foundation for Mental Health

CONTENTS

FIGURES

TABLES

TOMORROW'S PARENTS

A Study of Youth and Their Families

I: Some Conclusions as a Beginning

ʊʊʊʊʊʊʊʊʊʊʊʊʊʊʊʊʊʊʊʊʊʊʊʊʊʊʊʊʊʊʊʊ

PARENTS TEND TO DOUBT their lasting influence upon teen-age sons and daughters. Pundits have written lengthy discourses on the loss of parental control in the lives of children. Social scientists debate whether families have suffered a diminution in functions or have only changed emphases.

Twelve thousand eight hundred and ninety-two high school youth, the representative sample of the Texas Cooperative Youth Study, have pointed toward some suggestive answers to these questions and doubts. They document the conclusion that though families may perform fewer functions and do vary widely in what they have to offer, they remain the major agents in the socialization of the young and are, as they always have been, the paramount institution in society for the transmission of culture.

Basic attitudes of Texas youth toward society and toward people were linked with the educational level of their parents. Their concepts of authority in child rearing reflected their family background. Both their attitudes toward school and their academic competence were interwoven with their heritage. The pressures they encountered to conform to peer-group standards different from their own depended upon the subcultural orientation of their families and of the communities in which they lived. Even more important, the mental health of these youth, their own feelings of personal adequacy and social competence, could be correlated with the sociocultural status of their parents.

The word "culture" as used in this study is a sociological and anthropological term. In one sense, it is as broadly inclusive as the social heritage of man:

. . . it is the total legacy of past behavior effective in the present, representing the accumulation through generations of the *artifacts*, knowledges, beliefs, and values by which men deal with the world. It is the precipitate of *learned* human adjustments to the physical environment and to society . . . A way of visualizing American culture in this broad sense would be to answer the question: What is available to be learned by all the infants born in the society today? . . . Culture points to those common elements in behavior that are derived from individuals' having been reared in the same tradition.[1]

A more precise definition, and one more often utilized in this study, would be the following:

. . . a normative structure, a system of what Linton has called "designs for living." In this sense, culture is the "blueprint for behavior"—relatively standardized prescriptions as to what must be done, ought to be done, should be done, may be done, and must not be done.[2]

But families do not all have the same access to the total culture of the society to which they belong. Herein lies the elimination of danger of dead-level conformity. Herein lies the basis for the matrix of subcultures which make up any society. Here also is the source of cultural deprivation. Harry Estill Moore has utilized the concept of conditioned participation in culture to describe the variability in acquisition and in use of all that man has to offer his fellowmen from the past and in the present. He has defined this concept as:

Incomplete access to the culture of a region by a subordinate group, the degree of access depending upon the role assigned to and accepted by such partially excluded groups. Thus Negroes and some other ethnic groups are denied full participation in American culture, the degree of exclusion being limited by the status awarded such groups, the reaction to such status by the subordinate group and the accompanying attitudes on the parts of both dominant and subordinate groups; these elements making a conditioning process applying to both groups. Basic factors in terms of which this conditioning process operates seem to be ease of identification of members of the subordinate group through biological or cultural differences and traditions which define the appropriate role for members of each group. The groups

---

[1] Robin M. Williams, Jr., *American Society: A Sociological Interpretation*, p. 22.
[2] *Ibid.*, p. 23.

conditionally participating may or may not possess foreign culture traits with which to supplement their partial participation . . .[3]

"Conditioned" is used in this definition in the sociological rather than the classic psychological sense of Pavlov. It refers to a learned or acquired response to some social situation.

If Harry Stack Sullivan's definition of personality as the usual ways of behaving with other people is accepted, then adequate opportunities to learn about and share in "the *artifacts,* knowledges, beliefs, and values" of society is the bedrock of personalities adequate to function in that society. Perhaps it should be added that the better people learn the lessons concerning the proscriptions of the prevailing culture, the more acceptable is their behavior to the majority of their fellow men, and the better they "get along" in the day-by-day exigencies of life.

FAMILIES DIFFER

Families are not alike in what they have been able to acquire in cultural content to transmit to their children. Neither are they alike in their competence or ability to pass along a rich legacy. Differential access to the common heritage by families varies in Texas as in the nation as a whole.

Many parents have been limited by educational experience to the extent that they have lived with only minimal participation.[4] They have undergone no real involvement. Their work has been with their hands. They have earned so little that they and their children have been held at a subsistence level. Their lack of communication skills has cut them off from the vast stream of knowledge and ideas. The poverty of their backgrounds has been transmitted to their children in the form of poverty of opportunity and an inability to share fully in what may be readily available. One single reflection of this may be observed in the dropout rate in the public schools.[5]

[3] The theoretical formulation in this chapter is based upon Harry Estill Moore, "Definition of Conditioned Participation," *Dictionary of Sociology,* edited by Henry Pratt Fairchild, p. 57. Also see Ernest R. Groves and Harry Estill Moore, *An Introduction to Sociology,* p. 74.

[4] Gordon W. Allport, *Personality and the Social Encounter,* pp. 187–193.

[5] National Committee on Children and Youth in Urban Areas, *Social Dynamite: The Report of the Conference on Unemployed Out-of-School Youth in Urban Areas,* May 24–26, 1961.

The Texas study offers evidence that children of culturally handi-
capped parents do have a harder time remaining in school; yet the
general community interest carries many of them along. Generally
speaking, each generation of children goes farther with formal education than did their parents. While over one-third of the fathers of
youth participating in this study had completed fewer than eight
grades, and while one-fourth of them earned family incomes from
semi-skilled or unskilled labor, their sons and daughters were in high
school. These youth were, by their very presence, opening the door
to wider cultural participation for themselves and for the children
which they will bear. Nonetheless, the reflection of their family status
was distinct in its imprint upon their attitudes and their conceptions
of themselves.

Conversely, when families have had wider experience and broader
opportunity to participate in the common culture, their children show
it in their school achievement and personal adjustment. Where they
know, understand, and operate in the context of the more generally
accepted norms, rules, standards, goals, and values held in their
nation, their attitudes are more positive and they conceive of themselves as socially more adequate. Where fathers of high school youth
had completed some years or all of secondary education and were
employed in skilled, white-collar, ownership roles in their occupations,
then their children displayed less conflict with their peers and in
relationships with other family members. In addition, they expressed
greater hopefulness about the future and gave evidence of more adequate achievement in school. As could be expected, the higher the
educational and occupational level of parents, the greater the freedom
of access they have to all of the varied elements of the culture of the
society in which they live.

MANY FACTORS GOVERNING PARTICIPATION IN CULTURE

While rewarding acquisition of culture is largely conditional upon
educational and occupational attainment by parents, other factors also
enter the picture. The philosophy of free access to culture is empty
unless it is accompanied by availability of cultural resources. Place
of residence may determine opportunity. Rural areas, small towns,
neighborhoods in larger cities, regions within the state, are all diverse
in their accumulation of cultural assets and liabilities.

Where social, intellectual, and economic assets are abundant, ethnic or racial attitudes may prohibit their utilization. Religious beliefs may color the acceptance of what is available. Marital status displays divergent effects in different social classes. Sex membership assures differences in participation and reaction even in families of similar class orientation.

No matter what the availability of cultural resources, the ability and the capacity of parents are essential elements in the restraint upon or release of potentials of their children.[6] In other words, the personalities of parents are, themselves, psychocultural forces in the lives of their youngsters.[7] The personality orientation and cultural participation of parents are important elements in the sifting process which determines what experiences are available for their children.

Other elements in the family also play a part in the socialization of the children. Children and youth who are reared by both biological parents exhibit certain distinctions from those who grow up in a family with either a stepmother or stepfather. Youngsters who are brought up with either their mother or father alone as head of the house do not always respond like others. Furthermore, those young people who have grown up in institutions display real distinctions no matter how hard their houseparents have tried to simulate the more normal home-family situation. Some youth have been only children and others have shared with numerous brothers and sisters. These are not alike in how they feel about people or themselves. All of these are variations in family pattern or structure. Culture is indeed transmitted through the family itself, but when the nature of the family pattern varies, the process of communication within the family setting may be altered. This study of nearly thirteen thousand Texas youth will prove this point.

While the Texas Cooperative Youth Study did not set out to prove that family adequacy depends upon levels of participation in the culture, as the data were analyzed it became increasingly evident that youth are literally *of* their families.

POINTS IN RÉSUMÉ

The Texas study was specifically designed to gather information pertaining to personal and social attitudes, problems, concerns, and in-

---

[6] Talcott Parsons and Robert F. Bales, *Family, Socialization and Interaction*
[7] James S. Plant, *Personality and the Cultural Pattern*, Chapters I and II, pp. 3–43.
Process, pp. 16–17.

terests of average high school youth. Because of the ample number of cases available in the over-all sample, some twenty-four detailed sub-studies were possible. In the most general terms, findings from these studies may be summarized in fifteen propositions.

1. The family is easily the most important influence in the development of youth. The attitudes, problems, concerns, and interests of youth can be understood only in the context of the families and homes from which they have come.

2. As youth cannot be separated from their families, so families themselves cannot be understood outside of their place and participation in their culture.

3. The United States as a democracy assumes that all families have free access to the richness and variety of its culture, and that the cultural content of the nation is readily available to all families for use in the development and sustenance of their offspring. While this principle of equality is an ideal, the Texas Cooperative Youth Study indicates that even in America it is still more utopian than real.

4. Differential access to social and cultural resources varies by subcultural groups. The educational level of the father, with its occupational consequences, is the one most important factor in determining the socioeconomic group membership of the family. The education and occupation of mothers are important but not in the determination of family status.

5. As subcultural group membership of families varies, so do the attitudes, problems, and concerns of youth from these families. Few universal youth attitudes or problems were discovered.

6. Place of family residence by region and by community size, as well as educational and occupational level of fathers, indicates differential availability of and diversified access to culture, as expressed in attitudes toward and in recognition of problems by youth.

7. The differential aspects of culture available to each sex are definitely discernible in the attitudes of youth. However, their concerns and problems were not sex linked when expressed in general terms.

8. Family type by size and parental arrangement serves as a determinant in the impact of various aspects of culture upon youth.

9. Attitudes and problems of high school married youth vary by sex and by subcultural membership of the parental family.

10. Racial group membership remains a powerful factor in avail-

ability of the dominant culture to families of teen-age youth. Subcultural groups among the Negroes offered distinctive variations within the race itself, in addition to the distinctions observable between the two major races in the total culture.

11. Religious denominational choice is indicative of both status and rural-urban differences in families.

12. High school boys and girls expressed paramount interest in the study of personality and interpersonal relations, but they differ greatly in their amount of interest in homemaking, in child rearing, home management, and household skills—indicating again the sharp distinction held among youth between man's work and woman's world.

13. The Texas Cooperative Youth Study adds powerful documentation to the recognized need to keep *all* youth, of *every* place of residence, of *each* racial, ethnic, and subcultural group, in school through high school whenever potentialities make it possible. In certain subcultural groups, schools are supplemental to adequate family participation in culture. For others, the schools must literally open the door to cultural variety and richness if personalities are to be developed to meet the demands of the times and of parenthood in the future.

14. The case for the educated parent is irrefutably made by youth through their own revelation of themselves as products of the families. Their conception of their own adequacy, their fundamental attitudes toward their society and their fellowmen, the quality of their personalities, their promise for the future of their nation, are literally products of the richness or the poverty of participation of their families in what culture has to offer.

15. The need for education in the schools for family life stands shoulder to shoulder with the demands for education for scientific advance, technological competence, and dependable citizenship. Without healthy personalities, capable of creating and adapting to change, neither scientists nor technologists can produce what is needed to enhance man himself.

II: The Story of the Study

THE TEXAS COOPERATIVE YOUTH STUDY arose out of concern for *all* youth. However, there appeared to be a particular need for information about young persons who are functioning more or less effectively in everyday activities in their homes, their schools, and their communities. Relatively little data were available concerning the wide variety of young persons who constitute high school populations in all manner of communities—large or small, rural or urban, or somewhere in between. From comprehensive information about this age group, it was hoped, better insight could be obtained which would prove helpful in meeting problems of all teen-agers as well as those of less fortunate and more troubled youth.

High priority has been placed upon the study of juvenile delinquency over a long period of time and with increasing intensity in the past decade. Mass media are continuously headlining deviant behavior as a major social problem. The relationship of families and home life to troubled youth is stressed. Collection of data on personal and family attitudes, problems, and interests of high school students, it was hoped, would accumulate needed evidence of positive as well as negative factors which affect the lives of young persons.

Indeed, the newer approaches to juvenile delinquency itself are based more and more upon the belief that mediation of the problem may lie in the development of a deeper level of participation by youth in the rich resources available in their cultural heritage. In addition, it is felt that increased opportunities for development of feelings of personal adequacy and competence may well improve relationships of youth to society as a whole. Both participation in culture and feelings of personal adequacy (or, as this study will refer to it, self adequacy) are increasingly understood as derived from the quality of socialization afforded children in the home and in the community. The community is seen not only as the setting for family life, but as a complementary and supplementary resource in furnishing sufficiency in the lives of the young toward development of psychosocial maturity.

Improvement of family and home living through programs of education for homemaking has been accepted as feasible and practical for decades for both youth and adults. The applied science of home economics was developed on this premise. Teachers in homemaking have brought to focus research and clinical studies made in the physical, life, and behavioral sciences on problems of home and family. Departments of home economics education in Texas colleges and universities, with the Division of Homemaking Education, State Department of Education of the Texas Education Agency, had hoped to instigate a cooperative research program related to youth and their families since the mid-thirties. The Depression and World War II served to postpone its accomplishment.

Following World War II, problems of curriculum revision faced colleges, universities, and high schools alike. Homemaking teachers in public schools had been using a tentative curriculum for home and family education during the war years. A series of concerns and interests of high school youth had been formulated by teachers and supervisors in this field of study. A new state-wide curriculum committee was in process of preparing an up-to-date guide in homemaking education in the mid-fifties. This group needed basic research data on youth and on what these young persons considered their *own* problems, attitudes, and interests in family life at home.

The Hogg Foundation for Mental Health of The University of Texas had long maintained an interest in mental health and the family, in children and youth, and in community environment conducive to healthy personality development. Miss Ima Hogg, a family donor to the Foundation, and Robert L. Sutherland, its director, had stressed the need for incorporation of mental health principles in the public school and college curricula in appropriate subject areas.

A youth study, such as envisioned by all concerned, was recognized as having wider applicability than for any one course area of education or for high schools alone. School administrators, counselors and guidance personnel, visiting teachers and school nurses would find such research data a valuable resource, since their work is so closely interwoven with families as well as with youngsters. Teachers of high school subjects such as social studies and health-physical education, to name only two, would have available from it new or reverified facts which would enliven their instructional programs. Staffs in colleges and universities charged with orientation programs, counseling, and guidance services, as well as with teaching the social and behavioral sciences would find information from such research pertinent to their endeavors.

Parents of high school youth, as well as other interested adults, are expressing increased concern about adolescence. Organizations such as civic clubs, Congresses of Parents and Teachers, federations of women's clubs, and church and community leaders are seeking new information to make their programs more relevant. All of these people have expressed the desire to know more about young people in order to improve their own roles as parents and community leaders in relation to developing opportunities for youth. For them all this study was made. For them all this book has been written.

From the beginning, it was realized that only a widespread survey-type study could furnish the desired information. It was hoped that with the gathering of a mass of data from youth themselves, some beliefs could be verified and others modified, new facts uncovered, inferences drawn, speculations advanced, and even some hunches offered, which would be worthy of consideration. At no time was this action study thought of in terms of hypotheses to be verified. No attempt was made to write this book as a statistical monograph, although details on the development of the study and the analytical methodology are given to indicate the source and validity of the findings.

THE STUDY PLAN

Merger of these divergent concerns about young persons took place in a series of conferences between representatives of the Homemaking Education Division of the Texas Education Agency, departments of home economics education in some sixteen colleges and universities in the state, and the Hogg Foundation for Mental Health of The University of Texas.

From the earliest discussions of a possible study, particular stress was laid upon the need for more information on the problems, concerns, and attitudes of teen-agers in school. Out-of-school youth were out of reach for this investigation. In addition to providing data on personality development, personal and family relations, and family factors in mental health, a large-scale state-wide collection of information would make possible an increasingly functional approach to curriculum planning in education for home and family living in high schools. Moreover, general education as a whole would find some assistance in several curriculum areas.

Facilities for research in most of the colleges and universities involved were limited. Pooled efforts offered promise of advantages for all concerned. The opportunity to increase the number and quality of research workers in the field of mental health and the family through the training experience on the project was not the least of these. The Texas Cooperative Youth Study emerged as a large-scale, state-wide, cross-sectional investigation, limited in scope to questionnaire-type data to be gathered in high schools in approximately two periods of classroom time. Professors of home economics education and area supervisors of Homemaking Education from the State Department of Education became the field research team. Through the effort of these teams, including thousands of miles of travel to collect data, information was finally gathered from 182 high schools throughout the state in the spring of 1956. A low percentage of unusable instruments from the 12,892 ninth, tenth, eleventh, and twelfth grade students who participated may be credited to the efficiency of these field workers and, no less, to the sincere interest and earnest efforts of the high school students. Cooperation of principals, homemaking teachers, and counselors in the individual schools was all that could have been desired.

THE DEVELOPMENT OF INSTRUMENTS FOR THE STUDY

Instruments for the study were of paramount concern to the Central Study Committee. Development of new questionnaires and inventory materials was decided upon because of the nature of the data desired. The instruments had to be fairly objective and simple in format to obtain reliable, valid information from large groups of individuals. The items employed had to be phrased in the language of youth. They had to be focussed upon sensitive problem areas and attitudes without offending the respondents or unduly provoking negative attitudes toward the study on the part of parents or teachers in the communities where the data were to be collected.

After carefully examining inventories, questionnaires, and check lists that have been used in the past by other investigators, the planners decided that a fresh approach to the whole problem was needed. Professors of home economics throughout the state were requested to collect and submit statements from youth dealing with their concerns and problems and their attitudes toward personal family living. Most statements were actually obtained directly from the youth themselves. Under competent adult leadership, numerous small groups of teen-agers discussed openly the kinds of problems they encounter in all aspects of personal and family living which could be phrased in simply stated items. Many hundred such statements were collected from members of the Texas Association of Future Homemakers of America. Statements obtained in this manner were particularly helpful because they were formulated in terms used by youth.

All told, over three thousand statements were collected in this way. These provided a basic pool for the writing of items to be included in the preliminary forms of the inventories. In addition to items contributed by teachers and students, statements were obtained by a systematic examination of existing inventories, questionnaires, and check lists. Some items were included from scales developed by Joseph C. Marks, John Anderson, W. F. Brown, Wayne H. Holtzman, R. B. Cattell, and the Cornell University study of college-student attitudes, and two or three items from Leo Srole's anomie scale.[1] In many

---

[1] Most of the items on child-rearing attitudes used by Marks and others have a long history dating back to research by Baldwin, *et al.*, at the Fels Research Institute. In the present study only those items were taken from Marks' scales which differentiated significantly between the mothers of schizophrenics and the mothers of normal individuals. See J. C. Marks, "The Attitudes of the Mothers of Male Schizophrenics toward Child Behavior," in *Journal of Abnormal and Social Psychology*, Vol. 48 (1953), pp. 185–189. See also W. F. Brown, "Motivational Orientations and Scholastic Achievement"; A. E. Suchman, R. M. Williams, Jr., and Rose K. Goldsen, "Student to Soldier"; J. E. Anderson, "Prediction of Adjustment over Time," in *Nobles County Every Child Survey, 1949–1950;* R. B. Cattell, *Junior Personality Quiz;* Rose K. Goldsen, Morris Rosenberg, Robin M. Williams, Jr., and Edward A. Suchman, *What College Students Think;* Leo Sroles, "Social Integration and Certain Corollaries: An Exploratory Study," in *American Sociological Review*, XXI (December, 1956), 709–716.

instances, unpublished materials were provided by other research workers throughout the country.

The Major Categories

A preliminary sifting through of the written statements revealed that most of the items fell into one of two major categories. One kind of statement could best be responded to by a five-point continuum varying from "strongly agree" to "strongly disagree." The other could best be answered by indicating "true" or "false." Consequently, two different forms were constructed. The first was called "Attitudes toward Personal and Family Living," for which the response continuum was that used in the typical attitude questionnaire—a five-choice scale running from "Strongly Agree" through "Undecided or Uncertain" to "Strongly Disagree." The second form was entitled "Concerns and Problems in Personal and Family Living," for which a new type of response continuum was constructed. This was comprised of five choices, four of which could be answered "true" and the fifth, "false or does not apply to me in any way." The first four, in addition to indicating the truthfulness of the statement with reference to the respondent, required the student to indicate whether the given statement was of greatest concern to him, of much, of little, or of no concern to him. Thus the usual true-false dichotomy was combined with an "importance" scale for revealing the degree of concern admitted by the young person for the problem or issue implied in the item.

A third form was developed along the lines of a check list to determine interest in a variety of topics that might be considered appropriate for curriculum planning in education for personal and family living. In the preliminary edition of the "Personal Interest Check List," the youth was instructed to place an X in the space preceding each statement which refers to something he would like to study in school.

THE THREE FORMS AND THEIR CONTENT

Form I ("Attitudes toward Personal and Family Living") contained 150 items in the preliminary edition. Of the items, 28 were taken from a scale developed by Joseph Marks for differentiating the parents of schizophrenic children from the parents of normal children. These items dealt primarily with the extent to which an individual accepted or rejected authoritarian child-rearing practices. In addition, 13 were selected from the *Inventory of Student Attitudes* by Brown and Holtzman. These items differentiate between high- and low-scholarship groups among high school students and at the same time measure general attitudes toward education. Several more items were taken from inventories developed by John Anderson of the Institute for Child Welfare, University of Minnesota, and by staff members of the Social Science Research Center at Cornell University. The majority of the items, however, were written from the materials submitted by teachers and youth throughout the state.

The early edition of Form II ("Concerns and Problems in Personal and Family Living") consisted almost entirely of statements developed specifically for the Cooperative Youth Study—a total of 115 items. The preliminary version of Form III ("Personal Interest Check List") was comprised of 89 statements covering a wide variety of topics ranging from "Cooking for two" to "Jealousy as a personality problem."

In addition to these three inventories, a "face sheet" was constructed calling for vital information about the personal history, family structure, and socioeconomic status of each young person. The number of items in the preliminary edition of this general information sheet were kept to a bare minimum consistent with the purposes of the study.

THE TESTS OF FEASIBILITY

After several informal tryouts of these preliminary versions of the instruments using youth in the local schools, they were given to 696 home economics teachers at annual conferences in August, 1954.[2] Each teacher was provided with one copy of the face sheet, Forms I, II, III, and an IBM answer sheet for recording responses. In filling out the face sheet and Forms I and II, the teachers were asked to assume the role of a typical high school student, either a boy or girl. In responding to Form III, they were asked to revert to their true selves

---

[2] These teachers were attending state in-service education conferences sponsored by the Division of Homemaking Education, Texas Education Agency, under the direction of Ruth Huey. Without their careful and painstaking work the research instruments would have required infinitely more revision after pretesting in high schools.

and check the statements about personal and family living which they felt were important enough to be included in any over-all curriculum plan for homemaking courses at the high school levels. In the instructions, special emphasis was placed upon the importance of criticizing the wording and appropriateness of each individual statement in all the inventories. Teachers were instructed to cross out, change words, or add items wherever they felt that alteration was indicated. These qualitative remarks proved invaluable in the later refinement of materials.

Since the teachers responded from their own personal point of view in filling out the "Personal Interest Check List," data obtained from this form provided information regarding the attitudes of home economics teachers toward curriculum content for homemaking courses at the high school level. However, the main purpose of giving these preliminary forms to this group of teachers was to gain the benefit of their collective wisdom in refining the instruments for more systematic use in the main study. In addition, focussing attention on the proposed study at the annual conference of home economics teachers whose cooperation would be needed to carry out the main project, gave these teachers a deeper understanding of the Cooperative Youth Study than anything else that might have been done.

As a further check on the feasibility of the general approach, these preliminary instruments were given to several hundred students in grades seven through twelve in central Texas.[3] As with the teachers, the students were encouraged to write in comments and suggestions for improving the instruments. Item analyses were carried out early in the fall, 1954, including frequency distributions for each item and school grade. Analysis of these first results in conference with a group of advisory consultants [4] revealed several important points that were pertinent to the planning of next steps in the study.

It was obvious that the same set of instruments could not be used throughout all six grades. A number of the seventh and eighth graders had considerable difficulty in understanding many of the items, par-

---

[3] Test runs were made by home economics faculty members from Prairie View A. & M. College, Southwest Texas State College, Stephen F. Austin College, Texas College, Texas State College for Women, Texas Technological College, and The University of Texas.

[4] Advisors to the Central Work Committee were Carson McGuire, Harold G. Stevenson, Lucy Rathbone, and Robert L. Sutherland.

ticularly those in Form II, dealing with personal problems. Since most of the students in grades nine through twelve had no difficulty in filling out the forms, it was decided to limit the main study to this segment of the school population, putting off indefinitely the study of seventh and eighth graders.

The general format and most of the items in the three instruments weathered the preliminary testing with fair success. The greatest amount of revision was necessary for Form II, "Concerns and Problems in Personal and Family Living," and for the face sheet containing general information about the respondent. Several days were spent in revising the instruments at a special conference of home economics faculty members from throughout the state which was held in Fort Worth early in November.[5] Both Form I and Form II were reduced to ninety items apiece, while Form III was kept at eighty-nine items. Plans were also made at this meeting for the classification of items and the development of scales; for conducting a pilot study in the spring semester, 1955; and for setting up a network of cooperating agencies to make possible the large-scale collection of data in 1956.

The Clustering of Items and Development of Scales

Although it is possible to work directly with responses to individual items in a study such as this, there are several reasons why it is generally more desirable to build up clusters of items or scales that reflect more or less uniformly the same underlying attitudes or traits. Responses to individual items are often relatively low in reliability and are influenced by such extraneous factors as the particular wording of the items. By combining into a single scale a number of items that have a common core of meaning running through them, it is possible to increase greatly the reliability of the measure while also sharply reducing the effect of extraneous factors present in the individual items. Rather powerful statistical techniques are available to assess the extent to which such scale scores can be depended upon for drawing conclusions about the underlying attitudes and traits being measured. And finally, one can greatly reduce the number of variables to be analyzed by condensing several hundred items into a

[5] Invaluable assistance to the study was given by Miss Beulah I. Coon, specialist in research and special studies, Home Economics Education, United States Office of Education at the two research conferences in Mineral Wells, at the Fort Worth conference, and at other advisory meetings throughout duration of the study.

dozen scales, thereby making the expensive operation of data analysis far more efficient.

It is not enough, however, merely to sort the items into a number of predefined categories, for each of which some kind of score is computed by arbitrarily weighting the member items. One must fully justify the item clustering on both rational and empirical grounds before moving on merrily to any analysis and interpretation of results. Two general approaches were utilized in developing and verifying the scales employed in the Cooperative Youth Study: (1) a rational approach utilizing a number of expert judges independently classifying items according to the content evident in them; followed by (2) an empirical cross-checking of the item clusters by analyzing the item intercorrelations obtained from the actual responses to the items given by a large number of high school students.

THE CLASSIFICATION OF ITEMS BY JUDGES

Each item in the revised versions of Forms I and II was typed on a small card, and seven copies were made of the complete card deck. Each set of items was mailed to one of the home economists who was active in the study, together with detailed instructions to sort the cards into a number of categories according to similarity of content. The judge was told to shuffle the card deck before starting the task so that every item would have equal likelihood of appearing early or late in the series. It was suggested that the judge first compare for similarity the content of the first and second items in the shuffled deck. The third card was then compared with the first two and a decision made as to whether all three items would be likely to measure the same underlying attitude, whether they were all different or whether two belonged together while the third fell into another category. Each of the seven judges[6] went through the entire deck of items in this manner until they were satisfied that the classification made good sense. The judges were then asked to define briefly the nature of the attitude or trait represented by each cluster of items, returning these judgments to the Central Work Committee for tabulation and integration with similar data from the other judges.

[6] Original sorting of items was done by Gladys Babcock, Wayne H. Holtzman, Ruth Huey, Onah Jacks, Bernice M. Moore, Josephine Pazdral, and Gladys Short.

THE CROSS CHECKING OF ITEM CLUSTERS

Examination of the categories evolved by the seven judges working independently of each other revealed a common core of twenty item clusters. These subscales formed the basis on which a second set of eight judges sorted all the items in Forms I and II.[7] This time each judge was given the tentative names and definitions of the twenty subscales derived from the earlier experiment, and was asked to sort every item into one of the predefined categories. To avoid forcing the issue, a "miscellaneous" category was provided into which the judge was encouraged to put any item which could not be properly placed in one of the twenty subscales. Each judge was also informed that all

TABLE 1: *Initial Categories for Sorting Items in Forms I and II*

I. GENERAL ATTITUDES (Items from Form I)
  1. Orientation to Society
  2. Authoritarian Discipline
  3. Parental Invasion of Child's Privacy
  4. Other Child Rearing Attitudes
  5. Conservatism in Heterosexual Mores
  6. Criticism of Education
  7. Criticism of Youth

II. PERSONAL ATTITUDES—Family (Some items from Form I; most from Form II)
  1. Family Cohesion
  2. Resentment of Dependency
  3. Fairness of Discipline
  4. General Family Tensions
  5. Resentment of Family Life Style
  6. Financial Troubles

III. PERSONAL ATTITUDES—Self (Some items from Form I; most from Form II)
  1. Fatigue
  2. Aspiration Failure
  3. Social Isolation
  4. Social Ineptness
  5. Social Inadequacy
  6. Social Conformity
  7. Other Adjustment Items

[7] Sortings by the eight judges were made possible by Florence Scoular, North Texas State College; Jessie Bateman, Texas State College for Women; and Willa Vaughn Tinsely.

of the items in seven of the subscales (general attitudes) should come from Form I, while the majority of items in the six subscales dealing with the family and in the seven subscales dealing with the self should come from Form II. The tentative names and definitions of these twenty subscales are presented in Table 1.

A conservative point of view was taken in making final decisions about the subscale identification of each item and about which categories should be dropped. Unless a majority of the eight judges independently agreed in placing an item within a particular category, the item was dropped from further consideration in scaling, although it might be retained for analysis as an individual item. In many cases the item classification was unanimous, testifying to the compelling face validity of most of the categories. In this manner, a total of fourteen scales was obtained, six in Form I and eight in Form II. The names ascribed to these scales and the number of items originally in each are given in Table 2.

TABLE 2: *Fourteen Scales in Forms I and II, and the Number of Items Originally Included in Each Scale*

FORM I
1. Orientation to Society (9 items)
2. Authoritarian Discipline (9 items)
3. Criticism of Education (10 items)
4. Criticism of Youth (7 items)
5. Family Problems (7 items)
6. Self Inadequacy (10 items)

FORM II
1. Family Tension (20 items)
2. Personal Adjustment (26 items)
3. Social Inadequacy (12 items)
4. Resentment of Family Life Style (9 items)
5. Social Conformity (4 items)
6. Social Isolation (4 items)
7. Financial Troubles (5 items)
8. Resentment of Dependency (6 items)

No attempt was made to develop scales for the items in the interest check list, Form III. Revision of this instrument was handled separately by a special committee.[8] Care was taken to see that all major

---

[8] The committee for revision of Form III consisted of Gladys Short, Josephine Pazdral, Onah Jacks, Gladys Babcock, and Ruth Huey.

areas of homemaking education were adequately represented. Categories used for this purpose were (1) the house and its equipment, (2) management (time, money, and household), (3) family economics, (4) feeding the family (including nutrition), (5) clothing the family (including purchase, care, and construction), (6) care of family members, (7) skills in child rearing, (8) personal, family, and community relationships, (9) vocational opportunities in homemaking field, and (10) personal and family health.

A Pilot Study in Twelve Texas Communities

Having developed scales on a rational basis for the instruments to be used in the main project, the planners still needed to verify the scales and determine their measurement characteristics on an empirical basis before moving ahead with large-scale data collection and analysis. During the spring of 1955, the revised versions of the inventories and the general information sheet were employed in a pilot study of over two thousand teen-agers in twelve different Texas communities representing a wide variety of sociocultural backgrounds. In addition to providing important data for item analysis and verification of the scales, this pilot project served as a valuable dress rehearsal in every respect for the main testing program. The organization of a network for coordination and administration of the instruments, the development of a central staff for the scoring, coding, punching, tabulating, and statistical analysis of huge chunks of data, and the establishment of a conceptual framework within which to formulate hypotheses about youth that could be adequately tested by empirical findings—all grew out of the 1955 "shakedown cruise" for the Cooperative Youth Study.

THE GIVING OF THE TESTS

A total of 2,163 teen-agers—1,063 boys and 1,100 girls—in fifteen different junior and senior high schools throughout Texas participated in the 1955 pilot study.[9] The breakdown of the sample by sex and participating school is given in Table 3. The number of incomplete or unusable answer sheets was surprisingly small, varying from none in some classrooms to 14 per cent in one rural school. It was apparent from even a casual inspection of the quality of returns that with

[9] See the Acknowledgments for the listing of participating colleges and universities who were responsible for data collection.

careful administration of the instruments, highly satisfactory results could be obtained.

TABLE 3: *Junior and Senior High Schools Participating in the 1955 Pilot Study*

School	Boys	Girls	Total
South Junior High (Waco)	66	82	148
Lakeview (San Angelo)	76	67	143
Kyle	29	25	54
Blum	30	16	46
Douglas	13	12	25
Gunter	20	42	62
Oakwood	28	14	42
Aldine	230	240	470
Pickard (Brenham)	60	73	133
Herman (Houston)	16	18	34
Bragg Morris (Lindale)	16	17	33
Emmett Scott (Tyler)	77	119	196
Moore (Waco)	96	80	176
San Angelo	199	217	416
University (Waco)	107	78	185
Total	1,063	1,100	2,163

Because the total sample was heavily loaded with urban high schools, a smaller sample of 1,024 students was drawn for purposes of item and scale analysis which more closely resembled the high school population of the state as a whole. Such background variables as size of school, school grade, sex of respondent, status of parents, and father's occupation were coded and punched on IBM cards along with every item on Forms I, II, and III.

THE SCORING OF THE SCALES

Prior to further analysis, simple frequency distributions were computed for background variables and each item in the inventories. For the purpose of combining items to obtain scores on the attitude scales in Form I, each item to be included in a scale was assigned numerical weights of 0, 1, or 2, according to the degree of agreement-disagreement indicated by the student's response to the item. Cutting points for this three-point weighting system were chosen so as to equalize as much as possible the frequency of occurrence of responses scored 0, 1, or 2 in the pilot sample.[10] In other words, the distribution of five choices for each item was split roughly into thirds by combining adjacent categories, and the resulting three categories were weighted 0, 1, and 2.

For example, more individuals tended to agree than disagree with Item 3, "Most children should have more discipline than they get." Consequently, weights of 2, 1, 1, 0, and 0 were assigned to "Strongly Agree," "Agree," "Undecided or Uncertain," "Disagree," and "Strongly Disagree," respectively, in scoring this item for the Authoritarian Discipline Scale. On the other hand, many more individuals agreed than disagreed with Item 10, "I usually get fair treatment at home." Weights of 0, 1, 2, 2, and 2 were assigned to the five choices ranging from "Strongly Agree" to "Strongly Disagree" in scoring this item for Family Problems. In this manner, responses to Item 10 of "Uncertain," "Disagree," and "Strongly Disagree" are given a maximum weight of two points. The scores on all six items in the Family Problems Scale are added together to give the individual's score on this scale. Each of the six scales in Form I was scored in a like manner.

The higher the score on a given scale, the more clearly has the respondent expressed the basic attitude reflected by the items which constitute the scale. With such a scoring system, the possible range of scale scores is from zero to an amount equal to twice the number of scorable items. On the nine-item Authoritarian Discipline Scale, for example, the total possible range of scores is from zero to eighteen. That is to say, if a person expressed the most extreme agreement with all nine statements (getting a weight of two for each item), his scale score would be 18.

The Internal Consistency of the Scales

One approach to determining the internal properties of a set of scales is to compute the intercorrelations among all the items in an instrument and to examine the total inter-item correlation matrix for

[10] This procedure maximizes the item variance, statistically speaking, which in turn maximizes the amount of information retained in the scale score when a five-point response continuum is collapsed to a three-point weighting system. The three-point system was selected because this was the maximum number of allowable weights that will permit use of a Model 805 IBM scoring machine without involving more than one run of the answer sheets through the machine.

clusters of factors which will account for most of the common variance in the correlation matrix. One would expect to find the intercorrelations among items within a given scale to be higher than those among items which do not belong to the same scale, if there is a high degree of internal consistency, homogeneity, or unidimensionality in the scale.[11] A related approach which involves working with the variance-covariance matrix among items rather than the correlation matrix is the Loevinger-DuBois method of developing homogeneous scales.[12]

A short-cut procedure was adopted for ascertaining the extent to which the items in each of the a priori scales as developed by the teams of expert judges, do in fact cling together and yield measures of essentially the same thing, thereby justifying the pooling of items to obtain scale scores. The six scale scores in Form I were computed, using the pooled numerical weights as described earlier. Correlation coefficients were computed between each item and the scale score of which the item was a part.[13] One can reason that the higher the correlation between a scale score and an item in the scale, the more similar is the meaning to be assigned the item and scale, and the more the particular item contributes to the scale.

[11] Factor analysis of the inter-item correlation matrix is a statistical technique for determining a small number of dimensions (factors) which, when properly combined, can account for all of the important communality or common variance among the items as reflected in the correlations (B. Fruchter, *Introduction to Factor Analysis*). The labor involved in such an analysis with the large number of items in Forms I and II (90 each) is very great unless one has access to late-model, high-capacity electronic computers. At the time of this analysis in 1955, no such computer was available at The University of Texas. A special kind of factor analysis which starts with a priori scales and works with item-scale correlations and interscale correlations has been recently formulated by Wherry and Winer. (See R. J. Wherry and B. J. Winer, "A Method for Factoring Large Numbers of Items," in *Psychometrika*, Vol. 18 [1953], pp. 161–179.)

[12] P. H. DuBois, Jane Loevinger, and Goldine C. Gleser, *The Construction of Homogeneous Keys for a Biographical Inventory.*

[13] The correlations were computed by the tetrachoric method. Fourfold tables were compiled by splitting both the scale and item distributions near the median values. Item-scale correlations as evidence of internal consistency have been widely used in the test and attitude measurement literature. While they are a convenient, economical approach to the problem, the interpretation of item-scale correlations is not as clear, nor is the method as theoretically elegant or statistically powerful as the more time-consuming approaches of factor analysis or the Loevinger-DuBois Method.

THE FINAL SCALES

Form I

The results of this item-scale analysis for Form I ("Attitudes toward Personal and Family Living") are presented in Tables 4 through 9. The items within each rationally defined scale are listed according to the size of the correlation between the item and the total scale score of which the item is a part. Thus for each scale, those items which appear at the top of the list tend to define operationally the nature of the scale, and those items at the bottom of the list, which also have low correlation coefficients, contribute relatively little to the homogeneity or uniformity of meaning of the total scale. Some slight correlation between any item and its scale score is to be expected purely because the item appears in both variables being correlated— once by itself, and once in combination with other items as the total scale score. Such part-whole spuriousness is negligible with a large number of items, but must be taken into account when the scale is rather short (say, six or fewer items).

I ORIENTATION TO SOCIETY

For the first scale, called Orientation to Society, the two items best defining the meaning of the scale are numbers 48 and 64, "These days a person doesn't really know whom he can count on," and "In spite of what some people say, the life for the average person is getting worse, not better." Taken together with other items in this scale, these two make it fairly clear that individuals who get high scores on Orientation to Society (those who agree with these statements) have a pessimistic outlook on life and a somewhat disillusioned mistrust of mankind. When taken at face value, a high score is evidence of a negative orientation toward society.

TABLE 4: *Orientation to Society*

Item Number	Item Content	Item-Scale Correlation
48	These days a person doesn't really know whom he can count on.	.74
64	In spite of what some people say, the life for the average person is getting worse, not better.	.61
32	It's hardly fair to bring children into the world with the way things look for the future.	.58
49	When you get right down to it no one is going to care much what is going to happen to you.	.58
14	People always get into trouble when they haven't anything to do.	.53
63	We ought to worry about our own country and let the rest of the world take care of itself.	.48
80	If you don't watch yourself, people will take advantage of you.	.48
37	A person should insist on his own rights no matter what the cost.	.42
*54	One's reputation depends mostly on the people one goes with.	.32

* Indicates item dropped from final version of the scale.

II AUTHORITARIAN DISCIPLINE

Most of the items in the second scale, Authoritarian Discipline, were taken from earlier studies of attitudes toward child-rearing practices by Marks, Baldwin, and others.[14] Only those items from Marks' study which significantly differentiated between the mothers of schizophrenic individuals and the mothers of normal persons were included in the Cooperative Youth Study. Although this significant

[14] J. C. Marks, "The Attitudes of the Mothers of Male Schizophrenics," pp. 185–189; A. L. Baldwin, Joan Kalhorn, and Fay H. Breese, "The Appraisal of Parental Behavior," in *Psychological Monograph*, Vol. 63 (1949), No. 4 (Whole No. 299), pp. 1–85; E. S. Schaefer and R. Q. Bell, "Patterns of Attitudes toward Child Rearing and the Family," in *Journal of Abnormal and Social Psychology*, Vol. 54 (1957), pp. 391–395.

finding of Marks concerning "schizophrenogenic" attitudes is of some interest in its own right, it does not follow that individuals with high scores on Authoritarian Discipline are themselves likely to be schizophrenic. Care should be taken to avoid any such interpretation of scores in the present study.

TABLE 5: *Authoritarian Discipline*

Item Number	Item Content	Item-Scale Correlation
50	Too much affection will make a child a "softie."	.72
97	Children need some of the natural meanness taken out of them.	.64
90	If children are to grow up and get somewhere in life, they must be continuously kept after.	.57
79	Children who always obey grow up to be the best adults.	.56
25	Too much freedom will make a child wild.	.56
55	Strict discipline develops a fine strong character.	.55
17	A high school student should take the school courses which his parents decide would be best for him.	.42
71	Children should always be punished for being bad.	.35
3	Most children should have more discipline than they get.	.28

Several of the items in Authoritarian Discipline have fairly high correlations with the total scale score. The person with high scores on this scale is very likely to be one who values strict discipline, believes a child should be "toughened up" by withholding affection, and values unquestioning obedience to authority. That this attitude is not a highly generalized, simple one among high school students is evidenced by the low item-scale correlations for Items 3, 17, and 71.

III CRITICISM OF EDUCATION

All of the items in Criticism of Education were taken from a scale developed by Brown and Holtzman for assessing motivational and attitudinal factors in academic achievement.[15] Individuals who agree

[15] W. F. Brown, "Motivational Orientations and Scholastic Achievement."

with these statements are more likely to be poor students than are those who disagree. In general, the items in Criticism of Education are more homogeneous than the items in the two previous scales. All but one of the item-scale correlations is above .53. The six items with highest loadings (22, 34, 60, 69, 92, and 94) involve specific criticism of teachers as being too rigid and narrow-minded, too punitive, unfair in homework assignments, and generally lacking in an understanding of student needs and interests. A person with a high score on Criticism of Education is likely to be quite hostile toward formal education in general and toward schoolteachers in particular.

TABLE 6: *Criticism of Education*

Item Number	Item Content	Item-Scale Correlation
22	Most teachers are too rigid and narrow-minded.	.72
92	The main reason students cheat is because of the ridiculous assignments most teachers make.	.72
69	Most teachers have special favorites instead of showing equal fairness and impartiality toward all.	.68
34	Most teachers lack understanding of the needs and interests of their students.	.66
94	The illustrations, examples, and explanations given by most teachers are too dry or technical.	.65
60	Generally speaking, students cannot be expected to like their teachers.	.62
84	It is almost impossible for the average student to do all his assigned homework.	.60
52	Generally speaking, football coaches contribute more to school life than do the teachers.	.58
82	Students are not given enough freedom in selecting their own topics for themes and reports.	.53
5	The sole purpose of an education should be to equip students to make a living.	.42

IV   CRITICISM OF YOUTH

Only six items constitute the scale called Criticism of Youth, and only one of these (43) has an item-scale correlation above .60. These items were all formulated from statements submitted by youth themselves in the early stages of test development. While they apparently have a real meaning to most youth and might be of considerable value when analyzed as individual items, when added together as one scale they lack sufficient homogeneity to warrant a high degree of confidence in the meaning of the scale scores. In spite of its somewhat borderline nature, the scale was tentatively retained for further analysis in the main project because so little is known about teen-ager attitudes in this area.

TABLE 7: *Criticism of Youth*

Item Number	Item Content	Item-Scale Correlation
43	Silliness is one of the worst faults of most teen-agers.	.61
68	Most teen-agers have not yet learned to control their tempers.	.54
91	Teen-agers gossip too much about each other.	.50
101	In our community, more youth disrespect public property today than ever before.	.47
85	A girl who gets into trouble on a date has no one to blame but herself.	.46
7	Too many boys and girls think they have to drink to be smart.	.44
33	Whenever a girl marries she should drop out of high school.	.24

V   FAMILY PROBLEMS

The fifth scale in Form I, Family Problems, consists of a small number of items dealing with attitudes toward the family. A much larger number of similar items makes up Family Tension, a scale in Form II. The six items in Family Problems were included in the attitude inventory partly because Form I was suitable for use with adults while Form II was not, and partly to determine the degree of individual consistency in scores on the family scales in the two different instruments, Forms I and II.[16] Only one of the items (44) has a really low item-scale correlation, the others having loadings ranging from .57 to .65. While too short a scale for more than a rather crude analysis, especially since the degree of homogeneity is only fair, Family Problems was retained for further analysis in later studies.

TABLE 8: *Family Problems*

Item Number	Item Content	Item-Scale Correlation
1	I can always count on my family for help when I get in trouble or have a problem.	.65
42	My family never gives me any privacy.	.63
10	I usually get fair treatment at home.	.62
38	Members of my family feel hurt every time I want to go out with others instead of with them.	.60
98	Our family never seems to plan anything ahead of time.	.57
44	We have enjoyable times together during meals in our home.	.34
°89	I worry about my family.	.22

° Indicates item dropped from final version of the scale.

VI SELF INADEQUACY

The last scale in Form I, Self Inadequacy, was composed of items very similar to those used in many of the well-known objective personality inventories.[17] In every case, however, the items were derived from statements submitted by youth themselves, and were retained in Form I for the same reasons as Family Problems. The items most heavily loaded on Self Inadequacy (27, 70, and 6) involve admission

[16] It was contemplated that Form I would be given to a large sample of high school teachers concurrently with the collection of data from youngsters in the main project during spring, 1956.

[17] Starke R. Hathaway and J. Charnley McKinley, *Minnesota Multiphasic Personality Inventory;* R. B. Cattell, *Junior Personality Quiz.*

of feelings of inferiority and lack of self-confidence. Since the homogeneity of this scale is only fair at best, considerable caution should be exercised in drawing interpretations from scale scores except, perhaps, at one or the other extreme of the frequency distribution.

TABLE 9: *Self Inadequacy*

Item Number	Item Content	Item-Scale Correlation
27	I just never seem to get anything done.	.65
70	I often feel as if I don't really belong anywhere.	.60
6	I lack confidence in myself.	.57
2	I dislike eating away from home for fear I'll do the wrong thing.	.54
9	I often have the feeling I will say something wrong.	.54
18	I find any discussion of sex embarrassing.	.47
86	Most of the time, I am still tired when I get up in the morning.	.46
81	Young children always make me nervous.	.44
40	Some of my friends say that I am disagreeable and hard to get along with.	.30
*31	I'm never satisfied unless I do a perfect job.	.01

* Indicates item dropped from final version of the scale.

Form II

Four of the eight scales in Form II ("Concerns and Problems in Personal and Family Living") were scored in a manner similar to that used for the scales in Form I, with one minor difference. Instead of adjusting the cutting points to the shape of the frequency distribution, exactly the same cutting points were used for every item. A response of "False" was always assigned a weight of 0; "True, but of no concern," and "True, but of little concern" were each assigned a weight of 1; the remaining two choices, "True, and of much concern," and "True, and of greatest concern," were each given maximum weights of 2. This change from the scoring method used in Form I was adopted for two reasons. First, the nature of the five response choices is quite different, with an important shift in meaning from "False" to "True" as one moves from the first to second category. Second, most items in Form II were uniformly skewed in distribution, with a predominance of individuals generally checking "False" and only a handful marking "True, and of greatest concern" at the other extreme of the response continuum. Such skewness is to be expected in a refined problem check list of this type, since many individuals will not admit any problem with respect to a given statement.

The remaining four scales in Form II were all too short (the longest containing six items) to justify combining adjacent choices to reduce the five-point continuum to three categories. Although such reduction greatly increases the efficiency of machine scoring, the resulting loss of information when the individual items are sharply skewed in distribution can be serious. Consequently, the last four scales in Form II, Social Conformity, Social Isolation, Financial Troubles, and Resentment of Dependency, were all scored by hand rather than by machine, using numerical weights of 0, 1, 2, 3, and 4 for the five choices. Thus, on Social Conformity, with four items, the highest possible score is four times four (number of items times maximum item-weight), or sixteen. Of course, very few individuals received this maximum score because of the more general tendency to check "False" in Form II than to check one or the other extreme in Form I.

Correlations between the individual items and the appropriate scale scores of which the items are a part were computed in exactly the same manner for Form II scales as was described earlier for those in Form I. These coefficients are listed in Tables 10 through 17 for each of the eight scales, with the highest correlation at the top of the list and the others arranged in descending order. The higher the correlation between a scale and one of its items, the greater the similarity in meaning of the scale score and the statement comprising the item. The higher the general level of such correlations, the more uniform and clear is the general interpretation of the scale score.

VII   FAMILY TENSION

Probably the best defined scale in either Form I or Form II, Family Tension contains twenty items most of which correlate highly with the total scale score. It is interesting to note that the seven items with correlations of .70 or higher all involve conflict and tension between the parents and the child about which the child has expressed some concern. The two items with correlations above .80 capture very well the essence of Family Tension—"My parents quarrel and fight much of the time," and "My parents never have time to help me."

TABLE 10: *Family Tension*

Item Number	Item Content	Item-Scale Correlation
204	My parents quarrel and fight much of the time.	.86
176	My parents never have time to help me.	.81
220	Our family seems to have more problems than others in our neighborhood.	.77
210	My parents often object to the kind of boys and girls I go around with.	.76
221	Dad always seems too busy to pal around with me.	.75
196	Everyone in my family seems to be against me.	.75
201	My parents seem to change from day to day in the way they treat me.	.70
235	I am never able to discuss personal problems confidentially with either of my parents.	.68
200	My parents do not agree about religion.	.68
174	I like one of my parents much better than I like the other.	.67
182	My parents usually disagree about things I am to be punished for.	.66
213	If we didn't feel so crowded in our house, we'd be much happier.	.62
170	Family problems are never talked over with me.	.60
160	My mother is always nagging me to help around the house.	.59
206	I feel that I have often been punished when I didn't deserve it.	.55
216	My parents never take part in school affairs.	.54

TABLE 10: *Family Tension—Continued*

Item Number	Item Content	Item-Scale Correlation
152	Mother is really the boss in our family.	.48
181	Dad makes all the decisions at our house.	.48
185	Arguments in my family always upset me.	.47
215	I have to take care of the younger children in our family.	.45

VIII   PERSONAL ADJUSTMENT

The twenty-three items in Personal Adjustment deal with inner conflict, worry, and feelings of personal inadequacy that, for the most part, are not specifically centered around social adjustment and interpersonal relations, since these latter topics are covered in separate scales. When taken as a whole, this scale is not as homogeneous as Family Tension. The item-scale correlations range from .43 to .74 for Personal Adjustment, the average value being about .55. Similar correlations for Family Tension range from .45 to .85 with a mean value of .64. Examination of the item content in the two scales would lead one to expect this kind of difference. The items in Family Tension are focussed on the family, whereas problem areas covered under Personal Adjustment range all the way from "I would like to get married as soon as possible" to "I don't sleep well."

In spite of the relative heterogeneity of Personal Adjustment when compared to the other scales in Form II, the scale was retained in essentially its original version for several reasons. There was no clear basis in this limited analysis for rejecting any one item as being clearly foreign to the others. Even the several items with rather low item-scale correlations were not sufficiently distant from the rest of the items to alter appreciably the meaning of Personal Adjustment if dropped from the scale. Moreover, Personal Adjustment would inevitably turn out to be more heterogeneous than other scales in Form II because of the sorting method used by the judges in scale construction. Wherever a focussed problem area emerged as defined by at least four items, a separate scale was born, leaving the residual for likely inclusion under the more general rubric of personal adjustment.

TABLE 11: *Personal Adjustment*

Item Number	Item Content	Item-Scale Correlation
168	I would like to get married as soon as possible.	.74
179	I work hard but never get anything done.	.69
226	I don't sleep well.	.64
162	I can't seem to make other people understand I really like them.	.61
178	I can never figure out what grownups want me to do.	.61
224	People sometimes tell me I am a snob.	.60
187	I feel tired all the time.	.58
219	I'm never chosen by teacher to do any special task.	.56
177	I get mad and do things I shouldn't when I can't have my way.	.56
218	I never seem to be able to get anywhere on time.	.55
165	Sometimes I feel things are not real.	.55
163	Others always look better than I.	.54
194	My going steady presents real problems in petting.	.54
189	I wonder if for my age I am normal in my physical development.	.53
155	I'm often asked to drop out to let someone else have my place.	.52
161	People gossip about me behind my back.	.52
203	It's hard for me to live up to the reputation of others in my family.	.51
172	I don't seem to live up to my religious teaching as well as others do.	.50
153	Sometimes I feel I have been very wicked.	.48
192	I think about sex a good deal of the time.	.49
214	Sometimes criticism gets me down.	.47

TABLE 11: *Personal Adjustment—Continued*

Item Number	Item Content	Item-Scale Correlation
234	I am prejudiced against some people.	.46
157	I'm teased a lot by other boys and girls.	.43
*232	Being out with people who get drunk scares me.	.39
*191	I have trouble getting a job after school.	.36
*151	I see boys and girls at school whom I'd like to meet but I never get a chance.	.28

* Indicates item dropped from final version of the scale.

IX SOCIAL INADEQUACY

One of the most specific of the major scales in the problem inventory is Social Inadequacy. Feeling ill at ease socially is a particularly acute problem for a great many youngsters as they struggle to grow up and be accepted as adults. Certainly it is no surprise that a number of the statements submitted by youth touched on this sensitive area.

TABLE 12: *Social Inadequacy*

Item Number	Item Content	Item-Scale Correlation
197	I am always afraid in a crowd.	.83
199	I'm afraid people will laugh at me because I'm not sure I know how to act.	.83
227	I don't feel sure how to act on dates.	.79
238	I often feel uncomfortable when I'm around others my age.	.77
230	I feel ill at ease at parties.	.73
180	I have trouble making friends easily.	.73
233	I avoid meeting the parents of my dates.	.71

TABLE 12: *Social Inadequacy—Continued*

Item Number	Item Content	Item-Scale Correlation
173	I am often unable to look at people when I'm talking to them.	.69
158	I can't carry on a conversation in a group.	.68
195	I am never sure what I ought to wear to be dressed right for the occasion.	.64
183	I never feel I know what clothes make me look best.	.63
207	Often it seems that I hurt people's feelings without meaning to do so.	.56

Without exception, the item-scale correlations for Social Inadequacy show a relatively high degree of uniformity in meaning. A person getting a high score on Social Inadequacy is very likely to feel awkward, ill at ease, embarrassed, and unsure of himself in social affairs, and to be unable to make friends easily.

X RESENTMENT OF FAMILY LIFE STYLE

Everyone has a characteristic way of living that is reflected in eating and sleeping habits, home environment, choice of companions, work, and recreation. In a similar manner, the family adopts a style of life that permeates all of its daily activities. Resentment of Family Life Style contains nine items that focus on conflict between the dominant family life style and the wishes of the respondent. Most of the item-scale intercorrelations for this scale are highly satisfactory, indicating homogeneity and relative ease of interpretation. Definition of the scale is self-evident from the content of the more highly correlated items in Table 13. A person with a high score on Resentment of Family Life Style is very likely to be an individual who is ashamed of his family, particularly of the model set forth by his parents, and who wishes they behaved differently. Moreover, it indicates that the home setting and the way of living in the household have a negative impact upon the youth.

TABLE 13: *Resentment of Family Life Style*

Item Number	Item Content	Item-Scale Correlation
222	My parents don't like to have me bring friends home.	.73
156	I am ashamed sometimes of the way my parents behave.	.72
164	Housekeeping in our house is disorderly.	.71
167	Some of my family members do not know good table manners.	.69
208	My parents always say their way is the best way when I try to tell them things I learn in school.	.69
171	My parents rarely go to church.	.60
202	Keeping our house in order is more important to mother than having fun in it.	.54
228	My parents avoid discussing sex with me.	.53
237	I have to do most of the cooking and housekeeping at home.	.49

XI SOCIAL CONFORMITY

In addition to the four major scales described above, Form II contains four very short scales, each of which has highly uniform internal characteristics. Because they each contain only a few items and the scale score always includes the item with which it is being compared, the general level of the item-scale correlations will be spuriously high, and care must be taken not to overinterpret the apparent homogeneity.

Social Conformity contains four items that reflect conflict between individual's personal code of conduct and the mores of his peer group as he perceives them. The scale was intended to deal with the issue confronting many youngsters today of compromising one's personal standards in order to be accepted by the gang.

TABLE 14: *Social Conformity*

Item Number	Item Content	Item-Scale Correlation
240	Sometimes I tell dirty jokes when I would rather not.	.82
209	Sometimes I feel I just have to lower my standards to be popular.	.74
212	If you don't drink in our gang, they make you feel like a sissy.	.66
186	Some people think I'm a prude because I don't like dirty jokes.	.60

XII SOCIAL ISOLATION

A critical problem for some individuals that becomes acute in adolescence is the feeling of being rejected by others, of being isolated socially. The four items which define Social Isolation deal specifically with this issue. In spite of the greater part-whole spuriousness in the item-scale correlations for a scale containing only four items, the high degree of homogeneity of Social Isolation is impressive.

TABLE 15: *Social Isolation*

Item Number	Item Content	Item-Scale Correlation
231	Others like me to help with their lessons but they never give me a date.	.82
225	Even when I am with people, I feel lonely most of the time.	.82
205	Others my age do not talk to me much.	.72
190	I want to be accepted by the gang but they won't have me.	.68

XIII FINANCIAL TROUBLES

Four of the items submitted by youth were repeatedly sorted by judges into the same category, resulting in a tentative scale called

Financial Troubles. While the family as a unit may be economically secure, a teen-age member of the family may have acute financial troubles of a real or fancied nature quite independent of the family's total income level. Financial Troubles was developed specifically to measure the degree of concern admitted by the respondent for problems of spending or saving money.

TABLE 16: *Financial Troubles*

Item Number	Item Content	Item-Scale Correlation
175	I can never save any money.	.73
229	Our family always seems to be in debt.	.70
239	Our family watches what it spends so closely it spoils our fun.	.69
169	Members of our family argue about buying things on credit.	.64
*159	I always have to ask for money for things I want to do.	.35

* Indicates item dropped from final version of the scale.

XIV RESENTMENT OF DEPENDENCY

A critical problem for many teen-agers is their struggle for independence from the family in those activities which mark the adult person. No study of youth problems would be complete without inclusion of some method for measuring the degree of parental pressure perceived by the adolescent in "feeling his oats." Consisting entirely of statements proposed by youth, Resentment of Dependency contains six highly homogeneous items. The nature of the scale as defined by item content in Table 17 is self-evident.

TABLE 17: *Resentment of Dependency*

Item Number	Item Content	Item-Scale Correlation
154	My parents treat me as if I do not know right from wrong.	.81
223	My parents never really trust me.	.80
198	My parents are strict about my going out at night.	.75
184	My parents won't let me drive a car even though I know how.	.74
193	Mother won't let me help because she says I never do anything right.	.70
188	My parents often pry into my private affairs.	.67

THE RESULTS OF PILOT STUDY

Generally speaking, results of the pilot study in 1955 were highly successful. The collection of data from several thousand youngsters was carried out without a single incident, thanks to the excellent cooperation of school authorities with homemaking teachers in their schools and the professors of home economics from adjacent colleges and of the youth who patiently worked through the questionnaire materials. The number of answer sheets incorrectly submitted was trivial, and the information given on the face sheet was clearly interpretable. The amount of internal homogeneity for most of the fourteen scales was sufficiently high to justify moving on immediately with the large-scale collection and analysis of data for the main study in 1956.

III: The Accomplishment of the Major Study

THE SUCCESS of the 1955 pilot study was most encouraging, and steps were taken immediately to complete final versions of the instruments, to design sampling procedures, and to work out the administrative organization and details for collecting data on a large scale in the main investigation planned for spring, 1956. Activities of the research staff were augmented by frequent meetings of the Central Study Committee and by a two-day conference of key home economics professors, consultants, and the staff of the Division of Homemaking Education, State Department of Education, at Mineral Wells, Texas, November 7–9, 1955. By early February, 1956, final plans for the study were completed, and by May, 1956, the last of over thirteen thousand youngsters turned in his set of research instruments. All major hurdles had been successfully overcome, and the long, exhaustive program of data analysis began in June, 1956.

Designing and executing this massive program of data collection constituted a major aspect of the Cooperative Youth Study. When the decision was made to move ahead with the main study, three tasks remained to be completed: final versions of the instruments needed to be worked out; the sample of schools to be studied needed to be drawn; and the administrative organization for collecting the data needed to be set up. Each of these steps will be described in turn.

THE FINAL VERSIONS OF THE INSTRUMENTS

For the most part, the form of the inventories weathered the pilot study very well, and only a few changes seemed desirable. Special attention was given to Form III, the interest inventory, by participants in the Mineral Wells conference. Nine new items were added to round out several areas of homemaking activity which were not adequately represented in the earlier version of Form III, making a total of 98 items in the final form. In addition, the response categories were extended from two to three—from a simple check list format to three degrees of interest: strong, mild, and none at all. It was hoped that the use of three choices for each item would yield a more sensitive indication of interest patterns than the simple check list. Since analysis of Form III would be largely limited to individual items, the additional sensitivity was important.

New items were also added to Form I, the attitude questionnaire, by a committee [1] which made an intensive study of item content in both Forms I and II. The committee discarded 5 items because they did not belong to any scale and were not of great interest in their own right, and added 16 new items, making a total of 101 items in the final version of the questionnaire.

Form II was left completely intact. After carefully examining all items in the problem inventory, the committee decided that no changes in item content were necessary. The final version consisting of 90 items is identical to that used in the pilot study.

Adding new items to an instrument always raises doubts about their adequacy unless further pilot testing is undertaken. Arrangements were made to administer Form I to freshmen in home economics courses at The University of Texas, and to give Form III to youth in the San Marcos public schools.[2] Completed answer sheets for Form I were obtained for 149 freshmen. Similar data for Form III were obtained for 96 boys and girls in the ninth through twelfth grades of San Marcos public schools. In each case there appeared to be no difficulty on the part of any youngster in understanding and answering the new items. As an additional check on the adequacy of

---

[1] Members of this committee consisted of Anne Arbuckle, Walter Hanak, Onah Jacks, David Proctor, Gladys Short, and Gladys Babcock, chairman.

[2] Test runs at the University were conducted by Gladys Babcock, Anne Arbuckle, and David Proctor; those in San Marcos were conducted by Onah Jacks.

these items, the frequency distributions of responses were compiled and studied for any signs of marked skewness. Every item appeared to be satisfactory for inclusion in the final forms of the instruments.

Considerable attention was also given to the content and format of the face sheet which was to be used for obtaining such vital information as the family structure of the respondent, the occupation and education of his father and mother, and the nature of living conditions in his home.[3] The Student Information Sheet was kept as simple and objective as possible. The items were presented in a form that could be rapidly coded by clerical personnel once the sheet was filled out. In its final form, the Student Information Sheet could be properly filled out in only two or three minutes.

The Student Information Sheet, the attitude questionnaire (Form I), the problem inventory (Form II), and the interest inventory (Form III) are presented in their final form in Appendix B. To facilitate later analysis of the information collected, a special IBM answer sheet[4] was provided, together with electrographic pencils, for each student to use in recording his responses to the 289 items in Forms I, II, and III.

Defining the Sample of Youth

It was agreed that the main study in 1956 should be based upon a representative sample of youth throughout the entire state of Texas within the grades nine through twelve. While it would have been desirable to obtain data on youth of these ages who had dropped out of school, the cost and difficulty of locating such individuals and securing their cooperation was simply prohibitive. Therefore, it should be kept in mind that the population studied consisted of all youth officially enrolled in grades nine through twelve of Texas public schools in the spring term, 1956.

What should be the basic sampling unit in a study of this scope? Obviously it would be foolish to attempt to collect data from the entire population of high school youth in Texas, and some scheme for sampling a small proportion of the population would have to be devised. Since the basic unit of study is the individual and his responses to the inventories, rather than the classroom or the school, the ideal

---

[3] Drs. Herbert and Lois Stoltz made a number of helpful suggestions concerning the face sheet, for which the authors are most grateful.

[4] IBM Forms I. D. T. 1100 B 107 and 1000 B 108.

method of sampling might be to draw up a list of names composed of every youngster in the state who is enrolled in the ninth through twelfth grade. From such a list, every *nth* individual could be randomly selected for inclusion in the sample, where *n* is the ratio of the total population size to the size of the sample. But such a plan is totally unrealistic. Simply compiling the list of names would be a frightful task.

Another way in which the individual might serve as the sampling unit would be to decentralize the job of picking every *nth* student in every school in the state. While feasible if only a few hundred cases are to be studied, such a method is totally impractical and prohibitive in its cost when the number of cases to be studied runs into the thousands. Moreover, the advantage of using instruments that can be administered to large numbers of subjects at a time would be completely lost by any plan which employed the individual student as the unit to be sampled.

The largest and most convenient sampling unit, of course, would be the entire school. One could quickly build up a large sample by collecting data from every student in a score of different schools spread around the state. But the resulting sampling bias due to the heavy clustering of many individuals within each sampling unit would seriously limit the generalizations that could be made about the entire population of Texas youth. Since the purpose of the Cooperative Youth Study is to obtain useful information about individuals rather than schools as a whole, defining the primary sampling unit as the entire school would be quite inappropriate.

The method finally chosen employed the classroom as the sampling unit. It was estimated that a 5-per-cent sample (one out of every twenty students) would yield over ten thousand cases, a sufficient number for the kind of subgroup analyses that were envisioned. Estimating the average classroom size to range from ten students for rural to thirty for urban schools[5] meant that nearly 700 classrooms would have to be sampled, about 170 classrooms in each of the four grades to be studied. This number is sufficiently large that the clustering effect would be trivial, and analysis could proceed as planned with the individual as the focus of study.

[5] Since most of the rural high schools in Texas in 1956 had fewer than 100 students, the number of rural classrooms sampled was much higher, proportionately speaking, than the number of classrooms in metropolitan areas.

Stratification of the Sample

The state as a whole was broken down according to three major categories: (1) region of the state; (2) classification of the school as white or Negro; and (3) size of the community. The five subdivisions of the state were defined in terms of economic and geographic features. East Texas (Region I) is primarily rural with a heavy Negro population and is generally considered more like the Deep South in culture than is any other part of Texas. The Gulf Coast (Region II) is bursting with new industry, shipping, oil refining, and rapid urbanization. The Valley (Region III) is noted for its subtropical agriculture, large Mexican-American population, and a blending of Spanish and American ways of life. Central Texas (Region IV) ranges from San Antonio through the capital city of Austin and the teeming metropolitan areas of Fort Worth and Dallas to the Oklahoma border on the north. West Texas (Region V) covers the vast, far-reaching lands of the Great South Plains, west to El Paso and north to the Panhandle. The particular boundaries employed for defining these five regions are illustrated in Figure 1.

Stratification according to race was desirable because of the traditionally segregated school systems in Texas. Although in 1956 this segregation was rapidly breaking down in many parts of the state, notably Regions III, IV, and V, the vast majority of classrooms were still segregated into white and Negro systems.

The third major stratification of the state consisted of community size: small, medium, and metropolitan. Small communities were rural areas and villages with estimated population less than 2,500. Metropolitan communities were defined as major urban areas in counties having estimated population of 100,000 or more in 1955. The county boundaries, rather than city, were taken for selecting metropolitan areas since the metropolitan complex always extends to suburban and other areas adjacent to large cities. A total of seventeen counties qualified as metropolitan communities by this definition. These major urban areas are marked in Figure 1. Since some communities within each of the seventeen counties were distinctly rural in spite of the metropolitan area nearby, a special category (non-urbanized metropolitan) was developed containing all rural schools within the metropolitan counties. Communities which were excluded from the above categories were classified as medium-sized towns and cities.

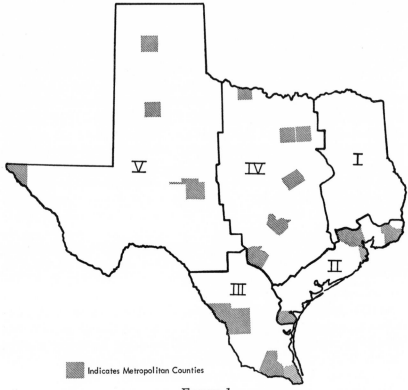

FIGURE 1
Seventeen Metropolitan Counties and Five Regions of Texas

Consideration of all possible combinations of the three major stratification variables yielded a total of fifty-six strata, or population cells,
within each of which a 5-per-cent sample was to be drawn. Since
there were no Negro high schools left in the Valley (Region III),
after the recent desegregation, five of the strata proved non-existent
and had to be dropped from further consideration, leaving a total
of fifty-one.

Random Selection of Classrooms

After the entire state had been divided into fifty-one strata from
which to draw a sample, the next step was to work out a method for
selecting a sufficient number of classroom units at random in each of
the four grades, nine through twelve, to yield approximately 5 per

cent of the total number of eligible students within each of the strata. Every accredited public high school in the state was placed in one of the fifty-one categories according to the size and location of the community that it serves and whether or not it was white or Negro. From 1955 population estimates,[6] the approximate number of individuals needed from each of the fifty-one strata was calculated so as to yield a 5 per cent sample. By using an estimate of average classroom size varying from ten students per classroom in rural areas to thirty students in large cities, one can easily estimate the approximate number of high schools to include, since only one classroom in each grade is to be included within any given school.

To illustrate how this sampling was done, consider one of the population strata, white schools in rural communities of East Texas (Region I). The name of every high school in Region I was listed on a small card, together with the estimated size of the school from extensive tables containing the average daily attendance for every school in 1955.[7] These cards were then sorted into four piles, according to whether the school served a small or medium-sized community and whether it was white or Negro. There were no metropolitan areas in Region I, as defined in this study. From the school population figures, it was estimated that 718 students, equally divided among the four grades, nine through twelve, would be needed to yield a 5 per cent sample of eligible white students in rural East Texas. If the average classroom size was 10 students this meant that seventy-two classrooms—eighteen in each of the four grades—would have to be drawn in the sample in order to get approximately 718 students. From the complete set of cards containing names of high schools in this particular population stratum, eighteen were selected at random to comprise this part of the sample.[8]

Using this procedure, a stratified random sample of high schools

---

[6] According to figures cited in the *Texas Almanac*, 1955.

[7] These tables of average daily attendance were generously made available by the Texas Education Agency through Ruth Huey, Director of Homemaking Education for the Agency.

[8] In many of the larger Texas communities, the junior high school system prevails, with ninth grade in a different school than tenth through twelfth. Choice of the particular junior high school was left up to local option, once the high school and community had been randomly selected. In many cases there was only one junior high school which fed students to the selected high school, while in others a choice had to be made locally.

throughout the state was compiled. Since it was highly likely that some schools would fail to cooperate in a study of this nature, a smaller number of schools was drawn at random in a similar manner to serve as a panel of alternative schools in case one of the first drawn would not participate. In this manner, a total of 182 school systems was randomly selected as the primary sample. The names of the schools which participated in the study and the number of youth drawn from each are listed according to the fifty-one strata in Appendix C.

PROCEDURES FOR COLLECTION OF THE DATA

Fortunately, from its inception the Cooperative Youth Study was conceived of as a truly collaborative endeavor involving nearly a dozen different colleges and universities, the Homemaking Education Division of the Texas Education Agency, and the Hogg Foundation for Mental Health. Administrative centers for collection of data were established on a regional basis throughout the state, with the Hogg Foundation assuming responsibility for central coordination and data processing.[9] For the most part, approaches were made by faculty members of these centers to the school administrators whose cooperation was needed in making arrangements for administering the instruments to selected classrooms in accordance with the randomly selected sample. In some instances contact with school administrators was made by area supervisors of the Texas Education Agency or by a member of the technical staff from the central committee at The University of Texas.

Detailed procedures were developed for conducting the initial interview with the school principal or superintendent to insure his understanding of the project and to encourage his participation. Convincing the authorities in several hundred school systems that the project was worthy of support was no small undertaking, especially when all these schools had been randomly selected in the first place. In most instances school authorities gave their wholehearted cooperation. In those oc-

[9] Administrative centers for the collection of data were established at Mary Hardin-Baylor College, University of Houston, Prairie View A. & M. College, Texas College, Texas State College for Women, Sam Houston State Teachers College, Texas Technological College, and The University of Texas. Mable McBain of Houston and Gertrude Barkley of Commerce, Texas, served as research associates to assist in the collection of data where the high school load was particularly heavy and the college and university staffs limited.

casional situations where it seemed unwise to press the issue further, an alternate school from the substitute list was included to round out the sample.

Within each school, the research associate and school principal selected the particular classroom within each grade that was to be included in the sample. In most cases, a home room class or one of the classes in a required subject such as English was chosen. Several alternative procedures were allowed to provide flexibility in the scheduling of the testing sessions. In some schools all individuals selected from the several grades met in a single assembly for several hours, completing the various inventories and questionnaires in one session with short breaks for resting between instruments. In most schools several sessions were required to fill out the instruments. The detailed suggestions for administration of the research instruments are given in Appendix D.

At many of the schools cooperating in the study, an attempt was also made to collect data from some of the teachers as well as the students. Only Forms I and III were given to teachers to fill out, since the Student Information Blank and Form II were inappropriate for adults. Participation by a teacher was purely voluntary, and the individual teacher's anonymity was strictly preserved. Background information obtained for purposes of analysis consisted of the teacher's school, age, sex, place of birth, and the names of school subjects currently taught.

Through this extensive network of study centers, research associates, and local school personnel, it was possible to obtain complete data for all but seven of the fifty-one cells in the stratified sample.[10] The resulting sample of almost thirteen thousand youth is a remarkably accurate representation of high school youth in the Texas public schools during the spring term, 1956. Only about 2 per cent of the answer sheets proved to be incomplete or incorrectly filled out. The overwhelming

---

[10] Most of the cells for which no data were obtained are of no significance. Five of them contained such small Negro populations that they were omitted. For example, the proportionate, stratified sample called for three Negroes from San Angelo and four from El Paso. The other two missing cells are metropolitan Webb County (Laredo) and medium-size schools in Area III. The number of students required for these two cells combined, in order to meet the proportionate sample requirements, is 148. Altogether, 216 schools cooperated in the study, 169 high schools and 47 junior high schools. A list of these schools is given in Appendix C.

majority of students responded sincerely and eagerly when asked to participate in the study.

PREPARATION OF THE DATA FOR ANALYSIS

While research associates throughout the state were administering the materials to youth in hundreds of classrooms, the central research staff in Austin made plans for the handling and analysis of the huge batches of data that would soon be flooding the office. Trial runs with data from the 1955 pilot study simplified the task greatly. The steps in preparation of the data for analysis consisted of (1) scoring the fourteen scales in Forms I and II, (2) coding the pertinent information on the face sheet and converting raw scale scores to standardized scores, and (3) punching the coded information on IBM cards for efficient analysis by high-speed machines.

Scores on each of the fourteen scales were obtained by summing the appropriate weights of the individual items within each scale as described in Chapter II. To obtain the raw scores for most of the scales—all those involving items with a three-point weighting system—a standard IBM Model 805 scoring machine was used. The last four scales in Form II, Social Conformity, Social Isolation, Financial Troubles, and Resentment of Dependency, were all scored by hand rather than machine, using numerical weights of 0, 1, 2, 3, and 4 for the five choices. Although hand-scoring so many thousands of papers was a tedious undertaking requiring a special staff of temporary clerks, the brevity of these four scales made it essential to utilize all the information present in the item responses.

Coding of the information in the face sheet and answer sheets also required a large, temporary staff of trained assistants, for the most part advanced students in sociology, psychology, and education. The coding key developed for this purpose is given in Appendix E.

The first thirteen columns of the IBM card were set aside for identification—geographic area, size of community, school identification number, type of school, size of school, grade, sex, race, age, and a three-digit number for identifying the individual student. The next thirty columns contained additional coded information from the Student Information Blank dealing with such characteristics of the respondent as sex, age, place of birth, status of parents, family structure, education and occupation of father and mother, size of home, and religion. Most of the data from the face sheet could be translated directly into numerical form for keypunching. Several variables, how-ever, did require some care and experience to code properly. Notable among such variables was occupational level. After a review of the various systems of classification for adult occupations, it was decided to use the scheme proposed by Centers.[11] Rather similar to that used by the U. S. Bureau of the Census, Centers' scale of occupational level fits nicely into the ten digits of a single IBM column. Farm laborers were assigned a code number of zero; major executives of large busi-nesses or ranches were given a code number of nine; and the re-mainder were spread out in between.

In addition to personal information from the Student Information Blank, scores from the fourteen scales in Forms I and II also had to be coded by hand before they could be punched on cards for analysis. All raw scores were converted to approximate standard scores so that the frequency distribution for any given scale would have a mean close to five and a standard deviation close to two.[12] The frequency distributions of scale scores obtained in the 1955 pilot study were used as a basis for setting up the conversion tables. Such standardized scores have several advantages over the raw scores. Although the distribution of raw scores may be sharply skewed in one direction or the other, standard scores are more normal in distribution, reducing the likelihood of any serious distortion in results obtained by such statistical methods as product-moment correlation or analysis of vari-ance. Furthermore, if all scale scores are converted to standard scores ranging from zero to nine, the number of IBM columns needed for punching fourteen scale scores is reduced from twenty-eight to four-teen, greatly simplifying later analysis.

After all the desired information had been coded in digital form, it was a simple, though tedious matter to punch three IBM cards for each individual in the study. Data from the Student Information Blank and Forms I and II were punched on Card A. Individuals' item re-sponses from Form III were punched on Cards B and C, together with

[11] Richard Centers, *The Psychology of Social Classes.*

[12] A normalized score with a mean of five and a standard deviation of two is often called a stanine score. The actual mean and standard deviation may differ from these values when the distribution of raw scores is badly skewed, truncated at one end, or drawn from a sample different from the one on which standardiza-tion was done. Procedures for converting raw scores to stanine scores are ably pre-sented in J. Guilford. *Fundamental Statistics in Psychology and Education,* p. 306.

the thirteen-digit identification number so that the different sets of cards could be collated if necessary. Altogether, nearly forty thousand cards had to be key-punched in order to store the basic data for machine analysis.

The use of scales in Forms I and II greatly reduced the necessity of working with individual items as in Form III. Nevertheless, some items of special interest in Forms I and II were not covered in any of the scales and could be analyzed only if punched on cards along with the rest of the data. Responses to fifteen such items [13] were coded and punched in the remaining columns of Card A, leaving eight blank columns at the end of the card to be used as needed in the analysis of data.

Ten months after the first school was approached to participate in the study, responses given by the last of the 12,892 students were coded and punched on standard IBM cards. At last the analysis could proceed as planned.

The Methods of Analysis

Several methods of analysis were employed. These were primarily statistical because of the extensive nature of the data. Some readers may wish to stop here and turn to Appendix A which is a detailed description of the analytical procedures upon which this book is based. Others may prefer to follow a reading of this chapter's brief sketch of methods with the discussion of findings. Again, Appendix A may be used for reference as each chapter is read or each new analytical method introduced. Choice of procedure lies entirely with the reader.

In the sample of the 12,892 cases which were scored, coded, and punched, several minor biases were present in spite of the precautions taken in defining the population and setting up strata throughout the state of Texas for the sampling of high schools. While such biases as were determined in the Texas data are found to be insignificant for many types of analyses, it was important to correct them if one was interested in saying something specific about the general high school population in Texas.

A sample of one thousand cases was carefully selected from the total sample in such a manner that each of the five geographic regions,

[13] Items 12, 16, 21, 29, 30, 33, 47, 53, 58, 62, 72, 85, 100, 168, and 192.

community types, and two racial groups contributed students in exact proportion to population figures obtained from the 1950 census. This sample of one thousand cases could be considered truly representative of high school youth in grades nine through twelve throughout the state of Texas during the spring of 1956, when data were gathered.

The statistical analyses of data were of two general types. The first was the usual descriptive statistics such as means, standard deviations, frequency distributions, and intercorrelations where pertinent for variables obtained on both the face sheet and the instrument scales. The second was a series of rigorously controlled analyses of variance—over two dozen sets of analyses. These were undertaken to test hypotheses about the relationships between personal-family background characteristics of youth and attitudes and personality characteristics as measured by the scales previously enumerated.

For the first type of analysis, the sample of one thousand cases provided an excellent, stable set of data from which one could generalize about the characteristics of youth in Texas high schools. For the second series of statistical studies, special samples were drawn from the entire pool of data in such a way that certain major variables were held constant or were systematically varied as independent variables in the design. In each case, the dependent variables or scores used in these analyses consisted of all fourteen scaled scores plus occasional selected items that had been stored on master IBM cards.

A matrix of 703 different correlation coefficients (all the possible pairs of thirty-eight variables) was developed. Reduction of this large correlation matrix to a small number of general dimensions was achieved by factor analysis. A similar, more rigorous analysis was done on the intercorrelations among the fourteen scale scores and seven background variables, using the principal components method of factoring and an objective rotation method for reaching a final solution. The results of the two analyses were quite similar. A total of nine factors was extracted by the principal components method, of which five had significant loadings on the scales from Forms I and II. Four additional factors were necessary to account for variation in the background information that was analyzed. The detailed results of these factor analyses are presented in full in Appendix A, together with other more technical material concerning research design and statistical methods.

IV: The Families and Their Teen-Age Children

ᴕᴕᴕ

YOUTH VIEWED APART from their families and the settings in which they live offer only segments of the picture. Youth cannot be considered as entities in themselves. Persons of every age are understandable only if seen within the breadth or limitations of their cultural heritage and their social settings. Such a picture will be painted from the background information furnished by the young people who participated in this study.

All families in the United States have much in common. Greater likeness is ever more noticeable as wide dissemination of customs, conventions, and manners take place through easy access to channels of communication. This in no way denies the fact that there still remain distinctive family life styles, beliefs, attitudes, values, and problems arising from subcultural group membership. Both availability of and access to cultural content is sifted through the "social envelope" [1] of racial, ethnic, occupational, educational, religious, and geographic groupings to which families belong.[2]

[1] This is a paraphrase and adaptation of the concept introduced by James S. Plant in *The Envelope*.

[2] Robert L. Sutherland, Julian L. Woodward, and Milton A. Maxwell, *Introductory Sociology*, p. 30.

A LOOK AT THE STATE AS A WHOLE

To gain a clearer understanding of these Texas youth, it is well to look first at the state of which they are a part. Texas, like numerous others in the nation, has changed markedly as it has grown. Only a little over a century ago, it boasted a total population of 212,592 residents.[3] This figure is now typical of single, medium-sized cities and is dwarfed by such metropolitan areas as Houston, Dallas-Fort Worth, and San Antonio. Mid-twentieth century found over 7,700,000 persons living in the state. Even more impressive was the addition of almost a million and a half residents between 1950 and 1957, bringing the total to 9,127,000. This was an 18.4 per cent increase in only seven years.[4]

Another spectacular alteration in the state scene was the increase by one-third in urban citizens during this same seven-year period. Some 6,416,000 men, women, and children lived in communities of over 2,500 by 1957. Urban areas by census definition claimed 70.3 per cent of the total population.[5] Exactly 2 per cent more youth in this study were urban residents than for the population as a whole. Probably this may be credited to the tendency of city youngsters to remain in school a few years more than their rural counterparts.

Not only has the population of Texas grown remarkably, but family size has also increased over the past two decades.[6] Just twenty years before the study was undertaken, the birth rate was 18.0 per 1,000 estimated population. By 1956, the year of collection of this data, it had increased to 27.7 per 1,000. During this same period, the death rate had dropped by some 3 per cent. Families were carrying the major burden of population increase even though immigration was sharing in the process of expansion.[7]

From the cross-sectional and representative sample of one thousand drawn from the 12,892 participants as described in Chapter III, information was obtained about the families which will serve as backdrop for interpretation of the responses of youth to the attitude and problem scales.

[3] *Texas Almanac,* 1958–1959, p. 95.
[4] *Ibid.,* p. 96.
[5] *Ibid.*
[6] Interdepartmental Committee on Children and Youth, "Families Are Larger," in *Children in a Changing World,* Chart 3, p. 5.
[7] *Texas Almanac,* 1958–1959, p. 401.

Native youth, as would be expected, made up the vast majority in schools in 1956. About half were living in the counties in which they had been born. Southeastern United States was the birthplace of about 4.5 per cent. The Mid-West had furnished 5.2 per cent. Western and northeastern sections of the nation had added 3 per cent each of these young citizens. Foreign born, predominantly of Mexican origin, accounted for less than 0.5 per cent.

Texas is noted for its distances and has, therefore, built a vast network of roads. About 90 per cent of the youth reported ownership of cars by their parents. Only a lone 1 per cent did not know whether an automobile was family property. Car ownership and economic adequacy are not too closely correlated in Texas. Transportation in an area as large as this state cannot be classified as a luxury.

TABLE 18: *Family Automobiles and Youthful Drivers* °

Does Family Own Car?	Are You Allowed to Drive?	Percentage
Yes	Yes	71.9
Yes	No	17.8
No	No	3.3
No	Yes	1.1
Unknown	Yes	
Unknown	No	
Yes	Unknown	0.4
No	Unknown	4.9
Unknown	Unknown	0.6

° Based on the 1,000-case sample.

Data presented thus far have given some indication of the complexity of the setting in which these youth were reared. Even more detail will serve as basis for clarification of some of the findings to be reported later.

Sons and Daughters of Twentieth-Century Parents

Parents of youth in the study were relatively young. Extremes in age were assumed to range from some in their early thirties to an even smaller number in the early sixties. Relatively few women under age fifteen bear children. Relatively few over forty bring infants into the world. Husbands are often somewhat older than their wives. Parents of high school youth are in their most productive years in their ability to contribute to the economic and social wealth of their society.

More children were found in these families than for the population as a whole within the state. Moreover, both parents and their children, with very few exceptions, were products of the twentieth century. They were quite literally families *of* a rapidly changing technological and scientific age. Reflected in them one would expect to find tensions due to intensified urbanization, high mobility, rapid communication, and incessant change, as well as the pressures of unremitting cold war. And no doubt these factors were reflected in the attitudes and problems of sons and daughters of these families, though not in an unusually high percentage of broken homes.

Intact Families in Abundance

Data from these secondary school youth revealed that over 77 per cent of them lived with both parents. Obviously the majority of marriages in these families had survived for sixteen years or better since the youngest age group consisted of only one-tenth under fifteen years. Divorce had taken place in about 10 per cent of the families; separations were limited to only 2 per cent and death had removed 5 per cent of the fathers and 3 per cent of the mothers. Full orphans numbered only one in a thousand cases.

TABLE 19: *Marital Status of the Parents* *

Parents' Marital Status	Percentage of Youth Reporting
Living together	77.4
Separated	1.9
Divorced	10.8
Mother not living	2.8
Father not living	4.9
Both not living	0.1
Unknown	2.1

* Based on the 1,000-case sample.

Family composition was anticipated to have meaningful bearing upon the attitudes and problems encountered in growing up. Almost 90 per cent of the youth lived with their own parents or one own parent and their full brothers and sisters, which is not far from the national picture. Half brothers and sisters were found in less than 5 per cent of the families, with a minimal number reporting one or more step-brothers or sisters. Both of these latter categories indicate remarriage of parents. A combination of half siblings and stepsiblings was found in so few cases they are hardly worthy of mention.

The number of youth living with grandparents, guardians, or in orphanages—all of these variations from nuclear family structure—was under 5 per cent. Represented in the random sample was a small number of students attending public high schools while living in two separate orphanages located in different communities.

Families—Large and Small

Family size covered a wide range and offered possibility for detailed comparison of youngsters from large and small families. Families with two or three children accounted for approximately 20 per cent each. Only children and families with four young members each numbered a little over one-tenth. Larger families, so often cited as preferable for child rearing by those who tend to see superiority in past culture patterns, accounted for 28.5 per cent. "Larger families" as here used included those with five or more children. High school youth in almost 5 per cent of the families had eight or more brothers and sisters—large families by any count! Older brothers and sisters were listed by almost three-fourths, and younger brothers and sisters were found alongside 84 per cent of these teen-agers.

TABLE 20: *Relationship of Youth to Their Siblings*

Number of Siblings	Percentages of Youth with				
	Older Brothers	Older Sisters	Younger Brothers	Younger Sisters	Both Brothers and Sisters
0	59.3	58.2	51.7	55.0	12.1
1	17.7	22.1	26.1	24.5	21.9
2	9.9	7.4	11.1	11.1	20.8
3	4.5	4.7	4.2	3.4	11.5
4	2.4	1.8	1.5	1.3	8.7
5	0.8	0.8	0.5	0.3	6.6
6	—	0.1	—	—	5.0
7	0.1	—	—	—	3.8
8	—	—	0.1	0.1	1.7
9 or more	0.1	0.1	0.1	0.1	2.7
Unknown	5.2	4.9	4.8	4.8	5.2

Whenever other than members of the nuclear family are found in homes, an important factor indicative of variations in cultural participation has been added. Since three-generation families in urban settings are still comparatively rare, grandparents in the household take on added significance. Lone grandmothers were found more frequently than lone grandfathers, a further indication of the differential death rate between men and women. A pair of grandparents was found living with less than 2 per cent of the families of high school youth. Dual grandfathers were encountered equally as often as two grandmothers within families.

A very few families had all four grandparents living under the same roof with their own children and their grandchildren. Complications appear inevitable when two different parental families of an elder generation are found in the same household with their son or daughter and their children's children. Divergent attitudes and behavior, not only of three generations, but of two distinctive families of oldsters would appear to furnish fertile ground for emotional involvement and social turmoil. Chances are good that economic inadequacy for any other type of care is also present, which would serve to add to intra-family tension.

Because of the paucity of information previously available on youth who reside with their parents and one or more grandparents, analysis of three-generation data held special significance. Some unexpected results will be recorded in a later chapter.

Only about one youth in twenty reported one or more relatives, other than grandparents, as household members. Even fewer indicated that outsiders lived in their homes.

Education and Occupation—Paramount Measures of Sociocultural Group Membership

Opportunities for broad participation in culture, for optimum growth and development, and for variety in experiences during formative years are intricately intertwined with the social strata in which families function. Opportunities, in turn, are largely derived from the educational and occupational level of parents. How important these variables were in the lives of youth will be continuously revealed throughout this report.

No formal schooling of any kind was reported for 2 per cent of the fathers of these high school youth and for an equal percentage of mothers. These men and women belonged to all ethnic and racial groups in the state. Access to the prevailing national culture, in the broadest sense, is conditioned for the lowest status group by lack of ability to communicate, limited knowledge, and poverty of perception, as well as minimal skills and consequent inadequacy of occupation and income.

TABLE 21: *Education of Parents as Reported*

Highest Level of Education Achieved	Fathers (%)	Mothers (%)
No school	1.9	2.2
Grades 1–4	8.3	3.5
Grades 5–8	26.6	20.6
Grades 9–11	23.6	27.3
High School	20.8	28.0
Some College	6.1	5.8
Junior College	1.3	1.3
4-Year College	6.8	6.0
Business College, County Veterans' School, or other	0.7	1.5
Unknown	4.3	3.8

Evidence that years of formal education are closely related to ability to earn and to available job opportunities has been pointed out in a study by the United States Department of Labor.[8] Median incomes from full-time employment in 1956, the year of this study, showed the closeness of the correlation of years in school to earning capacity. Men and women with less than eight years of academic training reported an average income of $3,120 and $1,811, respectively. Those who had completed eight years, or the equivalent of junior high school, earned $4,035 and $2,408. High school graduates, or those with twelve years of formal classroom experience, earned incomes of a little more than half again as much as did those men and women who had finished less than eight grades. Senior high school education can be measured as a tangible economic and cultural asset. Now high school graduation as minimum education is almost mandatory because of technological demands upon workers and the radical decrease in semi-skilled and unskilled jobs.

College women who had finished a full four years reported median

[8] U. S. Department of Labor, "Income and Education, 1956," in *1958 Handbook of Women Workers*, Table 3, p. 54.

incomes of $3,809 per year, as compared to $6,980 for men on the same educational level. These figures present the impact of years of school attendance on income for the nation rather than Texas. However, the proportional difference in income between educational levels should not be appreciably different for the state than for the nation as a whole.

The pervasive determining character of parental education as a socioeconomic factor in the family is well illustrated by the interrelationship among five variables: father's education; mother's education; father's occupation; size of the family; and number of rooms in the house. The occupational level of the father is, in part, a function of the father's education (correlation of 0.48). A slight negative relationship (about –0.20) exists between size of family and either education or occupational level of father or mother—larger families tend to go with lower education of parents. More important, the size of the family has no relationship to the size of the house in which the family lives. Only the educational and occupational level of parents show any appreciable correlation with the number of rooms in the house. Once again, this points up the importance of education as a vehicle for improving the socioeconomic status and the level of cultural participation of the family, whether in terms of material conveniences and comforts or in terms of "learned human adjustments" which make for ease in relationships, or as reflected in the attainment of goals held as of value in society.

One further important segment of parents supplied evidence of severe limitations in education. This group included 10 per cent of the fathers and 6 per cent of the mothers who had had less than four years in school, again at the poverty level of either cultural or economic assets.

These men and women lacked the fundamentals upon which to continue their self-education, save in rare and unusual instances. How educational level of parents, geared as it is to occupation, earning capacity, and involvement in culture, is closely allied to child-rearing practices has been reported in a recent study. Significant correlations between child training and education of mothers have been revealed by Sears, Maccoby, and Levin in their book, *Patterns of Child Rearing*. Physical punishment, withdrawal of love, use of ridicule, pressure for neatness and orderliness, and even rejection of children by mothers were found more often among women of lower educational attainment. The fewer the years in school which the mothers have had, the more likely they were to follow rigid child-rearing practices.[9] Whether the Texas study would lend substance to these findings was a teasing question. In addition, it is common knowledge among school administrators that regular attendance at school is largely dependent upon motivation of children and youth by parents. Support in keeping children in school has to do with parents' academic achievement and over-all attitudes toward education.

Even at the beginning of this report, these disclosures by high school students hold a hopeful note. A goodly number of children from parents of even this culturally limited group were still in school. In fact, they remained as students in the last four years of high school, a level of education their parents had been unable to achieve. Herein is illustrated a major strength in an open-class society. Young persons can and do begin their adult careers standing upon the shoulders of their parents who were denied educational opportunity for one reason or another. Because of the philosophy of the United States which includes *all* the children of *all* the people in its educational obligation and supports this obligation with compulsory attendance laws, a closed-social-class system remains on far distant horizons. A more selective or more exclusive policy for school attendance would tend to hold children to the same subcultural group membership attained by their parents—a concept which still runs counter to the democratic values and basic philosophy of this nation. This is especially true for Texas with the remaining vestiges of its frontier tradition.

Parent Occupations and Youth Opportunities

Texas is often described as a state with great wealth and astronomical incomes.[10] Facts deny this current fiction. Professions and large business enterprises, in reality, were the occupations of one in fourteen of the fathers of high school youth. Owners and managers of farms, men who owned or ran small businesses, and those in white-collar jobs, by way of contrast, furnished employment for about one-third of the fathers of these young persons. Even larger was the number of men working in semi-skilled or skilled manual occupa-

[9] Robert R. Sears, Eleanor E. Maccoby, and Harry Levin, *Patterns of Child Rearing*, p. 532. Also see Lee Rainwater, Richard P. Coleman, and Gerald Handel, *Workingman's Wife*.

[10] John Bainbridge, *The Super-Americans*.

tions—about four out of ten. The remainder of these male heads of households were farm laborers, tenants, or unskilled workers. Here again is an encouraging note. The 12.3 per cent known to be employed in the lowest socioeconomic bracket, the 1 per cent who were unemployed, and the 14 per cent whose occupations were unknown would not have been reported had not their sons and daughters been in school in the ninth grade or better.

TABLE 22: *Parental Occupations* *

Kind of Occupation	Fathers (%)	Mothers (%)
Farm Laborers	3.7	0.5
Unskilled Manual Laborers	7.8	2.3
Farm Tenants	0.8	0
Semi-Skilled Manual Laborers	13.4	10.2
Skilled Manual Laborers	22.0	4.4
Farm Owners and Managers	11.2	0.3
White-Collar Workers	10.9	13.9
Owners of Small Businesses	10.2	1.2
Professional Workers	4.6	3.4
Owners of Large Businesses	0.5	0.1
Homemakers (Mothers Only)	0	59.3
Unemployed	1.0	0
Unknown	13.9	4.5

* Based on the 1,000-case sample.

Whether full-time homemakers or working mothers make better parents is a subject for debate. Only 59 per cent of the mothers of these youth devoted full time to their homes. Employed in a variety of occupations were approximately 35 per cent of the women, with a little less than 5 per cent unaccounted for as to employment status.

Approximately 30 per cent of the mothers with children eighteen years of age or under were in the labor force in the United States at the time of this study, which indicates that some 70 per cent with children in this age range were full-time homemakers. When the percentage of youth who did not check the occupations of their mothers is added to the number of full-time homemakers listed in the Texas group, this still leaves a 7 per cent plurality above the national figure for mothers who were employed outside the home. Perhaps the larger number of mothers working outside the home in Texas may be accounted for by those in domestic and other unskilled services. Whatever the reason, over one-third of the mothers of these high school youth shared in earning the family income.

Mothers who were professionals or in large business enterprises were nearest in proportion to these same occupational classifications for fathers. School teaching, no doubt, claimed the largest number of professional women, and those in business enterprises were minimal. About half as many women as men were listed in the categories of white-collar workers, small business heads, and farm managerial and ownership positions.

Semi-skilled and skilled manual labor described the work of about 14 per cent of the mothers as compared to a little over a third of the fathers. The greatest difference in number for men and women in an occupational group was among the lowest income jobs. Over five times more fathers than mothers earned an income in this minimal bracket.

"Elbow Room" and Family Requirements

Size of home, it was surmised, would have an important bearing upon family living. Moreover, the size of home offers added evidence of family status. Family tension among youth was correlated with the number of persons living in their households. Family problems were also correlated with occupants in the home. However, problems of relationship were reported less frequently than family tension. "Getting on each other's nerves" is reality for those who must live in close quarters. It must be pointed out that some larger dwellings, especially on farms and in interstitial areas within cities, may afford adequate space while still falling within the definition of substandard housing.

TABLE 23: *Number of Rooms in Homes* °

Number of Rooms	Percentage of Youth
1	0.2
2	0.2
3	1.5
4	7.1
5	17.8
6	24.7
7	21.6
8	12.5
9	12.9
Unknown	1.5

° Based on the 1,000-case sample.

Number of rooms alone does not always signify opportunity for privacy or adequacy of space necessary for relaxed and comfortable living. "Elbow room," or the number of persons in proportion to the number of rooms in the house, is the determining factor. Families of high school youth averaged 4.86 persons per household, which is about 1.5 persons more per house than for the United States as a whole in 1955.[11] Texas is one of the seven states in the nation with the highest concentration of children.[12]

High school youngsters live in houses their parents can afford rather than in space sufficient for family size. The ideal arrangement, of course, would be to have a larger house for the larger family, but such is not the case. No correlation was found between the number of persons in the home and the number of rooms the house contained. The size of the house did correlate, however, with the socioeconomic level of the family as measured either by father's education or occupation.

"A place of one's own" is supposed to be of real significance to youth in their formative adolescent years. Opportunity for privacy and the possibility of occasional solitude are considered near essentials. Whether this was true or not was worth consideration. The information in Table 24 on the number of persons sharing a bedroom with high-school students offers background for later findings on this point.

TABLE 24: *Number of Persons Sharing Bedroom with Youth* *

Number of Persons	Percentage of Youth
0	57.5
1	29.3
2	8.3
3	2.6
4	1.0
5	0.1
6	0.3
7	. .
8	. .
9 or more	0.1
Unknown	0.8

* Based on the 1,000-case sample.

[11] *Statistical Abstract of the United States, 1956*, p. 49.

[12] Interdepartmental Committee on Children and Youth, "Families are Larger," Chart 4, p. 6.

From these variations in family life, in homes, in social and economic status, in cultural adequacy and inadequacy came the youth in this study. How they responded according to their backgrounds and their opportunities, and what they have reported as their problems, attitudes, and interests may prove of significance both to their state and their nation.

Youth Reflect Their Families

Young persons are not all alike any more than are their families. Even cursory observation reveals a variety of subgroupings. This study will add irrefutable evidence that problems and attitudes of youth can be neither studied successfully nor understood apart from the cultural context of their families and their other associates. Youth are within a given age range, say the early 'teens to the twenties. The majority share the common experience of some high school attendance. Moreover, they are exposed in varying degrees to the American value structure.[13] How these values are expressed in their lives remains a matter of the extent to which their families have had opportunity to realize the American Dream.

Before the dissipation of drudgery by the shift from physical lift to machine power, man passed through only three periods in his lifetime—childhood, maturity, and old age. Infants were born into large families and soon became the charge of older children. Children were put to work as soon as possible and were considered economic resources. Child labor still occurs in some social classes in the nation, particularly among agricultural laborers and migrant workers. Under heavy labor, persons deteriorated in early maturity and moved on into old age prematurely.

In contrast with the above, infants are today, more often than not, planned for and enjoyed.[14] What is demanded of children is conditioned by the knowledge parents have of the slow processes of physical, emotional, and social development as it extends into adolescence.[15] The years of youth hold sway for the majority of families from the

[13] Robin M. Williams, Jr., *American Society: A Sociological Interpretation,* Chapter XI, pp. 397–470.

[14] Ronald Freedman, Pascal K. Whelpton, and Arthur A. Campbell, *Family Planning Sterility and Population Growth,* pp. 220–226.

[15] Robert J. Havighurst, "Adolescence," in *Human Development and Education,* Part 3, Chapters 9–15.

early teens to the twenties before they become family earners. A long, relatively free period of growth and development is one of the luxuries of an urban and technological age. "Young adults" and "middle years" offer recognition of membership in other relatively new and discrete age groupings. Designation as elders does not usually come until the seventh decade.

In spite of significant variations in youth response by the socio-economic group membership of their families and other background characteristics, an analysis of certain items was made for the sample as a whole. From these were derived some common denominators for youth in the study.

YOUTH GIVE ANSWERS TO SOME BASIC QUESTIONS

No attempt was made to discover "youth in conflict" or "youth in trouble." This was not a study of deviation or delinquency. However, it is recognized that in a representative sample of 12,892 high school students, youngsters are found with a variety of problems. A number of trouble spots have been revealed in these simple percentages. Others remain hidden. On the whole, though, youth in this study should be seen as youngsters functioning well enough to remain as a part of high school student bodies. Otherwise their comments would not have been recorded.

Respondents were from all geographic regions of the state. They came from communities of varying sizes and locations. They represented the proportion of white and Negro youth in the population. They were in proper ratio to the number in their age range. Classes utilized were designated by school administrators as the most representative age-sex-grade groupings in the schools. This sample was as close to an accurate delineation of the total high school youth in Texas in 1956 as was attainable.[16]

Teen-Age Attitudes toward Parents

Most young persons appear to value their parents highly and are evidently thoughtful of their future. This came to light in the agreement among youth—73 per cent—that they feel it their duty to care for their parents when they grow old. A meagre one-tenth implied they felt no obligation toward elderly family members.

[16] See Chapter III for a description of the drawing of this sample.

When youth were questioned as to whether parents should sacrifice everything for their children, the majority did not concur. Over three-fourths disagreed with the idea that parenthood required complete selflessness.

Equality in responsibility between fathers and mothers in home-making and parenthood had widespread acceptance—80 per cent. Youth from modern families appear to believe in "togetherness" as far as their own homes are concerned. Less than one-tenth indicated that they retained the older idea of mother's assuming full responsibility for homemaking and major accountability for parenthood. The great majority felt that it was important for father to be other than "a guest in his own home." They expected him to share in household tasks, shopping, and other aspects of homemaking; but they were not as certain mother should contribute to dual wage earning for the family.

Approximately 40 per cent of the youngsters agreed that, "A wife shouldn't have to earn part of the family income." About one-third, however, implied by their disagreement that the wife should help supplement family finances. Those who agreed upon the principle of dual-earning approximated the percentage of youth whose mothers were actually employed outside the home. Whether these were the same youth was not statistically determined.

Youth Comment on Early Marriage

Whether high school marriages were considered a disaster or an opportunity by youth was investigated. Again, whether their responses to discrete items would serve as an accurate prelude to the findings from a more detailed analysis of the responses of married high school students remained a question. The final chapter in this study reveals the answer to this latter question. Popular opinion would seem to indicate that marriage has cut deeply into high school years. However, between 1950 and 1960, the percentage of teen-age youth throughout the nation who were married dropped slightly from 9 to 8 per cent.[17] The actual number of marriages has increased because of the increase in this age group within the population. The median age for brides had decreased from 21.5 years to 20.4 years and for grooms from 23.9 to 23.2 years between 1950 and 1956 for the nation as a whole. This

[17] Eleanor H. Bernert, "Demographic Trends," in *The Family and Social Change,* p. 48.

downward shift is part of a long range trend.[18] Only a fraction above 1 per cent of the students in the study reported themselves married, while 96.6 per cent indicated they were single. The remaining 2 per cent did not respond.

Contrary to the expectations of anxious adults, approximately 75 per cent of the students labeled as false the statement that, "I would like to get married as soon as possible." The one in seven who agreed that they would like to marry in the immediate future showed higher scores on the Family Problem scale. To them, escape from the parental family probably appeared desirable. However, when three-fourths of a representative teen-age population do not desire marriage in the immediate future, it may be assumed that there is no rush toward the altar among high school students.

The great majority of youth did not agree that "High school marriages only lead to trouble." They were relatively sure about this, though not to the degree of certainty they expressed regarding the lack of appeal of immediate marriage for themselves. About half felt that "trouble" was not necessarily concomitant with high school marriage. Almost a third were not certain how they reacted. Just under one-fifth agreed that this was a true statement.

In spite of current policies of some boards of education toward married girls in high schools, youth themselves do not support the idea that, "Whenever a girl marries, she should drop out of high school." Over two-thirds felt that married girls should be allowed to continue their education. Less than one-fifth agreed that the girl should quit school. This small fraction was approximately the same number who agreed that high school marriages could only lead to trouble. The undecided group was fewer in number on this query (15 per cent), about half as many as compared with those who could not decide whether high school marriages were fraught with problems.

Closely related to attitudes and concerns about early marriage, but of a somewhat different order was the item, "A girl who gets into trouble on a date has no one to blame but herself." The double standard appeared to hold for half of the high-school youth. They agreed that full responsibility rested upon the girl. By disagreeing with this statement, about a third indicated their acceptance of

[18] U. S. Department of Health, Education and Welfare, "Marriages: Detailed Statistics for Reporting Areas, 1956," in *Vital Statistics—Special Reports: National Summaries*, Vol. 48 (October, 1958), No. 16, p. 432.

mutual responsibility between the boy and girl for behavior on dates. The remainder were uncertain about how they felt.

Though little attention was devoted to questions concerning sex, two statements were included as relevant. Young persons were asked if they would agree, "It is not the duty of the parent to teach the child about sex." A resounding denial was voiced by nearly 80 per cent. The minimal one-tenth who agreed and the other one-tenth who were undecided were only small voices in opposition to an overwhelming majority.

To determine the concern of these youth with sex, they were requested to reply to the statement, "I think about sex a good deal of the time." Nearly half said this statement was false or did not apply to them. Another third answered that this was true but of little or no concern to them. Reticence in indicating their true feelings about this question might account in part for this response. Only slightly over one-fifth reported that they thought about sex a good part of the time, and that this did give them real concern.

Youth and Their Church Preferences

Religious faith of young persons and their attitudes toward church membership are areas for considerable speculation. Since these youth were attending public schools, listing of church preference was entirely voluntary. In spite of the optional nature of this item, over 90 per cent complied with the request by writing in the denomination of their choice. Their responsiveness thus laid the basis for an intensive series of analyses of differences in youth responses concerning attitudes and problems by denominational groupings.

TABLE 25: *Religious Preferences*

Denomination or Faith	Percentage of Youth Reporting
Baptist	41.3
Methodist	16.6
Catholic	11.5
Other (Small denominational groups)	9.1
Christian (Disciples and Church of Christ)	5.6
Presbyterian	2.8
Lutheran	2.8
Episcopal	1.0
Jewish	0.1
No Preference	1.8
Unknown	7.3

When high school students were confronted with the assertion that, "There is too little concern in my family for religion," their denial was positive. Three-fourths of them disagreed. Less than 10 per cent were undecided upon this point. The remainder did indicate they considered their families lax in religious interest.

Denominational differences were not considered to be insurmountable in marriage by the majority. The statement, "People of different religions should not get married," was agreed to by only one-fifth, with another fifth uncertain about it. The large majority of youth did not concur with this idea.

The Desire of Youth to Go to College

If the attitudes of young persons in high schools are relevant to the future enrollment trends in colleges and universities, then planning for expansion may be even more imperative than previous forecasts have suggested. Close to three-fourths of the youth agreed that, "Having an opportunity to go to college is very important to me." The word "very" in this statement should be noted. Only 15 per cent were not interested, and slightly over 10 per cent were uncertain or undecided.

The desire for higher education obviously over-reached the possibility of its achievement by all who wished it. Only about half of the high school graduates in Texas now go to college. Nonetheless, it is encouraging that in this era when stress is being placed on advanced study as imperative for the nation's future growth and security, as many as three-fourths of these high school students were concerned with more education than high schools afford. Assistance for many to be able to achieve their desire is more than a hypothetical need.

OTHER CHARACTERISTICS OF YOUTH

Close to the family in influence upon the processes of socialization and development during youth years are their schools and their work experience, at home or on jobs. The school is important not only because of its formal educational function, but also because of the climate of learning and the associations it furnishes. More and more attention is also being given to the quality of performance of students in school, particularly high school. Many factors influence such performance and also school attendance itself. Therefore, school size and student work load were considered important background information essential for interpretation of data furnished by youngsters.

When entrance to colleges or universities is taken into account, the size of high schools which these youth attended takes on even greater significance. Schools with under three hundred students took care of the educational needs of 46 per cent of the youth included in the study. The larger high schools, from seven to fifteen hundred or over, had an enrollment of 40 per cent of the group. The in-between schools of three to seven hundred accounted for only 14 per cent. James B. Conant has commented upon the problems which small schools encounter in giving adequate educational opportunity and college preparation to youth.[19] On the other hand, it should be recognized that problems of mass education exist when schools are very large. In Texas, it is the small and large high schools which carry the heaviest enrollment, with those in the middle range accounting for fewer students.

A little over one-third of the youth rode buses to and from school each day. The time indicated for travel ranged from less than twenty minutes for two-thirds to forty minutes or more for over a tenth.

Types of schools in which Texas youth were enrolled in the spring of 1956 were indicative of the changing social situation. White high schools accounted for 71 per cent of the students at the high school level. Negro schools had enrolled 12 per cent of the study total. Integrated schools were already taking care of 17 per cent of the high school population.

The age range in the four high school grades under consideration displayed a wide span—from thirteen to twenty years.

TABLE 26: *Age Range of High School Students*

Age	Percentage of Youth
13 and under	0.7
14 years	9.8
15 years	24.2
16 years	26.0
17 years	21.3
18 years	13.6
19 years	3.7
20 years	0.5
21 years	0
Unknown	0.2

[19] James B. Conant, *The American High School Today*, pp. 77–84.

Youth in the public high schools do not confine their activities to being students or to extra-curricular affairs. That they are "youth of leisure" is refuted by the report of three-fourths of the girls and two-thirds of the boys who gave an affirmative reply to the question concerning work at home. The over-all picture shows that 70 per cent of these young people spent sufficient time doing chores and other tasks at home to consider it "work." Employment for wages away from home, after school, was indicated by 39 per cent of the total.

Youth who helped support their families while attending high school included 7 per cent of the girls and 18 per cent of the boys. Of *all* students, 12 per cent shared in earning the family income, while 82 per cent indicated that they did not. The remainder gave no reply.

IN SUMMARY

These general results based on background data and individual items of special interest give a brief montage of youth and their families as they participated in the study. They were from homes established by oldtimers and newcomers, of varied ethnic origins, and of white and Negro races. Their parents ran the gamut in education from a minimal 2 per cent for both mothers and fathers who had no formal schooling to three times that number for each sex who had graduated from college. Occupations from which parents of these youngsters earned their family incomes ranged from unskilled labor to professions and large-business management. By far the majority came from families of the middle class, lower to upper. As later analyses will disclose, a close link exists between the attitudes, problems, concerns, and interests of youth, on the one hand, and the accessibility of cultural enrichment available through their families, on the other. Distinctive responses of high school students, because of the sociocultural experiences open to them, lend emphasis to a differential in adequacy among them for the adult tasks which they will face.

V: Where Youth Live and How They Respond

ʊʊʊ

SIMPLE GEOGRAPHIC DETERMINISM has long since been held invalid by social and behavioral science. However, the location and natural resources plus the culture of a region, a community, or even a neighborhood, shape the pattern of behavior of families and children. Adequacies and limitations of social institutions and socio-economic organization do contribute to distinctions

Texas makes no claim to be a microcosm of the nation. If it did, however, it could offer some documentation for this assumption. Its population is heterogeneous in origin and in its more recent immigration. The state has unusual breadth and diversity in its social and economic life. For these reasons, findings from this youth study may prove useful to other regions in the United States.

THE GEOGRAPHIC DIVISIONS OF TEXAS

The impact of an area upon youth responses can be best understood against a description of the five regions which are Texas. Moreover, such description will illustrate further the applicability of the data to many other parts of the country.

"The Old South" in Texas

East Texas was the home region of 13.2 per cent of the young persons. What remains of the "Old South" in attitudes and customs is to be found within its confines. What is developing as the "New South" is also illustrated within its boundaries.

Oil and gas have been discovered under the red soil of the area, with its forest cover of pine and oak, sweet gum and holly. However, East Texas is still primarily rural. Farms are "family farms" worked by owners, their tenants, and their "hands." As in the Deep South, former plantations have been broken into stock farms with less cotton and more pasture. Cut-over lands are being "planted" as new pine forests with grazing between the young seedlings. Though today's sawmills are mere shadows of their former size, lumber remains a steady source of income. This is particularly true since paper mills have been constructed.

Industries in East Texas are relatively young and few, but they are the hope of the region. No metropolitan areas are found within its confines, but it has a number of cities both beautiful and prosperous. Towns and villages show the economic inroads of city centers. Trade is no longer a matter of team-haul but is measured in terms of air strips or in automobile miles on fast highways.

About half the population is Anglo-Saxon of old-line stock. In this area also is found the largest proportion of Negroes to whites. As is true of its counterpart, the Southeast, some of its counties continue to lose population to the industrial Gulf Coast and to the more prosperous Central Texas region. East Texas remains traditional in many of its attitudes and in its politics. Cultural lag may be found in some of its economic and social developments, but decreasingly so. Financial limitations, outside of areas rich in oil and gas, show up in some of its schoolhouses and churches and in the level of family living.

The Industrial Coast

Next-door neighbor on the south to the rural region of East Texas is the booming, teeming, aggressive, industrial and metropolitan Gulf Coast. One-fourth of the youth of the state had their places of residence in this area which runs from the tip of East Texas along the Gulf of Mexico to Corpus Christi. Within the coastal strip is suburbia with its bedroom communities. This area has many active seaports, with oil and chemical industries dotting the landscape. Its latest acquisition is the National Air Space Administration's complex industry designed to probe the moon and the planets. National and

international trade are a crucial part of the region's economy. The
population is made up of native Texas whites, native Negroes, and
an ever-increasing stream of persons from other sections of the nation.
As one moves west toward Corpus Christi, the proportion of persons
having Mexican origin increases.

The Gulf Coast is the epitome of rapid urbanization and industriali-
zation. However, side by side with the cities and the industry are to
be found coastal-plains ranches of rich grasslands, rice farms of high
productivity, and petro-chemical establishments of tremendous size.
The old and the new are blending with all the growing pains which
accompany expansion and change. Traditionalism and conservatism of
the past attempt to hold firm against the inroads of the modern and
the different. Labor organizations have gained a hold even as business
and industry become more deeply entrenched. Here is a region in
which is found the mixed influence upon youth of city living, suburban residence, and the residue of rural life.

South Texas with Its Irrigated Valleys

The irrigated valleys of South Texas account for the smallest proportion of the youth population in the study. This region begins below
San Antonio and runs from the Winter Garden on the north to the
Rio Grande Valley on the Mexican border. Then it continues west to
Del Rio. Agricultural production of fruits and vegetables along with
some irrigated cotton is its economic base. Here is an "urban" agriculture with high income for owners and processors, and low and
intermittent pay for field and shed workers.

Many of the residents are of Mexican heritage, a fact which
accounts in part for the small proportion of young persons included
in the sample from this region. Youth from families of rural Mexican
descent tend not to finish high school. Indeed, until recently, few of
them ever entered the higher grades. Mexican braceros are imported
across the border each year as migrant laborers for seasonal work.
Negroes in South Texas are few and longer established than the
braceros. They are apt to be of a higher income level than many of
the Mexican laborers. This difference has also been true of Negroes
in San Antonio over many decades. However, there is a growing
middle class among the Mexican-Americans as members of this group
become established in small businesses and in the professions.
Ranchers in this area have been Texans for generations. Most farm

owners, processors, and business men are natives of the immediate area. Some have come from other sections of the state. A few decades ago the Middle West contributed many migrants who took advantage of irrigation to establish citrus groves, truck gardens, and cotton farms. Though many of the first families suffered financially, some stayed on to succeed in the second try.

Soil in the valleys is rich. Yield is abundant when water is available. Those who make a living there keep an eye on the weather which may bring rich harvests or disaster to gardens and orchards. Covering additional thousands upon thousands of acres in South Texas are the famous King and Kenedy ranches and many others of lesser fame. While this is an area of economic strength, it has the problems of every region with a large population of low earners and with language and ethnic differences in its social system.

The Center of the State

Busy, bustling Central Texas runs from San Antonio northward to the Red River. It encompasses the area from the pine forests on the east to the geological fault line west of San Antonio and Austin where it borders on the vast open lands of the hills and plains. Heavily populated, this section accounted for 41.8 per cent of the youth in the study.

People in Central Texas are remnants of early settlers under all six of the flags which have flown over the state. Their multiple heritage includes the Spanish and Mexican, the French, the German, Czech, and Swedish, the Anglo, and the Negro. And this does not exhaust the list. Old South and frontier West have left their marks on the peoples and their institutions. This is a region which is South and West, in fact.

Cosmopolitan natives and immigrants began building metropolitan centers early, as trade and shipping combined with military settlement. Crops were rich from the black wax soil found on the eastern border of this Central area. Cattle, sheep, and goats helped build ranches of substance on its western edge. The ranches brought growth to San Antonio, Fort Worth, and smaller cities. Waco, Dallas, and lesser cities to the north and east had their beginnings on the largesse of blackland farms. While Dallas and Fort Worth are only thirty minutes and thirty miles apart by super-highways, they are as distinctive as the New South and the Old West. Austin gained its strength as the state capital and as an educational and trade-association center.

Since World War II, industry and manufacturing have surrounded the metropolitan areas of Central Texas. Strong trade centers have been reinforced with new wealth. Commerce with Mexico and Central and South America is as old as settlement itself. The military has played an important role in this area. This has been true from the days of frontier Indian forts to the present. Large airfields and training camps are firmly established on its soil.

The Vast Western Lands

West Texas, with its many miles and fewer people, is the region from which 16.9 per cent of the Texas youth came. Ranches and oil fields vie for occupation of the rolling plains and broken country. Irrigated valleys surround El Paso, a city with a difference, and are important to the economy of the far western reaches of the area. Irrigated farms of hundreds of acres are to the north. They produce great storehouses of grains and cotton. A section with income among the highest in the nation is centered around Amarillo and Borger, where petro-chemical plants light the night sky like giant amusement parks.

West Texas is an area of rich lands and of waste lands. The people are of sturdy Anglo-Saxon and Scandinavian pioneer stock with a small scattering of Negroes and some residents of Mexican heritage. Migrant workers come in for the harvest season. At the same time mechanical cotton pickers and great combines work the flat fields. Young and healthy cities and prosperous small towns are set wide apart where space is at no premium. This is the true West of the Southwest.

These are the regions from which the youth come. These, in combination, with all their diversity, all of their problems of growth and deterioration, with all their complexities of change and readjustment, make up the state of Texas. The people are of every lineage of which the nation boasts. The families are of oldtimers and newcomers. They represent a variety of ethnic origins and the white and Negro races. They are a part of the regions in which they live, supported or deprived by the institutions which have been available for their growth and development. These regions of Texas are not too different from those which blend into the nation as a whole.

REGIONAL VARIATIONS IN YOUTH RESPONSES

Regional differences in youth responses were measured by comparison of gross mean scores on only four selected scales. These included Orientation to Society and Authoritarian Discipline, both attitude measurement. Problem scales included Family Tension and Resentment of Family Life Style. These particular choices were made for regional analysis because they were relatively independent of each other. They also covered the major variances noted in the correlation matrix and the factor analyses. The one-thousand-case representative sample of youth was used. No socioeconomic factors other than region were controlled. Perhaps it is well to note that while the regional differences indicated in Figures 2, 3, 4, and 5 are not very great, they do remain statistically significant enough to warrant some passing comment.

A Look at Their World—Orientation to Society

West Texas youth exhibited the highest degree of optimism and of confidence of any in the state as measured by the scale on Orientation to Society. Young persons in East Texas, on the other hand, were the least hopeful of the future and least trustful of people in general. Undoubtedly many variables interact to produce these regional differences.[1]

West and East Texas are contrasts in urbanization and mechanization. The former derives its higher income from irrigated lands, farmed with the latest equipment adapted to mass production, and has several areas of rich industrial development. The latter, in spite of the rapid changes which it is undergoing, retains older patterns of agricultural production and is less urbanized on the whole. The population of West Texas is of the predominant ethnic group with few Negroes and Mexicans. The eastern section of the state carries the largest proportion of Negro population, with the conditional factor

---

[1] Figure 2 is the first of many charts illustrating a significant relationship between a background characteristic or independent variable (in this case region of the state) and youth response or dependent variable (in this case mean scores on Orientation to Society). The general trend shown by the relationship presents a simplified illustration that can be quickly grasped once the standard form of the chart is understood. In these graphs the vertical axis consists of mean score on the response variable in question, while the horizontal axis designates the categories of the independent variable.

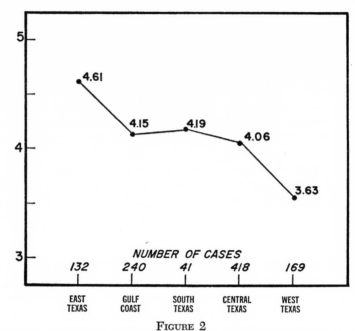

FIGURE 2

East Texas More Pessimistic in Orientation to Society than Other Areas

of minority status looming large among many of its peoples. The residue of the tragic contrast in East Texas between the historical status of the plantation owner, the tenant farmer of either race, and the field hand remains at least one source of a more pessimistic outlook on life among numbers of young persons.

Attitudes toward Authority

Concepts of discipline displayed a pattern in regional variation similar to that for Orientation to Society. The youth who were more authoritarian in their beliefs about child rearing were found in East Texas. Most democratic in the state in relation to authority were youth from West Texas. However, the degree of variation between these regions was not as marked as that discovered in attitudes toward the future and trust of people. Again, here are found evidences of contrast between the older, rural and the newer, urban areas; the more traditional east and the west, still in process of development; and the regions of lower and higher incomes. Here, also, is evidence

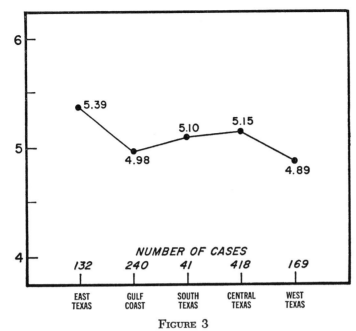

6

5.39

5.15
5.10
4.98
4.89

5

NUMBER OF CASES

4

| *132* | *240* | *41* | *418* | *169* |

| EAST TEXAS | GULF COAST | SOUTH TEXAS | CENTRAL TEXAS | WEST TEXAS |

FIGURE 3

Youth in East Texas Favor Authoritarian Discipline

of the differences in educational level found where minority peoples live in large numbers as compared with areas where few people of lesser status are to be found.

Family Tension

Tensions arising in families illustrated the least disparity between East and West Texas. Here is a shift noticeable between problems, on the one hand, and basic attitudes on the other. Families living under varied circumstances, arising from gross differences in economics and geography, appear to be able to achieve quite similar levels of satisfactory family interaction though their standards of life may be quite different.

Family Life Style

Resentment of Family Life Style proved to be another matter. This scale for the measurement of how youth react to the way the family lives in its home and behaves within the family itself, indicated a

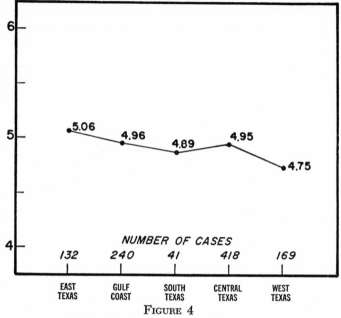

FIGURE 4

Family Tension by Geographic Regions

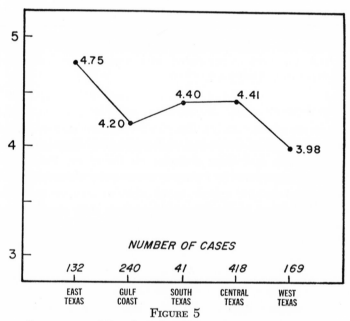

FIGURE 5

Resentment of Family Life Style by Geographic Regions

wide range of difference between East and West Texas, similar to the scale measuring an optimistic or pessimistic outlook on life. Actual income and differences in adequacy of appurtenances for comfortable living probably account for the variations in reaction of youth expressed in this scale. Young persons, who have attained the level of education necessary for high school attendance, are well aware of the adequacy or inadequacy of the way of life available to their families, and resentment over recognized inequities is not unexpected. However, it may well be that some of these responses, as well as others in this study, reflect comparative rather than actual inadequacies. A clear distinction could not be made between responses of youth faced with actual social, economic, and cultural poverty, and responses of those whose feeling of relative deprivation resulted only from a comparison of their own state and the state of those whom they would like to emulate. This is a limitation in some analyses over which the authors had no control.

Comparison of regional data in the Texas study, limited though it is in its significance, should offer suggestions to each region of the state in regard to its youth. Examination of assets and liabilities for the development of young people is the background for effective planning. Measurement of regional adequacy is, in final analysis, the quality of adults who emerge from youth reared in a given cultural setting.

THE IMPACT OF COMMUNITY SIZE

Rapid urbanization has been a major characteristic of the state and nation for half a century. No longer is there a clear-cut dichotomy between rural and urban in the United States. Science and technology, transportation and communication have produced what was once described as a "rurban" culture.

City living, formulated as it was out of migration from the country, carried residues of rural reactions and behavior. Rural residents have acquired an overlay of the urban in their way of life, their homes, their dress, speech, and manner. Until still other generations have passed, certain distinctions in attitudes and problems will probably remain, fading though they may be. The Texas Youth Study served to illustrate certain of the dual facets of American life. However, from the analysis of data, it was not possible to state that it is definitely better to rear children in the country than in the city. Each manifests strengths and displays weaknesses.

To determine if there were significant differences between young people from the larger and smaller communities, a sample of some 960 white youth was drawn. These teen-agers lived alone with their families. No roomers, relatives, or grandparents were in their homes. Age variation within the 9th, 10th, 11th, and 12th grades was controlled. Sex and grade level were maintained as independent variables. Number of children in the family was varied systematically from one to three (including the respondent). Community size was divided into rural and urban, using a 1950 census figure of 2,500 as the arbitrary cutting point. Father's education was examined in three categories: (a) eighth grade or less; (b) ninth to twelfth grade; and (c) some college education. Community size and its impact upon Negro students will be discussed in a later presentation.

Youth Attitudes Vary Little

Perhaps no better indication of the "rurban" way of life in the nation and in Texas can be found than in a comparison of the areas of similarity in youth responses. No significant differences were apparent between rural and urban youth in their Orientation to Society. Obviously other variables make the difference in determining the hopefulness or pessimism of young persons concerning the world in which they live. Authoritarian Discipline, as a method of child control, was equally acceptable or unacceptable, as the case might be, for future parents regardless of size of community. Family Problems were no more nor less acute because families chose to live in small or large population centers.

Some minimal distinctions were observable in the interaction between the number of children in the family and the size of community. Youth from larger families in cities were more critical of education than those in the country. And, youngsters in the country were slightly more disapproving of others of their own age in comparison with their urban counterparts. These variations are of passing interest here rather than of real importance in distinguishing between youth from communities of different sizes.[2]

Among the concerns of youth as measured by the scale scores for Self and Social Inadequacy and Social Isolation, no differences could

[2] See Appendix A for a full discussion of significance level as utilized in this study. In the present case, the rural versus urban difference was significant at the .05 level for Criticism of Youth and at the .01 level for Criticism of Education.

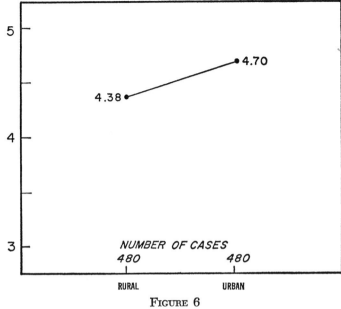

FIGURE 6
Community Size and Family Tension

be discerned in relation to the communities where they resided. Again, other factors affecting these measures of self-confidence appeared to be more important.

Tension in Cities

Increased tension is widely accepted as a major facet of city living. It is supposed to be a concomitant of complexity in environment. In general, urban youth did receive somewhat higher scores on Family Tension than those in rural communities.

It may be surmised with some validity that city youngsters would be a bit more readily aware of discrepancies in advantages which exist, or which they think exist, between urban families of different cultural orientation and backgrounds. Robin Williams has pointed out that subcultural groupings do not present any particular problems to society if these are not in "direct interaction" or "do not confront one another's differing orientations." [3] But large city high schools,

---

[3] Robin M. Williams, Jr., *American Society: A Sociological Interpretation,* p. 375.

whose populations represent varied sociocultural groupings, are settings for continuous confrontation among youth. Deprivation, real or imagined, does not go unnoticed. The "Haves" and "Have nots" are easily identifiable in classroom and on playground. Relative distinctions within the middle class itself may not be as obvious, but they often become tension producers within the home situation. The pressure of upward mobility is encouraged both by association among peer-group members and by classroom experiences. When parents cannot, or do not, measure up to the burgeoning expectations of their teen-age sons or daughters, difficulties may arise. While education and economics are paramount causes of emotional and social stress in lower-income families, these may not be of major importance among middle class youngsters. Relative adequacy within the middle-class family may appear to the high school student as *inadequacy* if his desires outreach his satisfactions in comparison to others whom he feels are afforded greater advantages than he.

Again, it may be noted that, while socioeconomic distinctions also exist in rural high schools for white youth, the range of difference usually is not as great. The poorest are not as apparently poor. Lower and upper middle-income families are not as far apart. Advantages available in rural settings are neither as widespread nor as discriminatory in their use.

City youth's awareness of the gulf between families with respect to participation in available culture may well be one element in the development of family tension. "Operation More" [4] in New York City and similar programs in other cities are attempts to break down excessive variations in opportunity for youth of widely divergent socioeconomic groups. Young persons from the more limited families in cities tend to be early dropouts from high school, and this would have some bearing upon the findings of the Texas Study.

On the other hand, family tension and poverty of opportunity are not the only teammates. Counselors frequently find themselves faced

[4] For a description of "Operation More" in the New York City schools see Harrison E. Salisbury, "The Shook-Up Generation," *The New York Times*, March 24–30, 1958, reprint, p. 10; later published in book form as *The Shook-Up Generation*. Also of importance is the New York City project described in Mobilization for Youth, Inc., *A Proposal for the Prevention and Control of Delinquency by Expanding Opportunities*, and that discussed in New York City Board of Education, *Demonstration Guidance Project: Junior High School, 43 Manhattan and George Washington High School*.

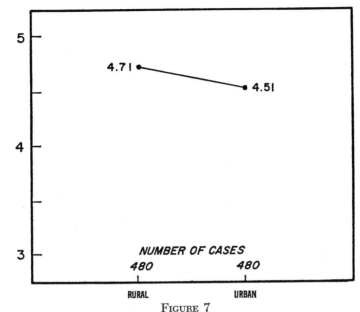

FIGURE 7
Rural Youth Show Higher Concern for Social Conformity

with the problems of middle-income families when teen-agers develop irritability and aggressive patterns of behavior over relative inequality in material advantages, real or imagined. In any event, urban and rural living, as far as youth are concerned, are not too different in the stress which may arise within the family.

Social Conformity

Youth, whether in city or country, live with pressures to conform to the standards and demands of their own age groups. They are, at the same time, faced with the necessity of living within the value pattern of their parents. In addition, youth need the support both of their peers and of adults as they develop toward young adulthood. They acquire their sense of inner security from belonging to the social-emotional world of their own agemates, but at the same time they require the approval of their parents. In the attempt to gain status in their own age groups, some will compromise ideals acquired earlier. Anxiety over the necessity of being a member of the "in group" sometimes is a price paid for participation with agemates.

Whether it is easier "to buck the gang" or "to be different" in urban or rural high schools was a question worth investigation.

Young persons in small communities found it a little more difficult to resist the demands of others of their age who behaved in opposition to their own values. Primary contact in small communities where "everybody knows everybody else" evidently creates greater fear of being left out. Social distance between classmates is more obvious. There are fewer groups to which one may belong.

Urban youngsters, on the other hand, have more choices of group membership. Their lack of acceptance by one particular clique does not mean that they may be "left out." Larger high schools offer social outlets with others who hold similar views to their own. Moreover, urban areas accept a wider variety in behavior than do most villages and small towns. "The anonymity of the city" or of the large high school, for that matter, usually does afford greater freedom of choice in behavior.

Personal Adjustment

Problems of personal adjustment are recognized as a part of the processes of maturation. Whether they are greater or less for youth in rural and urban areas is a subject for considerable speculation. Some contend that youth in larger population agglomerations are bound to encounter greater difficulty in their adjustment because of the size of the community, its multiplicity of choices and pressures, and because achievement of feelings of self-worth are complicated by intensity of competition. Others advance the argument that rural youth, faced with declining opportunities in smaller settlements and on the farms, would be forced to make decisions difficult to abridge. Moreover, in rural living, accessibility to cultural resources would be relatively limited in comparison to those available for urban youth. The realization that there is more to be had out of living than is readily available may well create personal problems which would be revealed in a study.

No clear-cut distinction was found in general between urban and rural youth and their problems of adjustment. Other variables had to be taken into account before differences became apparent. Even these were only of very minor significance. The more years rural young persons remained in school, the more their problems concerning their self-adequacy diminished. As they learned, so they evidently became

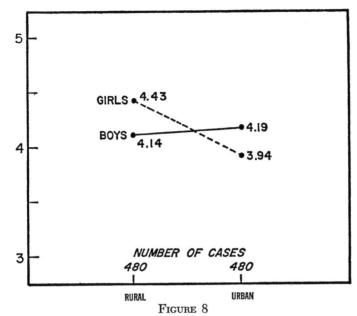

FIGURE 8

Relation of Personal Adjustment to Sex and Community Size

better adjusted. By the 11th and 12th grades, boys and girls from smaller settlements seemed to have been quite successful in gaining a sense of emotional security.

Sex differences in personal adjustment were discovered according to size of community in which young persons lived. Boys found little difference in personal stress whether they were urban or rural. Girls, on the other hand, found it more difficult to be at ease with self if they had been reared in rural settings. Young women in rural communities generally expect to acquire a more mature level of security through marriage. The measure of their personal adjustment is often expressed in terms of their desirability to the opposite sex. Opportunities for achievement after high school are often limited. If college or immediate marriage is not on the horizon, then a sense of personal failure may result. Many girls in small villages and towns are probably also aware of the relative poverty of their cultural experiences. Lack of self-assurance and ignorance about many aspects of life accompany limited opportunities. If these girls move into urban areas to find jobs and a greater market for their talents, they may become even more aware of the paucity of their backgrounds for self-determination and social adaptation. City girls from the very beginning have a wider range of avenues toward self-confidence and toward outlets for personal capacities other than through marriage.

Resentment of Dependency

Young persons of the predominant ethnic group from small communities expressed less resentment of dependence upon their parents than did those from larger centers or urban areas. Easy routes to personal freedom for high school youth are not as available in rural areas as in the cities. Vestiges of family-centered economy and the large family social system remain. Available jobs are usually on the family farm or in small business of family members or friends. Unlike their city cousins, youth from smaller communities are often forced to accept their places in the social and economic patterns of their families if they are to complete high school. They have little choice unless they leave home. Consequently, they appear to accept their dependence within the rural family system with better grace than do urban youth whose dependence rests more upon their parents and somewhat less upon a family-friend system.

Many teen-agers in metropolitan centers do not feel that they will necessarily complete high school. Jobs of sorts are more readily available, meager and insecure though many of them are. In fact, a phenomenon of 1960 compared to 1940 was the notable increase in the numbers of youth earning an income as they attended school.[5] Young persons who help produce a portion of the family income no doubt find it difficult to accept emotional and social dependence. If parental intervention is too strict, they can move into independent young adulthood after their sixteenth year when compulsory school attendance ends. This mobility is no doubt a factor in the dropout rate after the ninth grade in city schools. Of course rural high schools also lose students at this time, and many of them migrate to cities.

Youth from middle- and upper-class white families in cities are not necessarily less free from resentment of control. However, the etiology of their discontent is probably different. Families on these socioeconomic levels establish certain expectations for their children. Subtle, and some not-so-subtle, controls are exerted to assure their accomplish-

---

[5] Eleanor H. Burnert, "Demographic Trends," in *The Family and Social Change*, pp. 42–45.

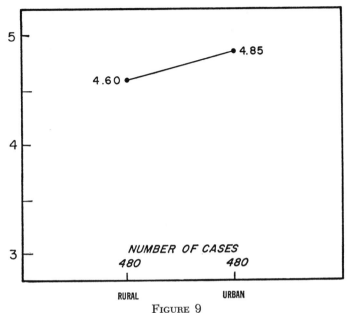

FIGURE 9

City Youth Show More Resentment of Dependency

ment. Financial support is a necessity if youth are to spend years in study toward business and professional careers. They may be old enough to become earners. They may be ready for more responsible and independent behavior. However, because of family definition of their future, real independence must be postponed. When parents dictate both the path to eventual freedom and the control of the purse strings, it is difficult for them to release their children emotionally. Some overt resentment is apparently hard to avoid.

IN SUMMARY

Rearing children in cities has some advantages if youth responses are examined. But so does rearing them in smaller communities and in rural areas if other measures are used. Neither is free of problems as indicated by youth themselves. In general, family tension was found only slightly more often in city families than in rural.

Resentment of dependence upon parents among urban youth was greater than in rural areas. On the other hand, pressures for conformity to peer groups holding values other than those of the youth who responded were discovered to be more intense in smaller than larger population centers. Girls in smaller centers of population found it more difficult to attain feelings of personal adequacy.

Community size, large or small, indicates some divergence in cultural patterns with different impact upon family life. However, it does not guarantee youth either more or less freedom from concern and problems. All it does assure is that these will not be entirely alike, though they were more alike than had been anticipated.

VI: Different and Yet Alike

ჄჄჄჄჄჄჄჄჄჄჄჄჄჄჄჄჄჄჄ

ROLE DEFINITION and performance of the two sexes are becoming increasingly alike in the United States. This is an important phenomenon arising from coeducation, technology, and democratic social organization. With this movement toward similarity, some people expressed anxiety over the possible loss of masculinity by men and the imposition by women of an undesirable "equalitarian togetherness." On the other hand, striking evidence is available that problems arise for both sexes from "culturally elaborated" distinctions imposed upon the biologically different. Youth in Texas, born into a variety of subcultural groups, of parents reared in the twentieth century, offer salient evidence about both culturally imposed differences and increasing similarities between the sexes.

Moreover, research is offering increasing evidence concerning adolescence itself. No longer can all youngsters between thirteen and eighteen be lumped into a single category and described as a unit. In fact, it is becoming more and more apparent that as children enter puberty, their behavior, attitudes, and problems are quite distinct from those of mid-adolescence. Even more striking are the differences discernible among older youth and the younger, even in a senior high school setting.

High school students, then, display differences because of their sex and likenesses in spite of their sex. Also, distinctions must be made concerning them regardless of sex because of their levels of maturation which become obvious at various age-grade periods in their secondary school life.

Sex-Differentiated Differences

Revealing variations in attitudes were apparent between boys and girls. Conceptions of the world in which youth live were not entirely alike. School and teachers impressed boys and girls differently. Adjustment to the demands of their own age groups was distinctive. To a lesser degree, they deviated in their reaction to family life style. Dissimilarities in absorption from culture and perception of culture patterns were consistent regardless of the subcultural groups with which their families might be identified.

Problems and concerns of young persons, as distinct from attitudes, revealed a contrasting picture. These were not sex-differentiated. Both boys and girls were found to have similar problems of behavior and similar concerns about relationships which they shared. Problems and concerns, it will be remembered, had to do with tension within families, personal adjustment, feelings of self or social inadequacy, conformity, and isolation. They also included resentment of family life style, dependency upon parents, and financial problems.

Why were differences apparent between the sexes in their basic attitudes, and why was no appreciable diversity discernible in their recognition of problems?

Attitudes are states of mind with emotional content. These tendencies toward action may be conscious or unconscious and are directed toward social values. Experiences with prevalent value patterns in the culture group to which persons belong are the sources of attitudes. These are, in fact, abstractions arising from numerous situations to which young people have seen their elders respond. They tend to express pervasive feelings of acceptance or rejection, hate or liking, abhorrence or acceptance, prejudice or tolerance—to name only a few reactions. Usually these feeling tones are not directed toward specific acts or problems or persons save in a generalized way. One tends to agree or disagree, with varying intensity, with statements of attitudes.

Problems are more personally oriented. These have to do with youth themselves and their evaluation of their own behavior or character. Concerns definitely relate to others with whom youth are closely and intimately associated. These "others" include the family, brothers or sisters, friends, and acquaintances. Problems are "interpersonal," as Harry Stack Sullivan has put it. They arise only between two or more persons, even if all save one is imaginary![1] Statement of a problem or of a specific concern requires more than agreement or disagreement. It does, or does not, apply to the person responding. It is or is not a problem to him, or he may be undecided. Moreover, the problem may be of little or great concern to him, or none at all.

Problems and concerns arise in everyday interaction. Boys and girls differ, but most of their experiences in or out of school are coeducational. Few are the problems of youth which may be clearly labeled either "male" or "female," save those which have to do with biological differences and limited social situations. Sons and daughters are treated very much alike at home. Schools teach and treat both sexes similarly. In fact, this similarity has been pointed out as one of the etiological factors of later problems of identity among mature women.[2] Similar behavior is expected of all high school youth. Their punishment for misbehavior is also increasingly similar. The wisdom of this is questioned by those who would have the sexes more dichotomized in treatment.[3]

Orientation to Society

Young men of high school age, no matter what their grade level, tended to express more pessimism about the world in which they live than did the girls. This finding was substantiated in numerous analyses.[4] Among the items which comprise this attitude scale were: "These days a person doesn't really know whom he can count on"; "In spite of what some people say, life for the average person is getting worse, not better"; and, "It's hardly fair to bring children into the world with the way things look for the future."[5]

Studies of other cultures do not contribute evidence that males carry inborn negativism or aggression to a greater degree than girls.

---

[1] For Sullivan's theory of the interpersonal nature of problems see Patrick Mullahy (ed.), *The Contributions of Harry Stack Sullivan*, pp. 18–20.

[2] Bruno Bettelheim, "Growing Up Female," in *Harper's Magazine*, CCXXV (October, 1962), 121–122.

[3] Urie Bronfenbrenner, "The Changing American Child: A Speculative Analysis," in *The Journal of Social Issues*, Vol. 17 (1961), pp. 6–18.

[4] The trends illustrating sex differences in Figures 10–14 are based on 1,440 cases in the sample described fully in Chapter X.

[5] See Chapter II for the scale on Orientation to Society.

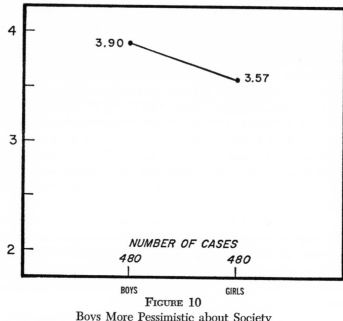

FIGURE 10
Boys More Pessimistic about Society

Current clinical studies in the behavioral sciences also do not substantiate this hypothesis.[6] It would seem then that the source for the differences in reactions of boys and girls displayed in this survey must lie in the culture in which they live.

Regardless of constant change in the status of women in the United States, men play the dominant role in economic, political, and social life. Boys in high school are moving rapidly toward maturity. In a few years they will assume leadership roles. Pessimism as a personality attribute among youth of either sex warrants consideration. The relatively greater cynicism expressed by boys in the youth study offers opportunity for speculation.

An intelligent appraisal of current dangers to civilization would give pause to either sex. Healthy anxiety is nothing more than realistic. Partial explanation for the more melancholy outlook for teen-age boys than for girls may rest in the inevitability of military service. These youth may subconsciously or consciously question the predictability

[6] Leon J. Saul, *The Hostile Mind*.

of the future. Their reasoning may be that if the world and its people are untrustworthy, whatever life may bring will hold more than its share of disappointment, if not tragedy.

Negativism, then, may be an adaptive mechanism for adolescent boys in an age of tenuous survival.[7] This would account in some measure for the oft-stated imperative to secure immediate gratification of personal desires. Tomorrow may never come for realization of long-term goals. Boys from subcultural groups where deprivation has been severe might be expected to find outlets for their insecurity through delinquency, youth crime, or other antisocial behavior. Boys from families of more substantial backgrounds may express their reactions through similarly inappropriate behavior, including vandalism and malicious mischief.

Boys are also limited in the range allowed them for expression of emotions. Aggression, and even hostility, have been granted as outlets for a variety of feelings, but other responses have been labeled "unmanly."

Note has also been taken by scholars interested in youth problems of the fact that high school boys find it difficult to develop a satisfactory masculine image because of their limited association with their fathers or other important men. They are in the company of their mothers many hours each day and are under the tutelege of women teachers almost entirely until they reach high school. Growing to young manhood in a predominantly woman's world offers problems of transition identification with adult masculine status.[8]

Moreover, Paul Goodman in his essay on *Growing Up Absurd*[9] points to the discontinuity in expectations between the irresponsibility for adolescent boys and the heavy responsibilities carried by mature men. Talcott Parsons has taken note of the role played by the mother in tacitly condoning, if not subconsciously abetting, socially immature behavior in her sons as an expected phase of "growing up."[10] Erik Erikson has described this same disruptive phenomenon as the

[7] Appreciation is here expressed to Dr. William C. Adamson, director, The Woods Schools, Langhorne, Pennsylvania, for his assistance with the tentative interpretation which follows.

[8] Bettelheim, *Op. cit.*, p. 122 n.

[9] Paul Goodman, *Growing Up Absurd.*

[10] Talcott Parsons, "Certain Primary Sources and Patterns of Aggression in the Social Structure of the Western World," in *Psychiatry*, X (May, 1947), 172.

struggle for ego identity in the face of an adolescent moratorium imposed upon boys by society.[11]

High school girls would seem to suffer less severe dislocation in feelings and behavior than boys if their relatively more optimistic attitudes as revealed in the youth study can be taken as an indicator. Identification as members of their sex is easier since they live with working models in their mothers and female teachers. They compete under similar circumstances in school. They may even carry some minor advantages if their teachers are predominantly women. Moreover, they are granted a variety of emotional outlets denied their brothers.

The future for young girls, they expect and hope, will include marriage. With marriage, many believe, comes a security which will preclude the necessity for sustained effort in a competitive world. Rarely, as Bettelheim has pointed out, do girls hear any suggestion that they may be expected to contribute or share broadly in the work of the world alongside men.[12] If marriage does not eventuate, they assume, they can fall back on a job or "a career." Mary Bunting has described young women with such assumptions as a sex of "unexpectations."[13] Relative complacency among high school girls apparently is concomitant with limited vision of future horizons even in a highly complicated world where millions of women carry joint responsibility with their husbands for earning, homemaking, and child rearing.

Still another interpretation concerning the optimism of girls in contrast to boys has been presented by Orville Brim in his book, *Personality and Decision Processes*.[14] He has pointed out that in his parent subjects, optimism is positively related to dependency. Optimism, he concludes, must be viewed as "defensive." Dependency upon other people, he indicates, causes anxiety and even fear about events in the offing over which there is little control. To allay this anxiety, such persons tend to adopt the attitude that whatever may happen,

[11] Erik H. Erikson develops his theory of "the psychosocial moratorium" in Helen L. Witmer and Ruth Kotinsky (eds.), *New Perspectives for Research on Juvenile Delinquency*, pp. 5–6.

[12] Bettelheim, *Op. cit.*, p. 121.

[13] Mary Bunting, "One Woman, Two Lives," in *Time*, LXXVIII (November 3, 1961), 68–73.

[14] Orville G. Brim, Jr., David C. Glass, David E. Lavin, and Norman Goodman, *Personality and Decision Processes*, pp. 106–107.

everything will work out for the best. Optimism and dependency tend to fuse together into "a nervous, rather than childlike trust in a beneficent destiny." Perhaps it should be remembered in this connection that dependence of girls is not only expected but required for a longer period than for boys. At any rate, this interpretation merits attention.

Neither sex, it would appear, has assurance of freedom from problems concerning attitudes toward society and their future in it. Differences in socialization of the two sexes and in expectations of them in relationships within the family can be safely assumed to have left their mark not only from data available in the study but from casual observation and from numerous other studies of sex differences.

Criticism of Education

No single scale was considered sufficient to determine basic attitudes of young persons. How they would react to formal education was presumed to be of major significance. School is literally the work life of youth. Further evidence of differential attitudes between boys and girls was disclosed. Boys displayed greater negativism toward school experiences, as they had about society in general. This sex difference appeared consistently in a number of analyses.

Scores on Criticism of Education measured not only attitude toward school but, indirectly, proficiency in scholarship.[15] Response to educational opportunity has peculiar pertinence in the evolving space age. The demand for educated persons has never been greater. Scientific talent and technological skill are at a premium. Moreover, schooling is fast becoming a determining factor between employment or unemployment. Success in school and liking for it are almost as important motivational factors for continued attendance as native endowment and parental attitudes.

The following statements are illustrative of this scale: "Most teachers are too rigid and narrow-minded"; "The main reason students cheat is because of the ridiculous assignments most teachers make";

[15] The scale, Criticism of Education, was devised primarily by William F. Brown and Wayne H. Holtzman. It is similar to the one utilized by the Brown-Holtzman Survey of Study Habits and Attitudes, although it has a different response format, using an "agree–disagree" continuum instead of the "rarely–almost–always" continuum of the Survey scale.

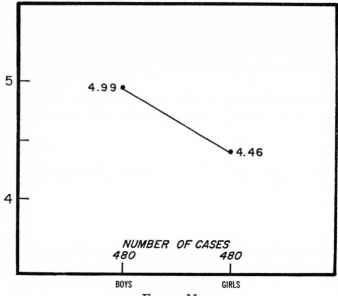

FIGURE 11
Boys More Critical of Education

"Most teachers lack understanding of the needs and interests of their students."

The fact that dropout rates among high school boys are higher than for girls is relevant to the obtained sex difference in Criticism of Education.[16] This differential between boys and girls has been attributed to the need for boys to leave school in order to earn an income. However, non-high school graduates are finding increasingly fewer jobs in the labor market. Many remain among the chronically unemployed. Fortunately, today more parents are able to keep their children in school. Dissatisfaction with school experiences for some may be subtly clothed with the garments of need to earn when reality presents a different picture.

Discouraged youth are not necessarily incapable of average or

[16] For a full discussion of current concern with the problem of dropouts from the public schools see National Committee on Children and Youth in Urban Areas, *Social Dynamite: The Report of the Conference on Unemployed Out-of-School Youth in Urban Areas.* See also James B. Conant, *Slums and Suburbs.*

better performance in school. Questions have been raised as to sources of existing discontent and low performance by high school boys still in high school. A preponderance of women teachers has been offered as one explanation, though the ratio of men to women is nearing equality. Failure by boys to understand or teachers to teach, and the relevance of the curriculum of high school to the demands of adult life have been credited as factors contributing to discouragement. The status factor in college preparatory work versus vocational training may make the latter appear unworthy of pursuit, even to those who never can expect to go to college. Lack of adaptation of methods, materials, and course content to the actual needs of boys has been suggested. Teacher definition of what constitutes a successful and good student may have real impact. Differences in maturation rates of the two sexes have been considered pertinent. Girls may be better able and more willing than boys to conform to teacher definitions and demands. Or perhaps school programs have been geared to the earlier maturity of girls so that boys have a harder time adjusting.[17]

A second important issue raised by sex difference in response to education has to do with girls and their academic careers. Girls appear to derive greater satisfaction from high school than boys do. On the whole, they make a better adjustment to school, as this and other studies have indicated. At least they make better grades, receive more academic honors, and get into fewer difficulties!

An informal study of June, 1961, graduates from all white high schools in Dallas documents this contention.[18] As indicated in Table 27, of the more than 4,500 graduates, three times as many girls as boys received highest honors. About half again as many girls as boys were in the list for honors. Only about one-fifth as many boys as girls were nominated by teachers for National Honor Society membership.

Even more telling was the statistical ranking of the graduating classes based on scholastic achievement. Though the schools noticed some slight modification in various subcultural sections of the city, the major trends remained the same. Evidence from tests of aptitude and intelligence indicates no such superiority of the female sex over the male, though sex differences in aptitude have been documented.

[17] Appreciation is expressed to Beulah J. Coon for this pertinent suggestion.
[18] William B. Helton and Ruby Morris, "A Study of Honors Received and Rank in Class of White High School Graduates, Dallas, Texas, June 1961."

TABLE 27: *Rank by Sex of Dallas High School Graduates, 1961*

Rank	Boys	Girls	Total
Quartile 1	350	806	1,156
Quartile 2	466	667	1,133
Quartile 3	621	518	1,139
Quartile 4	784	346	1,130

Nonetheless, there is still a continuing loss due to dropout of intelligent and able young women between high school and college, as well as in college prior to graduation. While this discrepancy between girls graduating from high school and those entering college is decreasing, loss during college years is high,[19] and the percentage who go no farther than secondary school is considered a real loss in human resources. Definition of the role of women and cultural conditioning at home and in the community apparently create a lack of desire or a lack of opportunity for girls to complete a college education.

When a family must make a choice between college education for sons or daughters, sons are usually chosen. Some parents tacitly consider college education for daughters, "who will only get married," an economic waste. This prejudice is evidence of culture lag which has real bearing on both the quality of parenthood and upon the availability of developed talent among women.[20] If immediate marriage, children, and homemaking in the traditional pattern were in the predictable future for all girls, such a situation would be relatively harmless. However, married or not, nine out of ten women will be employed outside their homes at some time in their lives. Employment and homemaking are a continuum rather than a dichotomy. The average period of work for women in the labor force is over twenty years.[21]

The problem of getting boys to complete their high school education and of motivating many of them toward further academic training is paramount. However, the problem of moving more girls through high

---

[19] See American Council of Education, *The Education of Women: Information and Research Notes*, No. 5, p. 2.

[20] See Chapter XIII, "The Case for the Educated Parent."

[21] U. S. Department of Labor, *1958 Handbook on Women Workers*, especially Part I, "Women in the Labor Force." See also U. S. Department of Labor, *Spotlight on Women in the United States, 1956–1957*, and U. S. Department of Labor, *Manpower Challenge of the 1960s*.

school and of sending a large percentage of them on into college would seem to be no less imperative. For the boys, the high school setting needs to be made more satisfying and more stimulating. Lack of achievement far outdistances lack of ability. Enjoyment and adjustment of girls to high school should be translated into motivation toward continuing their education.

Authoritarian Discipline

Authoritarian discipline was endorsed as the preferred method in child rearing by more high school boys than girls. This sex difference appeared consistently throughout the various analyses. Youth with high scores on this scale agreed with such statements as: "Too much affection will make a child a softie"; "Children who always obey grow up to be the best adults"; "Too much freedom will make a child wild." [22]

Man, in his traditional role, has been authoritarian. He has been expected to be head of the house. Evidence of increasingly equalitarian relationships between the sexes and with children is accruing. High school boys more often than girls, however, offer indication of a remaining lag between the old and the modern in conceptions of authority as they relate to children.

The authoritarian approach to child rearing is found more often in lower socioeconomic groups than in other subcultures in the nation. Even here women's attitudes tend to have been modified by education. More opportunities have been afforded them than men to study newer concepts of child development, family relations, and interpersonal behavior.

With their major responsibility for child rearing, women of the middle and upper classes, especially, have sought information for improvement in homemaking and child rearing. Some girls in high school have had courses preparatory for their roles as homemakers and mothers. Women, in addition, have long been regarded as the sex dominated by "tender emotions." Men have tended to equate these emotions with weakness and femininity. [23]

However, as the gap between women in various social strata has narrowed in their knowledge of effective relationships with their chil-

[22] See Chapter II for a description of each of the following scales: Authoritarian Discipline, Criticism of Youth, and Resentment of Family Life Style.
[23] Norman R. F. Maier, *Principles of Human Relations*, p. 95.

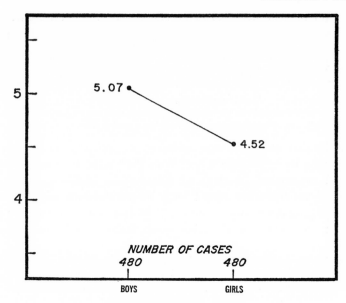

FIGURE 12
Boys Approve Authoritarian Discipline More than Girls

dren, so also is the discrepancy between men and women in their
attitudes undergoing modification. High school boys and college men
are being offered opportunity to study in the areas of personality
development, family interaction, and marriage. With the permeation
of behavioral scientific information to larger numbers of men as well
as women in all social groups, it can be expected that the divergence
between the sexes will tend to disappear.

Criticism of Youth

As a class, boys tended to be more critical of society and education,
and more authoritarian than girls. But it was the latter who turned
critical eyes on their peers. This sex difference was revealed in their
responses to such items as: "Silliness is one of the worst faults of
most teen-agers"; "Most teen-agers have not yet learned to control
their tempers"; "Teen-agers gossip too much about each other." All
of these, and other items, indicated negative criticism of those of their
own age.

Differences in role definition for the sexes may be responsible in

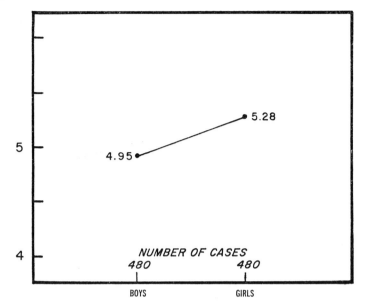

FIGURE 13
Girls More Critical of Youth

some measure for this finding. Girls are taught to be observant of social behavior. They are expected to adhere more closely than boys to a code of personal morality particularly as this relates to sexual relations and to drinking. They are inculcated with the necessity of protecting themselves from gossip as well as in behavior with the opposite sex. They tend to be more involved with problems and interests of their own personal and intimate world rather than with concerns of wider scope. Here again the factor of earlier maturation of girls than of boys may be of major importance. Because of these differences, it is not surprising that high school girls even in this day tend to be more critical of other teen-agers than do boys.

GRADE-LEVEL DIFFERENCES

Youth in middle adolescence in their first years in senior high school and those in the latter two years of this same developmental period offered evidence of increasing maturity. Early adolescence is usually considered a period with greater crises than middle or later teen years.

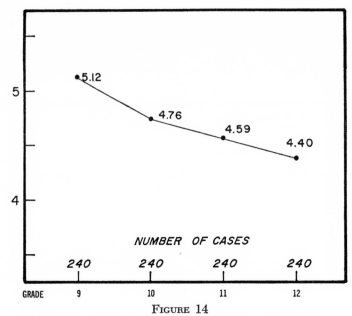

Figure 14
Younger Adolescents Favor Authoritarian Discipline

The Texas study was originally planned to cover the total period of youth from the earliest years of junior high through senior high school. However, as previously reported, it was found that the instruments could be used successfully only in the final four years of high school.[24]

Grade levels in this study were ninth, tenth, eleventh, and twelfth. Roughly these coincided with ages fifteen, sixteen, seventeen, and eighteen years. The sample totalled 960 cases. The distinctions between early adolescence when youngsters are thirteen or fourteen years old as contrasted with the responses of the eighteen- and nineteen-year-old youth no doubt would have been more vivid.

However, some significant trends were evidenced in the four grade levels, or age groupings, which were studied. Attitudes toward authoritarian discipline were worthy of note. Adolescents in the ninth and tenth grades expressed more rigid attitudes toward discipline than did older youth. A noticeable shift in perception of relationships with children was apparent even between the ninth- and tenth-grade

[24] For a description of the study design see Chapter III.

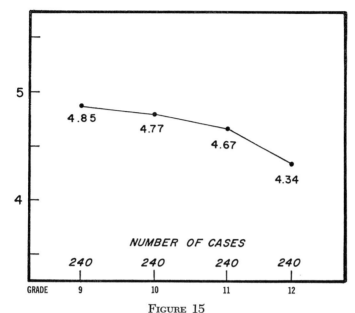

FIGURE 15
Younger Adolescents More Critical of Education

students. By the time these young persons were nearing graduation, concepts of democratic authority in contrast to authoritarian methods were well established.

Perhaps it was newness of the senior high-school setting, scheduling, and teaching methods, but youth in the three lower grade levels showed significantly different feelings about school and academic accomplishment from those of twelfth-grade students. As already noted, boys were more critical of education than girls on every grade level. The older the youth and the higher the grade achieved, the more at ease they were in school. The younger the adolescents, the more difficulties they had in being happy about school or its teachers.

A factor easy to overlook may be pertinent here. When boys and girls move into senior high school, many of them are already above the highest grade level attained by their own parents. Some may even be facing parental doubt concerning the advisability of their continuing their high school education. A goodly number of other youth in their first years of senior high school may be faced with lack of home support even if real resistance is not encountered. These young

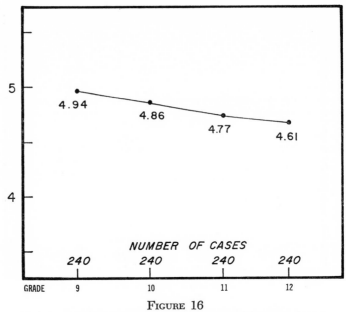

Figure 16
Younger Adolescents Feel More Isolated

persons must be self-motivated to continue. They must also struggle to become a part of a new world for which they have little or no background. In these instances, perhaps their critical attitude toward education is rationalization for poor performance because of pressures from parents to "get out and get going," or because of inferior preparation. Help is needed if some of these youth are not to fall by the wayside and increase the number of undereducated, incompetent young persons who are out of school.

Also, it is quite possible that, at this juncture, a goodly number consider the last two years of high school as "top dressing," special preparation for college. College is outside the reach of many students and is quite apart from their own upbringing. Such students might very well consider the last years of high school unnecessary for themselves. However, it should be remembered that 73 per cent of the youth in this study considered going to college personally important to them. Without high school graduation, college is removed from the realm of possibility, save in rare instances.

Grade-level differences in reaction to school experiences offer im-

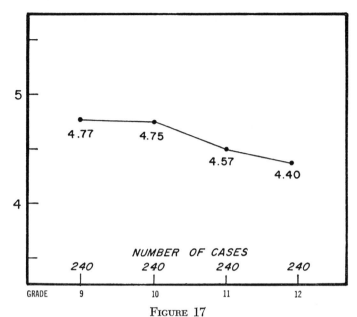

FIGURE 17
Younger Adolescents Feel Greater Need for Social Conformity

portant clues for those who would stem the tide of loss of potential talent, or of the dropouts who account for the increasing addition to the undereducated and unemployed.

Younger teen-agers indicated that they believed they were more isolated from their peers than other students. They also felt they faced more problems related to conforming to the behavior of their own age group than did older youth. To gain membership in their peer groups, the younger they were the more they felt impelled to go along with the crowd even if group behavior did not coincide with their own emerging values.

Newcomers to senior high school, it should be pointed out, find it easy to feel left out. The change from the greater intimacy of junior high or elementary school is noticeable. The move is usually out of a neighborhood institution into a community, if not a city-wide, high school. It involves demotion from the roles of "wheels" in smaller schools to near anonymity both in the classroom and on the playground. The need to prove oneself anew becomes imperative. Friends have to be made. Yet self-consciousness is high. There is an urgent need for belonging, not for isolation. The group which will help establish the sense of integration into the new social situation does not exist. These youngsters, with others, have to bring it into being. Perhaps dread of the move to unfamiliar surroundings and into new groups is among the more substantial reasons for the dropout rate between junior and senior high school among less assured or less well-motivated youngsters.

Feelings of isolation and the imperative need for conformity with the peer group decreased in the last two years of high school. A sense of ease within the situation, with teachers, and with fellow students evidently had been achieved. Sensitivity to real or imagined differences also tended to decrease with increase in maturity. The processes by which social acceptance is achieved both in the classroom and in the peer group should be considered by high school administrators whose aim is to hold all youth in school.

What can senior high schools plan to make the incoming youth feel as if they were not isolated so that more of them will tend to remain in school? How can in-school and at-home motivation of youth to remain in school be enhanced at every subcultural level and for both sexes? Here are important areas for experimentation and investigation to prevent both loss of talent and flooding of the labor market. Moreover, the undereducated, as later analyses will reveal, are indeed hampered in effectiveness for their roles as parents.

VII: Racial Group Membership and Youth Reactions

MEMBERSHIP in racial and ethnic groups, distinctive from the majority population, serves as an important conditioning factor in access to and availability of cultural resources. It determines in large measure what is obtainable for the development of children and youth.

General styles and patterns of family life achieved by subordinate groups are also conditional upon the degrees of likeness or difference of these persons to those of the majority. Family interaction, structure, and life style may be superficially similar but, at the same time, significantly different in subtle ways. Distinguishable racial and ethnic groups do remain, or are forced to remain, somewhat isolated from those of majority status. Their cultural participation may approximate but rarely has it equaled that enjoyed by the controlling peoples.

Negroes in Texas are a case in point. Many came as slaves during the period of Anglo colonization. They were an integral part of the economy of the Republic of Texas and remained within the state from its inception. In the last eighty-seven years the ratio of Negroes to white persons in Texas has been declining steadily. In the census of 1860 before slaves were freed, they made up almost a third of the population in the state. Each census from 1870 to the present time has shown a decrease. In 1957, the year following the collection of

youth study data, it was estimated that only about 11.4 per cent of
the total population was Negro.[1] Loss of this ethnic group has been
by migration, since the Negro birth rate has always exceeded the
death rate.

Traditionally, East Texas has been Old South. Many Negroes also
live in Central Texas and on the Gulf Coast. Few are to be found in
the valleys of South Texas or in far West Texas. Traditionally, again,
Negroes were field workers. They were unskilled laborers on plantations and farms. In recent decades they have become urbanized along
with the white population. Almost two-thirds of all peoples in the
state, it will be remembered, lived in communities of over 2,500 by
1960.

With the urbanization of Negroes has come rapid improvement in
economic opportunities and educational experiences. Also many other
advantages have accrued to the group along with upward mobility.
Prior to the Supreme Court ruling on desegregation, many cities had
made impressive strides in developing public schools which were
"equal but separate." Accreditation by the Texas Education Agency
is statewide. Therefore, standards for buildings, for programs of education, and for curriculum in Negro schools had been steadily improved just as they had in other schools. Only in some rural areas in
the spring of 1956 were there schools for Negroes which remained
minimal in every sense.

When data for the youth study were gathered, over a hundred
school districts had already begun the process of desegregation. San
Antonio, Austin, and El Paso were in the vanguard. Many of the
communities in the Rio Grande Valley and in West Texas had found
it economical to strip themselves of the dual cost of separate Negro
and white schools. In many of these latter institutions there had been
only infinitesimal Negro enrollment. Houston, Texas' largest city, was
well underway with its desegregation process. Negroes in the state,
therefore, were in a period of rapid transition in place of residence,
in occupations, in educational opportunities, in access to the total
culture. It is important in light of these changes to examine responses
of youth from one of the oldest and largest minority ethnic groups of
the state.

[1] *Texas Almanac,* 1958–1959, p. 95.

NEGROES IN THE YOUTH STUDY

Data were obtained from 1,849 Negro youths from the ninth through the twelfth grades in the total sample of 12,892. These data were gathered by departments of home economics education from Prairie View Agricultural and Mechanical College, Texas Southern University, and Texas College. Supervisors of Negro schools from the Division of Homemaking Education of the Texas State Department of Education cooperated with the colleges and the local schools in all phases of the study.

When the representative sample of one thousand cases was drawn from the total number collected, approximately 12 per cent were Negro youth. This percentage closely paralleled the proportion of Negroes in the population of Texas.

Data for Negro youth were sent to Prairie View Agricultural and Mechanical College where a faculty committee from the College, with representatives from Texas Southern University and from Texas College, worked together to plan for analysis and interpretation. For many years, Prairie View College has been holding an annual conference on education. When its 28th meeting was held, the conference was devoted to an examination of data from the Texas Cooperative Youth Study as it related to Negro youth and their mental health problems. Moreover, discussion by the assembled educators representing public schools, colleges, and universities, was devoted to steps which might be taken to meet the revealed needs of Negro students.

Analyses of youth data undertaken at Prairie View College were limited in scope and relatively simple in methodology. Time forced this decision upon the faculty committee. No attempt was made at sophistication in design or model. Nonetheless, some of the findings offered tentative bases for understanding Negro youth at this period in history.

A comparison was made of the total number of Negro youth included in the inclusive sample, numbering 1,849, as contrasted with the corrected representative sample of 1,000 which included a proportional representation of both white and Negro youth. Some of the results paralleled later findings in an analysis of variance made at the Collating Center. Others were not corroborated by the later study.

Negro youth, as reported to the Prairie View conference, differed from those in the representative sample of all youth by tending to get higher scores on several of the attitude scales. They were more pessimistic in world outlook, more accepting of authoritarian child rearing, more critical of education, more critical of youth, and they expressed greater resentment of family life style. Also, they showed more concern over family tension. They indicated more severe feelings of social isolation and they revealed that they suffered from pressures to conform to their own peer group.[2] The higher degree of resentment of family life style and of feelings of social isolation were not confirmed in the more rigorous analysis of variance undertaken later.

Selected background data from the Student Information Sheet were taken into account in another comparison made at Prairie View. Chosen were the following factors: sex, age, school enrollment, school grade, residence, father's occupation, marital status of parents, and the number of persons living in the home. Certain broad differences were discernable between Negro boys and girls, and between ninth- and twelfth-grade students. No attempt was made to ascertain the degrees of difference between the variable of sex and grade level and the scale scores. Only gross variations were shown.[3] With these limitations, the findings were used primarily as stimulus for discussion at the Prairie View Conference on Education in 1957.

Among the broad generalizations considered by the conference was the apparently greater complacency of Negro girls in a variety of problem areas when compared with boys. Negro men and boys are currently afforded greater opportunities both for upward and outward mobility than women of the same race. They come into more continuous and more varied contacts with the major ethnic group. Frustrations and limitations in opportunity are, therefore, likely to be more apparent to them. This sex distinction may not continue too much longer. Women and girls, as well as boys, of this racial group are being afforded greater educational and occupational opportunities. With these advances no doubt will come lessened tension among the men and a more realistic awareness among women of situational factors affecting their lives. As the marginality of this ethnic group in relation to the total culture decreases, so will problem orientation probably become more similar to that of men and women of the predominant race.

[2] The College Research Committee, *Improving Mental Health*, p. 12.
[3] *Ibid.*, p. 17.

RACIALLY DIFFERENTIATED VARIATIONS—AN INTENSIVE APPRAISAL

Sociocultural differences between Negro and white youth in families indicated need for a careful examination of their distinctions and similarities. Negroes in the valleys of South Texas and in West Texas were minimal in number when contrasted with the remainder of the state. Also many of the high schools of these two regions were in the process of desegregation when the data were secured. Consequently, an intensive study was made of Negro and white youth from only the other three regions—East and Central Texas, and the Gulf Coast.

Racial comparisons would be considered realistic only if families of both ethnic groups were similar in standards of living, educational level of parents, and occupational level of fathers. It was realized that even these controls would not provide entirely parallel samples because of the majority-minority status of whites and Negroes. This fact cannot be disregarded in its impact on family life and on personality.

Only intact families of both races were used. Cases were chosen from the total sample of Negro and white youth whose fathers had had no college education and were employed as unskilled, semi-skilled, or skilled workers. Community size was divided into rural (2,500 or less) and urban (over 2,500). A total of 228 cases were drawn to fill the 32 cells of the resulting factorial design. Systematically varied were race, sex, education of fathers, occupational status of fathers, and community size.

Negro youth obtained significantly higher mean scores than did white students for five of the 14 scales. Each of these five appeared previously in the list presented by the faculty committee for the Prairie View Conference on Education. Similarities between the races revealed in the remaining scales were not examined separately. They are elaborated throughout the study as a whole. The distinctions accentuated here are those more closely associated with race membership than with any other social characteristics.

Negro youth, and it should be recalled that these were high school students, were more pessimistic about society and their future in it than white youth. Even though they were members of a race in transition in socioeconomic status, they were quite evidently realistic enough to realize that years would elapse before they could expect their race to achieve equal status in either opportunities or personal

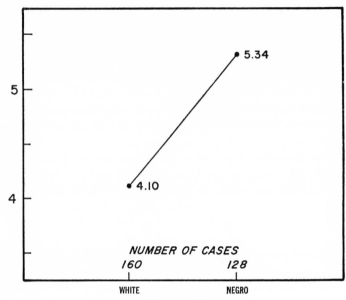

FIGURE 18
Race and Orientation to Society

acceptance with the majority group. Less hopefulness concerning the world and its largesse was not an unexpected finding.

Responses to Negroes as persons or as an ethnic group vary among the predominant race from the extremes of overt hostility and rejection to acceptance as peers. But what response will be forthcoming from whom is never certain. With unpredictability comes distrust. With inconsistency in relationships comes lack of confidence in other people. With hostility comes counterhostility. Though these patterns of behavior between the races are continuously decreasing and changing, enough vestiges remain to create in Negro youth a more pessimistic orientation to people as well as to society as a whole. Speculation is indeed interesting as to what two or three generations will bring in change of attitudes concerning society and people among Negro youth. In not too many decades, parents of all ethnic groups in the nation will have shared common educational experiences. Through this channel, if through no other, will be derived a broader share in participation in the culture as a whole and more equitable relationships between persons.

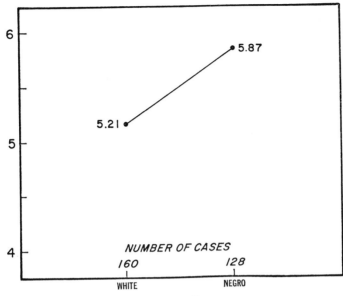

FIGURE 19

Race and Authoritarian Discipline

Young Negroes were more authoritarian than their white contemporaries in their concepts of discipline of children. Negro families, on the whole, remain more authoritarian than do those of many white youth. Authoritarian relationships between school administrators and teachers have been noted as well. Persons who have lived under restrictive and often autocratic control for generations accept this as their pattern of interpersonal relations with those of lower status or younger age. While the authoritarian approach to children and youth is often retained by Negro parents, there is also a recognized warmth of response between adults and their offspring. Authority over children in most Negro families rests with the mother rather than the father. From slave days, the woman in the Negro family has been the source of continuity and relative stability for the family group.

Family tension, problems of personal adjustment, and concern over conformity demands of peer groups were significantly greater for Negro than white students. Many Negro families have moved from country to city to increase their opportunities for economic and socio-cultural advancement. The majority now reside in urban rather than

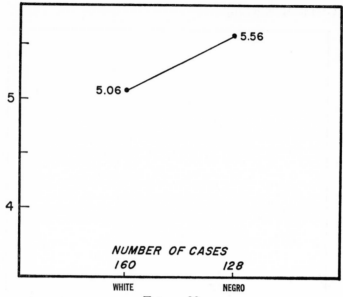

FIGURE 20
Race and Family Tension

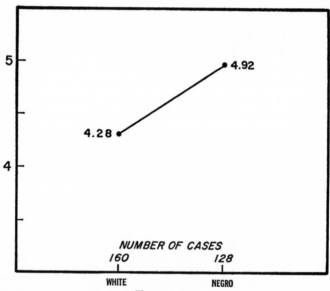

FIGURE 21
Race and Personal Adjustment

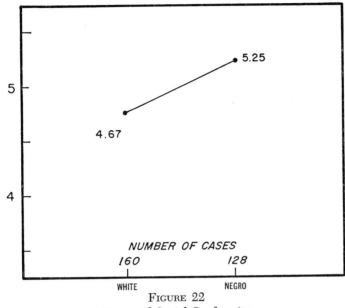

FIGURE 22
Race and Social Conformity

rural communities. The younger generation is increasingly better educated than the older. Therefore, it is small wonder that levels of
tension within families were reported high. Other ethnic groups who
have migrated to the United States have brought with them language
differences, and they have encountered conflict of cultures between
older and younger generations. Negro families, on the other hand,
exhibit the stress which accompanies upward movement from one
stratum to another within a given societal structure.

Negroes of the upper classes tend to hold more rigidly to standards
of similar subcultural groups of the majority than do many of the
whites themselves. Conventions are accepted as mandatory. Codes of
behavior are rigorously enforced by those who are attempting to
establish themselves in another stratum of society. Many of the youth
who participated in this study are already, or will become, members
of higher status groups among Negroes and in the total culture. Rapid
processes of upward mobility are reflected in more intense stress
among youth than among those who remain in more traditional
circumstances.

Forces within their own cultural matrix are revealed in problems of adjustment reported by Negro youth as well as those encountered because of color and minority status.

Young educated Negroes are well aware of the degrees of difference between their participation in what the predominant culture has to offer and that of white high school youth. Complications in absorption of these still acute distinctions into adequate personality adjustment are to be expected. On the other hand, many of these youth in transition no doubt are utilizing their tensions as motivation toward achievement of new status. In the long run, these latter young persons will serve to increase the participation in the predominant culture of their whole ethnic group.

Pressures for conformity to peer-group demands were also more apparent among Negro youth than whites. Many are faced with the necessity to meet standards of behavior set by their families as they move up the social ladder. Yet, these youngsters may desire to maintain contact with many others of their age group who do not carry similar ambitions.

Negro girls showed a slight, though insignificant, tendency to be more unhappy with school than did Negro boys. The reverse was found among white students. White boys were significantly more critical of education than white girls.

Traditionally, the majority of Negro women have not been well educated. Their skills have been domestic as were their occupations in the main. Some have worked as farm laborers. Nonetheless, because of the greater stability of their position as family heads, their status is often higher than that of Negro men. As Negro men have attained higher educational levels and entered more and better occupations, they have more and more assumed the same status as middle-class men in the total culture. Consequently, Negro boys may have become increasingly aware of what high school education means for them and their future, and their attitudes have become increasingly more accepting.

THE IMPORTANCE OF COMMUNITY SIZE FOR NEGRO YOUTH

Negro youth in smaller communities reflected the poverty of their opportunities. Frequency of contact between white and Negro groups in rural areas may also provide more intense interaction. In any event,

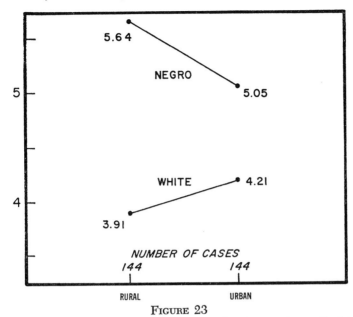

FIGURE 23

Interaction of Race and Community Size for Orientation to Society

negative response to society and distrust of people was definitely a part of the emotional pattern for many Negro youth in these communities. Moreover, these rural youth displayed greater feelings of self-inadequacy than did Negro young people living in metropolitan areas, a finding which did not appear among white youth. Migration of Negroes into cities has been large. Over two-thirds of them are now in urban residence. A selective factor has probably entered into the responses for those remaining in rural areas and smaller towns. They find themselves caught in the traditional relationships between the races. They are also probably trapped by their own inability to face a move from country to city. The quality of their education, regardless of years in school, has been inferior in many instances.

Rural economy has been declining within the total pattern of modern life. Wage levels, job opportunities, and even community services have suffered in many rural communities. Impact of these combined forces has been felt by all, but more intensely by the Negroes with their unequal share in the culture as a whole. Factors such as these

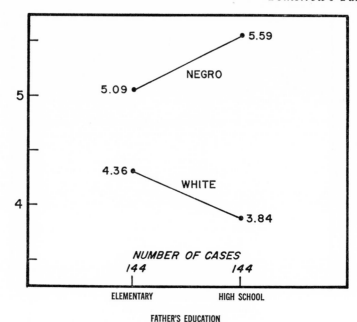

FATHER'S EDUCATION
FIGURE 24
Interaction of Race and Father's Education for Orientation to Society

also tend to combine to hold persons in status relationships which otherwise would be modified, in spite of the fact that the minority group would like to see them change.

Urban youth, Negro and white, were not far apart in the scores they made in relation to their orientation to society. Young people of the minority group became less negative as the size of the communities in which they lived increased. Opportunities are always more open in cities for Negro youth, and this fact was reflected in their more hopeful attitudes. By the same token, their relationships with people were evidently better since they were less distrustful of their fellowmen. White high school students, on the other hand, were less well oriented to the world when they lived in urban areas and were less trustful of people than their counterparts in the country. While city life appeared an open door to hope for the minority group, it evidently offered greater complexity in attitudes toward society for white teen-agers. Responses of high school students concerning the

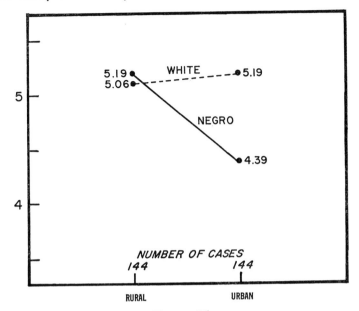

FIGURE 25
Interaction of Race and Community Size for Self Inadequacy

world and man displayed divergence that was significant between the two ethnic groups in rural areas. Whites were far more optimistic than Negroes in such settings.

In cities feelings of self-inadequacy were revealed as greater for white youth than for Negroes. Scale scores were higher for the majority group than for the minority in settings of larger size. Factors other than racial group membership would appear to be important in the insecurity evidenced by white city youngsters when compared to Negroes in the same age range. No significant differences in their conceptions of self-inadequacy were obtained between white youth who lived in rural or urban areas. Evidently these youngsters found compensating values wherever they lived which created greater similarity in their feelings of ease or lack of it.

Negro young people, as stated previously, suffered far greater doubt about their own competence when they lived in the country. To the Negro youth, city life made a great deal of difference in development of self-confidence. The contrast between experiences and opportuni-

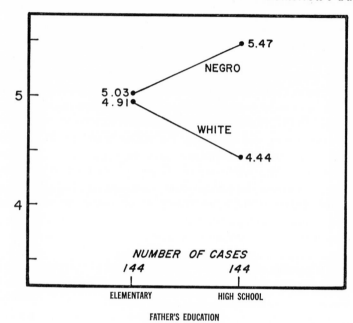

FIGURE 26
Interaction of Race and Father's Education for Social Conformity

ties available to Negroes in rural and urban areas was thus again highlighted.

Well-educated Negro families produced young persons of high school age who expressed greater negativism in their outlook on life than did those from poorly educated families—just the reverse of results obtained for white families. Among white youth, there was a definite decrease in negative orientation to society as the fathers' education increased. Negro youth from families of more adequate background also experienced greater pressures toward social conformity than did youth from homes of fathers with less than high school education.

Responses to the scales on Orientation to Society and Social Conformity by Negro young persons with better educated fathers could be products of frustration and conflict. Frustration due to limitations on continued upward mobility in the social and economic order is certainly present. Conflict over the attempt to remain a part of their own racial youth culture as they work toward greater acceptance in the total social matrix is also undeniable. Negro youth from less educated parents apparently face fewer problems of identification with their own culture. However, they, too, indicated pressures from their minority status. This interpretation in no way denies the reality of continuous and accelerating improvement in relationships between the two major ethnic groups in the nation.

Numerous young persons from the subordinate group, it may be assumed, carry the same or even greater motivation for advanced education as do the white youth. Every year of school that Negro youngsters complete increases their competence and adequacy in eventually obtaining the "good things of life." On the other hand, it must be realized that additional education may also develop goals for them which they probably cannot achieve fully within the current social order, even though they may have all formal prerequisites for such achievement.

Here is a classic example, among youth, of the concept of the culture lag. Means to attain higher goals are becoming more available for young Negroes through education. Reaching their potentialities in employment and social participation, however, still remains distant. Development of goals which can never be fully achieved no doubt contributes toward negativism in response to society and its future. At least it remains a problem which must be realistically faced by the educated Negro and by educators in general.

QUESTIONS FOR CONSIDERATION

The Research Committee for the 28th Annual Conference on Education at Prairie View College concluded its comparison of data from the Texas Cooperative Youth Study with a series of questions pertaining to Negro youth and their families. They suggested that certain problems demanded consideration. They also expressed the hope that programs of action would be developed to meet these essential concerns.

Among the major areas they listed for consideration were: (1) the influence of adult Negro family members upon their children and youth; (2) the success or failure of Negro families in meeting the psychological needs of their offspring; (3) the tension between Negro parents and youth and its contribution to feelings of personal and social inadequacy in the young; (4) the inadequacy of the sex education given Negro youth by their parents and this inadequacy as a contributing factor in emotional problems; (5) the impact of broken homes on the mental health of Negro youth; (6) the discrepancy existing between authoritarian discipline of parents and the emancipation of teen-agers in Negro families; (7) the lack of parental interest in the development of social skills as these influence behavior and acceptance of Negro youth in the larger culture; and (8) the prevailing child-rearing practices, with the aim of improving some aspects of the relationship between Negro parents and their children.

The improvement of the mental health of Negro youth was judged by Conference participants to require several approaches. Self-confidence as contrasted with insecurity should be developed among Negro youth to bring about improvement of self and social adequacy. Young persons, they recognized, require assistance from educated adults in the development of healthy attitudes toward themselves, as well as toward marriage and the family. Youth adjustment in high school appeared to have two major facets; satisfaction *with* school was seen as paramount in the development of attitudes which keep youth *in* school. The value of high school education was also stressed as essential to the evolvement of more adequate adult personalities within the group. Relationships between the sexes, the committee agreed, needed clarification and modification because of certain recognized characteristics inherent in Negro culture of the past. Finally, they suggested continuous work on problems of desegregation. They were aware of the lasting influence of segregation upon emotional and social adjustment in the lives of individual Negro youth.[4]

[4] *Ibid.*, p. 20.

VIII: Religious Denominational Preferences and the Answers of Youth

RELIGION in the United States has been a definitive aspect of its culture from early settlement. An essential motivation for colonization was demand for freedom of worship. Church affiliation has reached its all-time high since World War II.

A church of their choice was reported by 96.4 per cent of all persons in the nation in a recent sample survey conducted by the United States Bureau of the Census.[1] Baptists, whose membership cuts across all subcultural groups, were in greater number than any other. Nearly one-fifth of Protestant membership was among sects of this church. Methodists accounted for 14 per cent, with Lutherans numbering about half as many as Methodists. A few over one-twentieth were Presbyterian. All other Protestant denominations combined numbered approximately one-fifth of the population. Jewish congregations claimed 3.2 per cent. The Roman Catholic church was the faith of one-fourth of the persons in the nation. This church likewise has members at all socioeconomic levels.

Interest in religion was affirmed in a striking manner by youth in this study. Because these were students in public high schools, an answer to the question on church preference for background information was entirely optional. This particular query asked that each

[1] Editorial, "Ninety-six Percent Church Affiliated," *The Austin Statesman,* Saturday, August 1, 1959, p. 6.

student write in the denomination of his choice. Over 93 per cent named a specific church.

No answer was given by 7 per cent. The 93 per cent of youth who responded compared with the 96 per cent of the census sample of all ages for the nation as a whole. How regularly these young persons attended church was not known. Nevertheless, that this many teenagers identified themselves with a specific denomination is important in itself.

These young persons were also asked to respond to a series of statements related to religion, as has been previously reported. Perhaps it would be well to review the specific items. The first of these stated, "There is too little concern in our family for religion." Approximately three-fourths of the youth disagreed. They implied that religion did play an adequate part in their family lives. Less than one-fifth felt that their families were too limited in their concern for religion. Still fewer, one-tenth, were undecided as to how to answer this particular question.

A second proposition shed light on the nature of religious convictions of high school students. "People of different religions should not get married." Almost two-thirds disagreed, conveying the impression this was not a major consideration. However, 20 per cent agreed that this was true—a larger percentage than the combined Catholics and Jews in the group. Some members of sects other than these two evidently also adhere to the tenet of the hazard of interfaith marriage.

SUBCULTURAL VARIATIONS IN CHURCH AFFILIATIONS

In Texas, Baptist churches, the largest Protestant denomination, and the Catholic churches are more broadly cross-cultural in racial and ethnic group membership than others. Baptist churches run the gamut from the most urbane to the most conservative. They encompass rural and metropolitan populations as well as those in between. They include Anglo groups on all educational levels and a majority of the Negroes. Many members are from middle and upper income brackets. Yet numerous other affiliates, among both whites and Negroes, are from occupations which are unskilled both in city and country.

Catholic heterogeneity ranges from heavy membership among the Latin Americans through second generation families from many European countries. Some of the oldest Texas families of German and Irish extraction are in this group. Many members also count among their forebears early settlers from Spain and France. It is this church which carries the largest membership of those of Mexican heritage, the second largest racial minority group in the state.

Discussion of these two particular church groups has been detailed because they encompass a wide range in socioeconomic status, and they represent varied ethnic agglomerations. Moreover, their subcultural distinctions account for some striking implications as to religious affiliation and family life. They show up as important reflections of the cultural conditioning of certain groups and are indicative of differential participation in the dominant culture. Responses of young persons by denominations, it must be remembered, are not simple. They are confounded and complicated by other factors. They proved significant enough, however, to be worth careful examination.

Perhaps one other word of warning should be offered concerning data in this particular presentation. Reports of attitudes, problems, and concerns of youth are just what this implies. They are simply statements of how young persons of different church affiliations responded to the scales in the Texas Cooperative Youth Study. In no sense are these findings reported as critical of churches, or of their teachings. Nor do they even suggest that denominational affiliation is either the basic cause of attitudes, on the one hand, or of problems and concerns on the other. Instead, these divergencies should be accepted for what they are: a part of the wide cultural diversity made possible in the United States because of continuous adherence to freedom of religion as a basic principle. Information in this study stresses broad over-all trends. In no instance can generalizations be imputed as specific in application to any given congregation or church.

A Preliminary Investigation

For an initial analysis of the relationship of religious preference to scale scores, a 100-case random sample was drawn from each of the six major Protestant denominations, from Catholic students, from those stating no preference, and from those who left blank the question about church of their choice. An additional 100 cases were drawn from the remaining minor Protestant denominations. Since only 25 students of the total 12,892 indicated that they were Jewish, all of these were included.[2] A simple one-way analysis of variance or the comparable Chi Square test was carried out for these 1,025 cases on each of the fourteen scales for some of the individual items.

No attempt was made to control any background factors in this initial exploration. Consequently the results provided only tentative information about the impact of religious affiliation upon the lives of youth. Subsequent designs were constructed in which important variables were rigorously controlled in order to determine more clearly the relationship of church preference, per se, to the responses of the young persons.

TABLE 28: *Rank Order* * *by Religious Denomination of the Three Highest and Three Lowest Mean Scores on Eight Scales Showing Significant Denominational Differences (1,025 Cases in Sample)*

			Rank	
Scale	*Denomination*	*Mean Score*	*High*	*Low*
Orientation to Society	Catholic	4.52	1	
	Lutheran	4.23	2	
	Baptist	3.98	3	
	Jewish	3.68		8
	Episcopal	3.32		9
	Presbyterian	3.24		10
Authoritarian Discipline	Catholic	5.79	1	
	Christian	5.38	2	
	Other Protestant	5.19	3	
	Methodist	4.53		8
	Jewish	4.40		9
	Episcopal	4.23		10
Criticism of Education	Lutheran	5.24	2	
	Catholic	5.09	1	
	Baptist	4.99	3	
	Jewish	4.36		8
	Presbyterian	4.33		9
	Episcopal	4.16		10

* The higher the rank order, the more youth were aware of problems in the area under examination.

[2] The number of Jewish students was this small because members of this religious group live in urban areas. Relatively few reside in smaller cities and rural areas where the majority of the youth surveyed were located.

TABLE 28: *Rank Order by Religious Denomination of the Three Highest and Three Lowest Mean Scores on Eight Scales Showing Significant Denominational Differences (1,025 Cases in Sample)—Continued*

Scale	Denomination	Mean Score	Rank High	Low
Social Conformity	Other Protestant	5.94	1	
	Catholic	5.20	2	
	Christian	4.89	3	
	Episcopal	4.59		8
	No Preference	4.28		9
	Jewish	3.96		10
Self Inadequacy	Catholic	5.23	1	
	Baptist	5.05	2	
	Lutheran	5.04	3	
	Presbyterian	4.64		8
	Jewish	4.58		9
	Episcopal	3.88		10
Social Inadequacy	Catholic	5.56	1	
	Lutheran	5.43	2	
	Other Protestant	5.23	3	
	Presbyterian	4.88		8
	Episcopal	4.68		9
	Jewish	4.12		10
Family Tension	Catholic	5.52	1	
	Other Protestant	5.25	2	
	Episcopal	4.95	3	
	Methodist	4.80		8
	Presbyterian	4.66		9
	Jewish	4.20		10
Resentment Family Life Style	Catholic	4.91	1	
	Other Protestant	4.69	2	
	Christian	4.46	3	
	Lutheran	3.96		8
	Episcopal	3.86	9	
	Jewish	3.32	10	

No differences among youth across denominational lines were observable in their basic attitudes toward their peer groups. Their church choice was not coincident with their Criticism of Youth.

Church choice was evidently also unimportant in relation to feelings of social isolation, conception of problems with the family or finances, feelings of personal adjustment, or resentment of dependency.

Certain significant variations were obtained on the remainder of the scales as religious affiliation differed. When youth responses were ranked by the three highest and the three lowest scores on the eight remaining scales, some patterns became evident. The higher the scale score, it should be remembered, the greater was the difficulty encountered by young persons.

High school students who indicated their choice of churches as Catholic, Lutheran, or Baptist were the least optimistic about society and people. They were the more critical of education. They considered themselves to be less adequate. Some comment on this finding appears appropriate. Catholic and Baptist churches encompass the widest spread in socioeconomic groupings of any denominations within the state, as already indicated. Moreover, it should be recalled, the two largest minority ethnic groups are found within their respective memberships: Latin-Americans and Negroes. Lutherans are, in many instances, of relatively recent European background. Membership tends to be heavy among persons who maintain an in-group relationship with their own language and ethnic culture patterns. Many are rural and small-town residents, as are the Baptists. Each of these three denominations is relatively authoritarian, although they exercise their control over the behavior of church members in somewhat different areas.

Youth from Catholic, Christian, and "Other Protestant" denominations scored high in their adherence to authoritarian discipline as preferred in child rearing, in their problems of pressures for conformity to peer-group standards, and in their resentment of how their family members related to each other and lived within their homes. Christian churches, as utilized in this study, included both the conservative branch known as the Church of Christ and the more liberal Disciples of Christ. The latter group in the Christian churches is highly urban, while the former has heavy membership in smaller towns as well as in cities. "Other Protestant" churches included the smaller and more traditional denominations found outside the major church organizations. Among members of these are persons living in rural areas, small communities, and in working class neighborhoods in cities. This designation also encompassed religious bodies such as

Unitarian and Christian Scientist, to name only two others. Cultural dichotomies such as rural versus urban, orthodox versus modern, and upper-middle versus working class, with some ethnic considerations in addition, may account for the problems as revealed by high school youth.

Feelings of social inadequacy were most often recognized among youth from Catholic and Lutheran churches and those youngsters having no preference for a denomination. Why this may have occurred among Catholic and Lutheran youth has already been noted. Youngsters giving no preference for denominations might be assumed to include a minimal number from unconventional families in any status group. More than likely, however, this segment of the youth population was made up from youngsters of minimal socioeconomic background where membership in any kind of social organization by family members was outside their experiences. Paucity in social relationships, apart from the family and neighborhood, would help account for feelings of social inadequacy among children of such parents.

The responses to the scale measuring Family Tension deserves special comment because of the unusual combination of church groups whose youth received the highest scores. Young persons listing Catholicism as their preference, those indicating "Other Protestant" denominations, and youngsters from Episcopal families admitted to higher tension levels within their families. Youth from the first two groups might have been aware of increased tension because of contrast between the restrictions placed upon them and the freedom enjoyed by other youth from families belonging to churches with less restrictive regulations on behavior. Moreover, conflict between generations in ethnic groups with language differences (and many such groups are included in the membership of Catholic churches) no doubt may account for some of the family stress noted by these young people. Disparity between parental standards, where parents were members of the more orthodox Protestant denominations, and the standards of their high school aged children may also be assumed to have played some part in responses of these youngsters.

The more unexpected finding, of course, was the admission of high degrees of tension in families of Episcopal young people. Parents of these youngsters are usually better educated and their status in society often is considerably higher than others. It would seem logical to assume that stress in such families had arisen from parental pressures for achievement, from their high expectations for their young, and from demands for competitive performance on all fronts by their sons and daughters. While family tension had its origin in broad socio-cultural factors among Catholics and "Other Protestant" young people, it probably was generated within Episcopal families themselves out of parental expectations for youth performance, showing up here because of the status of members of the church.

Low scale scores, indicative of more adequate functioning, were consistently obtained by Episcopal, Jewish, and Presbyterian youth (save on the Family Tension scale for Episcopal young people). Students from Presbyterian families joined the three lowest scoring groups in Orientation to Society, revealing their greater optimism concerning the world and its people. These groups were least critical of education and thereby indicated their more effective scholarship as well. Methodist teen-agers, combined with Episcopal and Jewish, were the more democratic in their approach to child rearing. Youngsters with no church preference, along with Episcopal and Jewish, felt least pressure to conform to peer-group standards other than their own. Methodist youth replaced Episcopalians to score among the lowest in tension within their families, alongside Jewish and Presbyterian. Resentment of Family Life Style was minimal among Lutheran, Jewish, and Episcopal youngsters. Because Jewish, Episcopal, Presbyterian, and Methodist families are among those with parents who, on the whole, have had more formal education and whose incomes are higher, the participation in upper-middle-class culture experienced by their families was evident in the responses of their offspring.

Varied Reactions to Certain Specific Statements

Attitudes of young people toward the older generation are subject to speculation. Youth are often accused of lacking concern for their parents and of being indifferent to the teachings of their elders. That there would be variations as revealed by church groupings in relation to such attitudes was a foregone conclusion. In which direction distinctions would be found awaited evidence from youth themselves.

The ten statements submitted to special analysis with denominational preference taken into account are as follows:

12. Children should feel it is their duty to care for their parents when their parents grow old.

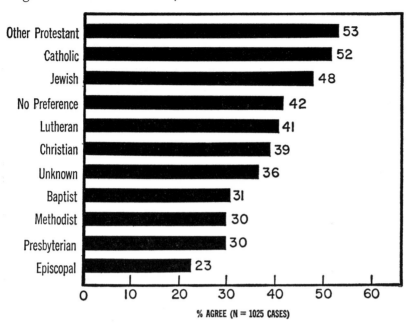

% AGREE (N = 1025 CASES)

FIGURE 27
Per Cent Who Strongly Agree that "Children Should Feel It Is Their Duty
To Care for Their Parents When Their Parents Grow Old"

16. High school marriages can only lead to trouble.
21. Parents should sacrifice everything for their children.
53. A parent has the right to read a high school student's letter
without first asking permission.
58. There is too little concern in our family for religion.
62. It is not the duty of the parent to teach the child about sex.
72. People of different religions should not get married.
100. Having the opportunity of going to college is very important
to me.
168. I would like to get married as soon as possible.
192. I think about sex a good deal of the time.

Young persons from Catholic families, from "Other Protestant" denominations, and those of Jewish origin agreed emphatically that it
was the duty of children to care for parents when they became elders.
Reflected in this attitude is the strong emphasis placed upon parental
authority and the family by the Catholic and Jewish faiths and by

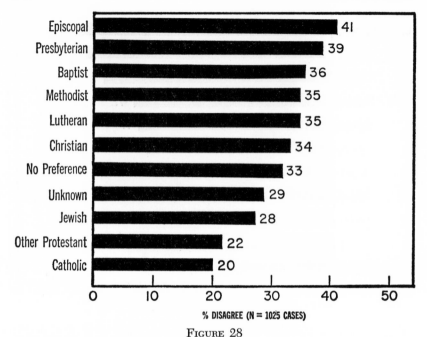

FIGURE 28

Per Cent Who Strongly Disagree with the Statement that "Parents Should Sacrifice Everything for Their Children"

churches in many smaller Protestant denominations. The admonition to "Honor Thy Father and Thy Mother" is taken quite literally in the teachings of these groups.

Episcopal youngsters expressed highest degree of disagreement with the statement concerning care of elder parents. Speculation as to the reasons for this leads in two directions. Again, a statement of possible reasons does not imply a causal relationship. In the first place, the possibility that children in Episcopal families will have to assume full responsibility for the care of their parents in later years is relatively remote. Generally speaking, persons belonging to this church are among those in substantial income brackets. Secondly, more equalitarian relationships between parents and their children are cultivated among members of this denomination and others of similar education and income. This does not mean, of course, that should necessity arise, these youth would be any less careful of their parents. However,

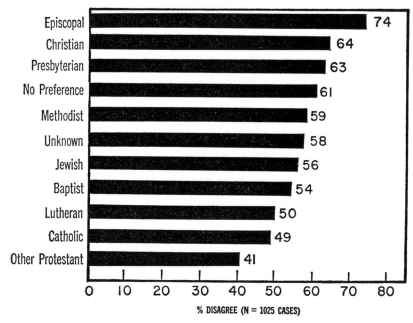

Figure 29
Per Cent Who Strongly Disagree with the Statement that "A Parent Has the Right To Read a High School Student's Letter Without First Asking Permission"

their reasons for assuming their responsibilities would be somewhat different: for instance, basic affection rather than duty.

Interestingly enough, those who agreed most strongly that parents should sacrifice everything for their children were youngsters from the same three denominations as those who were most sure they had a duty to care for their parents when they grew old. If youth expected parental sacrifice for their rearing, they also anticipated self-denial as adults for those who had given up for them when they were children. Again, the highest disagreement with the statement that parents should "sacrifice everything for their children" was among the students from Episcopal families. Evidenced in these findings are real divergencies which still exist on different sociocultural levels in the United States in concepts of relationships between parents and their children. Ernest R. Burgess and Harvey J. Locke, in a book subtitle,

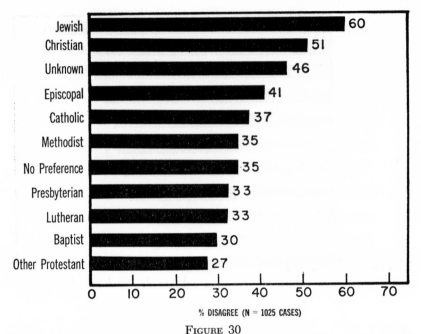

% DISAGREE (N = 1025 CASES)

FIGURE 30

Per Cent Who Strongly Disagree with the Statement that "There Is Too Little Concern in Our Family for Religion"

have highlighted the more traditional versus the modern in family life as "from institution to companionship." [3]

Consistent with the results of the two former analyses were responses to the statement, "A parent has the right to read a high school student's letter without first seeking permission." Approximately half of the Jewish, Catholic, and Lutheran young people felt it was all right for their parents to invade the privacy of their correspondence. "Other Protestant" youth were even more agreeable to having their letters read without permission. Episcopal youngsters were, by far, the least tolerant of such intrusion into their personal lives.

Family indifference to religion was denied emphatically by youth of the Jewish faith. Nor is this surprising when consideration is given to the careful inclusion of the total family in the worship and cere-

[3] Ernest R. Burgess and Harvey J. Locke, *The Family: From Institution to Companionship.*

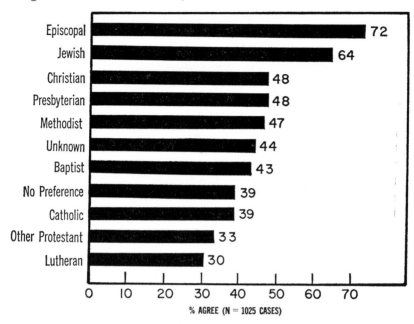

FIGURE 31

Per Cent Who Strongly Agree that "Having the Opportunity To Go to College Is Very Important to Me"

monials of this church. Members of the two Christian churches were second to Jewish youth in feeling that religion was given ample attention by their families. "Other Protestants" and Baptists were more numerous among the students who felt that too little attention was paid to religion in their families. Perhaps this response may be attributed to the fact that among these denominations are those who are, in the main, more fundamentalist. Church members, young or old, might well tend to feel that no matter how much attention was given to religion in family groups, it would never be enough. This might even be construed as an expression of the "Doctrine of Original Sin" expressed through the specific of family worship.

The two groups who agreed most strongly that going to college was very important to them were youngsters from homes of Episcopal and of Jewish background. Both of these churches include persons of high socioeconomic status and of value patterns which consider a college education as imperative to social and economic maturation. However, perhaps one observation may be offered. Episcopal families accept college education as an integral part of social status. Jewish persons, on the other hand, have stressed education as the major attribute for movement up the socioeconomic ladder. For the former it is an accepted criterion of social position. For the latter, it is a major technique for achievement.

Catholic, "Other Protestant," and Lutheran youngsters indicated they were least concerned with college education. In fact, percentages among these groups ranged from 39 per cent who were concerned among the Catholics to only 30 per cent among Lutheran young people. Again, among many of the Catholic youth, college has not been a part of the culture pattern or the level of expectation for their parents of more recent migration from Mexico. The possibility of college and its relation to improved status over that customary in their families is still discovered by relatively few of these young people even if they are attending high school. Here is a waste of talent that some communities are investigating and making an effort to overcome through guidance within high school itself. That "Other Protestant" denominations included youth who did not consider college attendance important or desired is not surprising. Smaller and more fundamentalist denominations are found more often than not in neighborhoods where college-educated parents are few. Explanation for lack of interest in higher education among Lutheran young people might lie in the rural residence of many of them or in traditional control of children by fathers who still consider "hard work" rather than education to be the road to independence and success.

The query as to whether people of different church background should marry brought no unexpected results.[4] Episcopal youth felt that intermarriage with other faiths was indeed compatible, as did Presbyterians and Baptists. The first two denominational groups consist, in the main, of urban persons, sophisticated and individualistic in their choice of behavior. Baptist youth were third in feeling that

[4] The frequency distributions of responses to Items 16 and 72 were sufficiently normal in shape to justify employing the more powerful technique of analysis of variance and F tests for examining differences among the religious groups, rather than chi square analysis as in the case of the other items. Consequently the findings refer to mean scores rather than percentages of agreement or disagreement for these two items. The conclusions are essentially the same. This difference in statistical method employed is also reflected in Figures 32 and 33 for Items 16 and 72, respectively.

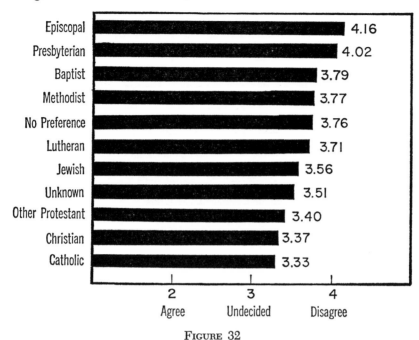

FIGURE 32

Mean Scores for Different Religious Groups in Responding to Item 16: "People of Different Religions Should Not Get Married"

church membership should not impede marriage to a member of another group. Baptist students, in contrast with Episcopal and Presbyterian, probably gained their independent viewpoint from church doctrine itself. Each Baptist congregation is a law unto itself and while certain conventional behavior is demanded of communicants, individual determination of conviction is stressed in other areas.

Catholics, who experience strong pressures against interfaith marriages as a matter of church dogma, were highest in agreement that "people of different religions should not get married." Even the Catholics, however, were more inclined to disagree than to agree with this statement. Next to the Catholics in this belief were youth from the Christian churches. This may be accounted for because of the cultural characteristics of the Church of Christ itself. Acute differences in practices of worship exist in this church even from the Disciples of Christ which stemmed from the same beginning. Where

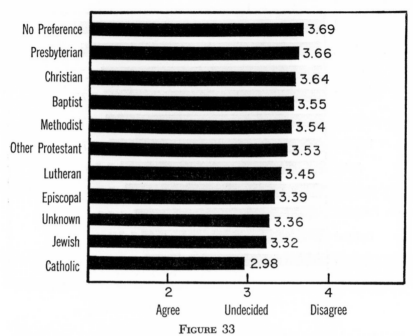

FIGURE 33
Mean Scores for Different Religious Groups in Responding to Item 72: "High School Marriage Can Only Lead to Trouble"

ritual and church requirements for members are unique from others, reluctance concerning marriage outside the group may be expected. "Other Protestant" denominations were third, again indicating the in-group qualities of more fundamentalist sects. Jewish youth ranked fourth among those who felt that intermarriage was undesirable, perhaps pointing toward a looser adherence to the practices of isolation from other faiths.

An examination of responses to the statement that "high school marriages can only lead to trouble" also brought forth evidences of religious differences. Youth, who expressed no preference for denominations, disagreed most with this statement. Their lack of adherence to the traditional as indicated by failure to indicate church membership was perhaps further expressed in their attitudes toward age of marriage. If a later marriage age is culturally accepted as preferable, then a divergent attitude toward age of marriage would further state

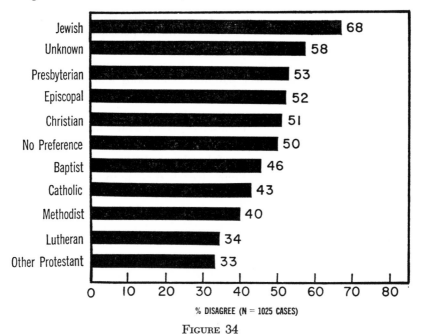

% DISAGREE (N = 1025 CASES)

FIGURE 34

Per Cent Who Strongly Disagree with the Statement that "It Is Not the Duty of the Parents To Teach the Child about Sex"

a break with established custom. Or perhaps a simpler explanation is all that is needed. The group of youth expressing no preference for a church probably included large enough numbers from socioeconomic strata where early marriage is a part of the pattern of the subculture. Presbyterian and Christian church youngsters were second and third in feeling that early marriage was not necessarily undesirable. For many families in the Presbyterian and Disciples of Christ denominations, subsidy of youthful marriages would not be impossible and their children know this. For some youth in the Church of Christ group, early marriage was likely to have been a family fact.

Expectations might be held that Catholic youth would accept early marriage with greater ease than others, but such was not the case. They, with the Jewish and the Episcopal youth, indicated that high school marriages were most undesirable to them. Again, differences in origin of these attitudes may be pointed out for consideration. Catholic youth expect to have children soon after marriage and in larger numbers. High school students of this church perhaps see early marriage as the inevitable assumption of adult responsibilities, and they desire to delay such obligations. Jewish and Episcopal youth, on the other hand, probably reflect parental aspirations which demand delayed marriage to accomplish educational goals. It should be remembered that these same two groups of young people held college as a most desired experience for themselves. High school marriages would, therefore, appear to these youth as both flaunting parental expectations and also as assumption of burdens which would prohibit accomplishment of what they, themselves, had come to hold as essential.

Jewish youth were most positive of all that it was the duty of parents to teach their children about sex. They outdistanced the denominational representatives nearest them by some 15 per cent. Young people from Presbyterian, Episcopal, and Christian churches and those with no church preference were next in agreement to the Jewish group that parents should assume teaching responsibility in this important area of living. The statement read, it should be remembered, "It is not the duty of the parent to teach the child about sex." Those groups of teen-agers who agreed the most with this comment were Catholic, Lutheran, and "Other Protestants." Again, these young people were voicing attitudes prevalent in their varied sociocultural groups—attitudes which have been, and in many instances still are, among those accepted by adult members of these churches.

Youth among denominations not specifically singled out for consideration fell between the extremes discussed above. The examples given were chosen to highlight teen-age responses to the ten items portraying parent-youth relationships and family life when measured against denominational choices.

INTERACTION OF RELIGION AND OTHER BACKGROUND FACTORS

Religious variables as already indicated cannot stand alone. They are inextricably meshed with other important background factors. Among the more important of these considered was fathers' education with its inescapable relationship to sociocultural group membership. In addition, it seemed probable that community size would be an element of relevance to religion as expressed in denominational choice. These and other lesser variations in places and ways of life were expected to influence youth responses to the study scales.

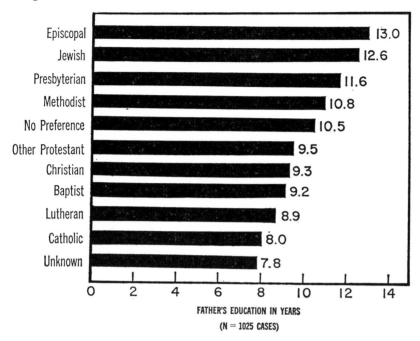

FIGURE 35

Religious Preferences of Youth Related to Father's Education

Fathers' Education—A Telling Factor

To test these hypotheses, and especially the impact of the schooling of fathers, an analysis of variance across religious groupings was made by fathers' education level. Striking differences did indeed exist by church preferences when fathers' education was the major consideration.

Previous studies have indicated that members of the Episcopal Church have superior socioeconomic status in most communities. Persons affiliated with the Jewish faith are also usually high in education and income. This latter group, small as it was among total students, consisted of families of many years' residence in the state. Jewish families are well established both in economic position and over-all social integration in many Texas communities. Fathers on the lowest educational level, as might have been surmised, were those of teen-agers who did not fill in information on religious preference. Closely following, in minimal years of formal education were fathers of Catholic students. By far the greater majority of youth of Mexican heritage, as has been noted, were Catholic. Average number of years in school for Catholic fathers was no doubt reduced by this factor.

Rank order by church preference of youth and educational level of fathers was: Episcopalian, Jewish, Presbyterian, Methodist and other less numerous Protestant denominations in that order. Below these came the Christian churches. Many members of the Church of Christ live in smaller communities and Disciples of Christ are more urban, as previously indicated. Baptists who ranked below the two Christian churches also have heavy rural membership and many Negro communicants. Catholic fathers were next to lowest in educational attainment. Those whose sons and daughters made known no religious preference were of lowest rank. Again, let it be stressed, Baptists and Catholics in this sample included minority group members.

Other Background Factors and Their Significance

Denominational preferences of youth appeared as of major importance for examination. Therefore, four separate factorial designs were constructed in order to control different variables as they might impinge upon religion. Geographic regions of East and South Texas were dropped. In the former there were few Catholics and in the latter, few Baptists. However, regional differences across the Gulf Coast, Central and West Texas were retained as an independent variable for systematic study.

Fathers' education was utilized as an independent variable at three levels in the first of these four factorial designs—elementary, high school, and some college. Community size included large (metropolitan) and small (all other). The fourth background variable was sex of the respondent.

Only four church preferences occurred with sufficient frequency to justify inclusion: Methodist, Christian, Catholic, and Baptist. A total of 576 cases was drawn to place two, four, or six cases in each of the 144 cells of this factorial design. Only white students from intact families who had no roomers, grandparents, or other relatives living in the home, were employed for this study.

Significant differences were revealed for these religious groups on about half of the scales concerning attitudes and problems of youth.

TABLE 29: *Significant Mean Scores on Seven Scales for Four Major Religious Denominations*

Religion	N	Orientation to Society	Authoritarian Discipline	Criticism of Education	Family Problems	Family Tension	Social Inadequacy	Social Isolation
Catholic	144	3.99	5.37	4.90	5.01	5.17	5.42	4.98
Baptist	216	3.74	4.60	4.89	4.46	4.72	4.99	4.89
Methodist	144	3.15	4.69	4.29	4.10	4.40	4.76	4.57
Christian	72	3.10	4.79	4.65	4.24	4.60	5.21	4.96

Catholic students were distinctly more negative toward society. They more readily accepted authoritarian discipline as proper for child rearing. Criticism of education by them was more acute. Family problems and tensions were reported with greater frequency. Social inadequacy as a problem showed up more extensively. These results were not entirely unexpected.

Minority status is two-fold in relation to Catholic youth in public schools. They constitute only a small segment of the population, a little over 10 per cent. Moreover, minority status is social reality for Catholic youth of Latin origin. This is also true for many rural Catholics whose origin was in dissenting minority groups of European background. Fewer years of education for fathers of Catholic students is also a contributing factor in the lack of optimism of their children.

Criticism of education indicates problems within the school setting. A language handicap in addition to minority status tends to produce difficulties in academic achievement. Feelings of social inadequacy are to be expected among young persons who recognize themselves as of a distinctive culture from the majority. Family problems and tensions are also to be anticipated among young persons where the patterns of family life differ markedly from those of the major group. Strain is inevitable between generations where authoritarianism and male dominance are indisputably accepted by elders but less dogmatically adhered to by the younger generation. Especially do young persons resent a parental control of their behavior which is different from that experienced by other youth.

The rapid economic and social mobility to middle-class membership by young persons of Latin origin who have been reared in Texas cities is notable. Educational level of these second and third generation children is increasing rapidly. With additional schooling, occupational competency and income have improved materially. The

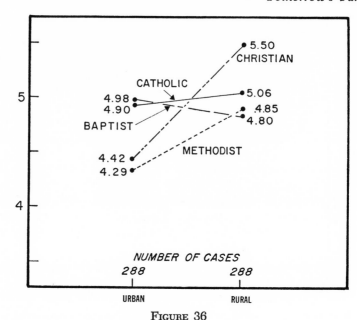

Effect of Community Size upon Social Isolation for Four Religious
Denominations

development of a middle class among persons of Mexican origin
throughout the south, central, and western sections of Texas is a phenomenon of the last two or three decades. This particular study was
made, of course, during this period of rapid change.

Methodist youth tended to show the least family tension and the
fewest problems of the four religious denominations. Membership in
this denomination is among the better educated, higher income, upper
middle class. These same students had the lowest scores on social
inadequacy and social isolation. Baptist youth and those from the
Christian churches placed in the middle between Catholic, on the
one extreme, and Methodist on the other.

Community size as related to religion proved significant in only one
instance. Youth of Christian or Methodist denominations showed
greater concern over feelings of social isolation in rural communities
than in the cities. For youth from Baptist and Catholic homes there
was no distinction between town and country. This rural-urban difference was particularly noteworthy for the Christian denominations.

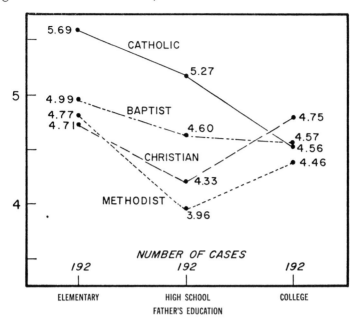

FIGURE 37

Effect of Father's Education upon Family Tension for Four Religious Denominations

This may be due in part to the fact that the rather fundamentalist Church of Christ is more common in the rural areas of Texas while its related denomination, the Christian Church, tends to be concentrated in the cities. As previously noted, worship practices of the Church of Christ are distinctive enough from those of the other Protestant denominations to create a sense of difference among their communicants, which may be carried over by younger persons into their social relationships. Such distinctive practices would be more apparent in rural communities than in urban where divergencies are less noticeable and, therefore, less compelling in their impact upon youth.

Fathers' education and the religious preferences of their offspring revealed another significant relationship. No differences were discovered between religious groups in response to family tension for youth with college-educated fathers. Democratic processes within the family and ease in interaction between family members is a part of cultural adequacy and middle-class status. Distinctions have already been noted for youth from families whose fathers had high school or elementary education.

A Slight Shift in Design

A second, related analysis was undertaken in which community size was dropped as a variable and East Texas was added as a region, since regional differences proved to be of little importance in the previous analysis. Although the increase in number of Catholic youth from East Texas was rather small, this rearrangement made it possible to include 640 cases to fill ninety-six cells. Aside from the change in geographic regions and dropping community size as an independent variable, this factorial design was identical to the previous one. The four religious groups included Methodist (240 cases), Christian (80 cases), Catholic (80 cases), and Baptist (240 cases). As usual, the fourteen scale scores were examined. In addition, comparisons among the independent variables were made on the ten individual items listed previously. These items all dealt with social or family issues that are often ostensibly handled in different ways by distinctive religious groups. Results essentially similar to those secured earlier were obtained for the fourteen scale scores with respect to variations among the four religious groups.

Catholic youth again tended to express greater negative orientation to society; more agreement with principles of authoritarian discipline; higher degrees of criticism of education; and more family problems and tension. Other religious groups remained in the same comparative positions as in the former study.

An interaction between religion and sex came to light in this particular design, which had not reached significance in earlier analyses. Boys who stated preference for the Methodist church tended to see themselves as having more family problems than did girls in this denomination. Methodist youth, it will be remembered, were those from homes in the upper educational brackets for parents. Also it should be recalled that boys in this particular status group for the sample as a whole, displayed more concern over family problems than did girls. Why this may be a valid difference between the sexes has been explored previously.

High school boys and girls from the Christian denominations displayed a reverse trend. Girls received higher scores on family prob-

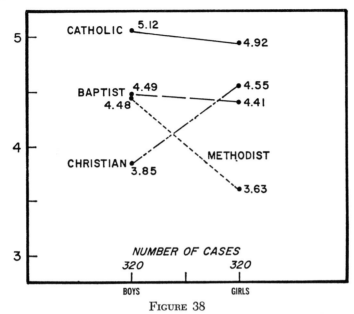

FIGURE 38

Effect of Sex Differences upon Family Problems for Four Religious Denominations

lems than did boys. No sex differences were noted for either Catholic or Baptist youth on the family problem scale.[5]

AN ITEM ANALYSIS FOR FOUR DENOMINATIONS

Differences across the four religious groups proved significant for only three of the ten items that were examined in this rigorous design. In each of the three items, outcomes for Catholic youth were similar to those presented earlier. The first of these items was, "Children should feel it their duty to care for their parents when their parents grow old." Catholic youth in both studies tended to agree more strongly than others that children should assume responsibility for

---

[5] In this particular analysis, the combined higher order interactions for family problems proved significant at the .01 level. Consequently, interpretation of the interaction between sex and religion should be approached with caution. It is possible that this is a chance occurrence in spite of its significance at the .001 level when tested against the within-cell error variance. Moreover, it does not appear in any of the other analyses of variance involving religion.

their parents. Emphasis is placed upon family unity by the Church as well as upon family stability couched in unquestioned adherence to parental and church authority and prohibition of divorce.

Youth from Baptist, Christian, and Methodist denominations expressed increasing disagreement, in this order, with the concept of care for the elderly in this design. Parents in these denominations place less stress upon filial duty and more upon strength in family relationships to assure care of elder family members. Even here, however, the great majority thought young persons should assist their parents in their later years.

As in the earlier study, highly significant differences between religious denominations were also discernible in response to "High school marriages can only lead to trouble." Most of the variation in group means could be accounted for by contrasting Catholic with the three Protestant denominations combined. Catholic youth agreed with this statement more frequently than did the Protestant young people. As previously indicated, agreement among the Catholics probably arose from their realization of the permanence of marriage in their church. To repeat again, Catholic youth have instilled within them the expectation of early parenthood and adult responsibility for children. Moreover, with the expectation of having several children, concern over sufficient income as it relates to family adequacy also probably looms as reality for these youth.

Answers to questions on interfaith marriages would be expected to show divergence between religious groups. To the statement, "People of different religions should not get married," the majority of Catholics responded by endorsement. Baptist young people took the middle of the road between Catholic and those who designated Methodist or Christian church preference.

As important as differences were the likenesses among youth from these four denominations. No significant variations in response were recorded to "Parents should sacrifice everything for their children." Three-fourths of the youth from all denominations had disagreed with this. Also, it might be expected that the more authoritarian churches, Catholic and Baptist, would accept the statement, "A parent has the right to read a high school student's letters without first asking permission." However, 82 per cent of all youth disagreed with this. The right of parents to invade youths' privacy was granted only by one-tenth of the youngsters in the over-all sample, regardless of denomination.

That no Protestant-Catholic division existed in answer to the question, "There is too little concern in our family for religion," would seem to dispel a prevalent myth: the lack of religious orientation in Protestant families, and only token adherence in Catholic families. Obviously youth in Texas feel that religion is an adequate part of the lives of their families.

The final series of statements revealed a noticeable lack of Catholic-Protestant division. Over 80 per cent of the boys and girls, regardless of church preference, disagreed with the statement that it was not the duty of parents to teach their children about sex. On the item, "A girl who gets into trouble on a date has no one to blame but herself," about half of the youth agreed and others were undecided or disagreed. It might have been expected that a higher proportion of agreement would be found among Catholic and Baptist youth because of their more traditional conception of masculine and feminine roles. But this did not prove true.

In response to, "I would like to get married as soon as possible," no difference between denominations was found regardless of the greater emphasis on marriage, family life, and children in the Catholic church. Also variations might have been anticipated because of the wide subcultural distinctions within the membership of the Baptist and Catholic churches in Texas. As will be remembered three-fourths of the youth responded that desire for immediate marriage did not apply to them. Again, in reply to the statement, "I think about sex a good deal of the time," no difference was found between the youth from the more conventional backgrounds and those from the less traditional denominations. Almost two-thirds of the young persons said this did not apply to them or was of little importance.

Indicative of the changing attitudes of all groups in the state were reactions to the statement, "Having the opportunity to go to college is very important to me." No distinctions in replies were recorded across religious lines. Ambition for higher education among today's youth is obviously quite generalized. It traverses religious groups, educational levels, and ethnic membership since three-fourths of all youth responded affirmatively to this question.

A SPECIALIZED COMPARISON

Baptist and Catholic youth were relatively close in their responses on several scales in both of the preceding studies. Because of the size of affiliations of these two denominations in the total population, it was decided that a special analysis should be undertaken focussed upon youth from these major churches. Over half of the youth population involved in the study were from one or the other of these two denominations. While the Baptist and Catholic churches are radically different, they do have similarity in their highly conservative approach to certain social practices and problems. Moreover, both hold allegiance to traditional patterns of family relationship, role definition, and behavior. Emphasis in the Baptist church is upon the more conventional from the point of view of social activities. Dancing, drinking, smoking, card playing are prohibited for Baptist membership. While this does not hold in the Catholic church, there is a conventional, theological adherence, equally prohibitive, in relation to intermarriage, family planning, and dissolution of marriages. Neither group belongs to the National Council of Churches. The Catholic church is rigid in its hierarchy. Baptist churches could almost be called inflexible in adherence to independence of congregations. However, while there are distinctions between the Baptist and other Protestant denominations, the social-emotional distance between Catholic and Baptist churches is indeed far wider. Comparison of youth, then, between these two major church organizations is one of likeness in authoritarian orientation. At the same time, vast differences in application of authority exist. Also even more extreme divergence in church organization prevails.

East Texas was omitted in this examination because of the small number of Catholics in the region. Since most Catholics live in the Rio Grande Valley, and many are of Latin-American origin, the South Texas region was included. However, all possible interactions between geographic regions and religion were carefully checked with regard to the linkage of Catholicism with Latin Americans in the Rio Grande Valley.

Only two levels of fathers' education were included—elementary and high school. This restriction was necessitated because of the small number of college men, especially among Catholic fathers in the Rio Grande Valley. Community size and sex constituted the remaining two background factors. A total of 560 cases was selected from intact white families to fill the 64 cells in this factorial design.

Differences between Catholic and Baptist youth were highly significant for most of the scales measuring both attitudes and problems. Catholic youth tended to be more negative in their social attitudes, more accepting of authoritarian discipline, and more critical of education. They were definitely troubled by pressures for conformity to their peer groups. Slight trends (significant only at the .05 level), were also noted in negative criticism of peers, in intensity of family problems, and in feelings of social isolation. There were no significant differences on other scales.

TABLE 30: *Significant Mean Scores on Nine Scales for Catholic and Baptist Youth*

Religion	N	Orienta- tion to Society	Authori- tarian Disci- pline	Criti- cism of Edu- cation	Criticism of Youth	Family Problems	Self Inade- quacy	Social Inade- quacy	Social Con- formity	Social Isolation
Catholic	280	4.46	5.80	5.41	5.38	4.98	5.50	5.65	5.16	5.06
Baptist	280	3.78	4.71	4.71	5.11	4.57	5.05	5.17	4.77	4.81

No important variations were found between Baptist and Catholic youth by geographic regions. However, many Baptist teen-agers in the Gulf Coast area come from families who have migrated from rural East Texas into highly industrialized urban centers. Catholic youth of minority group origin are numerous in the Valleys below San Antonio. Both of these categories of young persons expressed concern over personal problems more often than youth from the state as a whole. Because this difference was only significant at the .05 level, this trend should be viewed with some caution. Nonetheless, it does serve to indicate that problems may arise when young persons are in process of orientation to changing cultural conditions. Rural backgrounds are not adequate for easy assimilation into city living. Ethnic culture patterns of the Latins in South Texas are in process of modification toward majority group configurations. Personal and family adjustment is never easy for youth who are in transition from rural to urban culture, from social class to social class, or from the way of life of one ethnic group to another.

Youth responses concerning authoritarian discipline showed a highly significant interaction between community size and religious affiliation.

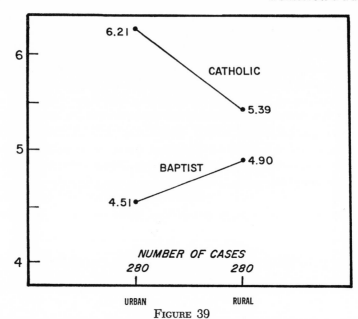

FIGURE 39

Effect of Community Size on Acceptance of Authoritarian Discipline for Baptist and Catholic Youth

Catholic youth in larger communities tended to be more accepting of authoritarian discipline in child development. The reverse proved true for smaller communities. Catholic congregations in larger communities are cohesive. Active members are in constant communication. The church is a major influence on many families. Not only is this influence exerted through religious services, but through many activities planned for youth groups at the church. Teachings of the correctness of authoritarian control by the church and in families are reinforced by close interaction between the clergy, the parents, and youth from like religious backgrounds. Catholic youth in rural areas and smaller communities in Texas are in less constant communication. They are fewer in number. Many of them live apart from each other on farms. Most attend public consolidated high schools and are in day-by-day association with many non-Catholics. Social activities tend to center around the school. They attend church for services and occasional social events.

Fathers' education level and religious affiliation also proved to be

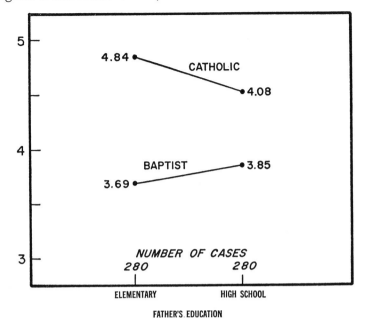

FIGURE 40

Influence of Father's Lack of Education on Youth's Negative Orientation to Society for Baptist and Catholic Youth

significant in their interaction. Catholic youth from homes where fathers had completed an eighth grade education or less tended to be more negative in their reactions to the world and their fellow men. They adhered more rigidly to principles of authoritarian discipline. This was in contrast to other youth of the Catholic faith whose fathers were better educated. Also this was in comparison with youth from the Baptist churches.

MATCHED GROUPS FOR RIGOROUS COMPARATIVE PURPOSES

Fathers' education in all previous discussions of interaction with religious affiliation was only grossly controlled. Groups were compared according to three levels of schooling—elementary, high school, and some college. In spite of this gross control, fathers' education still remained sufficiently uncontrolled in several instances to raise some question concerning the possibility of slight but significant confounding of religion and educational level. Some doubt existed as to the extent to which religious affiliation alone was responsible for differences on several of the scales of measurement. A final analysis of variance was carried out in order to control meticulously fathers' education and several other background variables. A sample was especially selected in which youth were matched exactly on four background factors: geographic region, community size, sex, and fathers' education. Included in this particular study were once again the Baptists, Methodists, Catholics, and the two combined Christian denominations. South Texas was eliminated to overcome difficulties of interpretation due to the heavy predominance of Latin Americans. Only intact white families were used. A total of 512 cases was drawn to fill the ninety-six cells of the factorial design.

Differences among the four religious groups in Orientation to Society were smaller than in previous analyses. Nevertheless, the F-ratio for religion still proved significant beyond the .05 level. Catholics continued to retain the highest scores on negativism toward society, followed closely by Baptists. Again, the broad range of subcultural group membership in these two churches was indicated. Also here was visible the more traditional approach to social behavior and management of family problems which are integral facets of authoritarian religious organizations. Teachings in both of these churches, as vastly different and as completely antagonistic as they are, approach social behavior from a "thou shalt not" point of view. Methodists and the two Christian groups obtained almost identical mean scores which were lower than for either Catholic or Baptist. None of the interactions between religion and sex, community size, or fathers' education proved significant for Orientation to Society.

Differences between the four religious groups were much more striking for the scale on Authoritarian Discipline. Catholics, again, had the highest scores. Baptists and the undifferentiated Christian groups were in the middle. Had the Church of Christ been distinct from Disciples of Christ, probably this third group would have fallen nearer the Methodists. Methodists were the most democratic in concepts of authority. Again, this gives indication of the total matrix of subcultural differences as represented by church affiliation within the state.

Catholics stood apart from the three Protestant denominations on family problems. These youth admitted to more difficulties in family relationships than did the Protestant groups. Attitudinal changes among Catholic youth of this generation who are being educated in the public schools may be evident through this finding. Conflict with parents over their relatively authoritarian approach to parent-child relationships is probably reflected. No distinctions were discovered in intensity of family problems between the Baptists, Methodists, and the two Christian denominations.

Similar results were obtained for family tension and social conformity as for family problems. Catholic youth in public schools were aware of tension between themselves and other family members. Pressures for conformity to behavior patterns of their peers were also evident. No other interactions than these proved significant between religion and background factors in this carefully matched sample.

A COMMENT IN CONCLUSION

To assume that religion and the teachings of denominations are the basic causes of problems and attitudes in the lives of young persons is obviously only a part of the picture. These carefully designed and intensive studies of the differences between youth as related to their designated choices of denominations, however, do point to religious orientation as an important factor among others which contribute to the responses they make toward themselves and their families.

IX: Patterns of Parenthood

FAMILIES in a technological and urban society find themselves only small segments within a complex culture. In contrast, the agrarian kinship groups of past generations, with their multitude of functions, might have been designated as "little societies." Socialization of children, in large measure, took place at home. Present-day parents, even if they would, could not impart to and interpret for their children all they need to know to become adequate adults in a complicated social system. Socialization of today's youngsters, as Talcott Parsons and Robert Bales have pointed out, requires more than any one family can communicate. Children have farther to go and more to learn. It takes longer to grow up and more help from many sources.[1] The family is only one facet of an intricate whole.

As a subsystem, rather than as a "microcosm of society," the nuclear family is limited or released in its cultural participation by the place it holds in society and by its residential location in region and community. Family members interpret and perceive cultural content according to the restrictions or freedom in sharing imposed by their sex, by their racial group membership, and even by their denominational allegiance. These social forces have been examined as they have impinged upon the acculturation of Texas youth.

[1] Talcott Parsons and Robert F. Bales, *Family, Socialization and Interaction Process*, pp. 18–20.

Intrafamilial factors, as well as those pertaining to the family and its place in culture, are also of major importance in the development of youth. By far the majority of high school students do live with both parents. However, different configurations of adults within the home are found in many instances. Rearrangements are brought about by death of one or both parents, by divorce, separation, and even by remarriage. Role definitions are thereby rearranged and the structure of the family itself is changed.

Moreover, the nuclear family is more often than not separated from the larger kinship group. Only two generations usually make up its membership. If parents of either the mother or father, or both, are in the home with growing children, new elements have been added. Three-generation families are different from two. Distinctive values, attitudes, and patterns of behavior of elders are imposed upon their own children as well as upon the children of their sons and daughters. Additional adults in the family setting intrude complex definitions of role, as well as intricate and delicate relationships. These various arrangements and distinctive role definitions for adults within the intimate family become conditioning factors upon youth. They relate to the absorption and perception of culture and in many instances tend to affect availability and use of resources.

Youth in the Texas study lived in families which ran the gamut of parental arrangements. It will be recalled that over three-fourths lived with both father and mother. Young persons whose parents were divorced numbered approximately one in ten. Those who had lost their mothers numbered 3 per cent; 5 per cent of the fathers had died. Some of these widowed parents had remarried, bringing a stepparent into the picture. Two per cent of the youth lived with a parent who was separated but not divorced. Only one in a thousand were full orphans. A minority of families included grandparents. Most of these had one or two elders in the home. An important few had three or four oldsters.

Adequate numbers of youth in each of these family constellations offered opportunity for study of varied adult-child relationships and their impact upon personalities. Comparisons were possible between those living with both parents and those living with only one. Youth with stepfathers or stepmothers were contrasted with those from complete biological family units. The few young persons who were residing in orphanages or with substitute parents were available for special consideration.

Children and youth reared in families with both parents have been considered to have superior cultural and emotional advantages. Lone parents, either mothers or fathers, are assumed to be less adequate in what they offer in opportunities or relationships for well rounded growth toward maturity. An old cliché, now subject to scientific questioning, holds that no matter the severity of conflict between parents, they should remain together at all costs for "the sake of the children." From ancient fairy tale to modern myth, the stepparent—especially the stepmother—has been pictured as the epitome of tragedy to children. Sweeping generalizations demand investigation when sufficient data are available.

Social scientists recognize that problems of child rearing are critical if youngsters must be removed from the family. The cultural adequacy of an institution, no matter how superior, is essentially different from a family in a home. Social workers have tended to shift their recommendations from institutional care to foster home placement. In addition, they now give careful consideration to the possible effects of taking children from even severely limited families. Removal to foster homes or institutions may not always bring an improvement in relationships and response even if the physical or social environment is more adequate. For additional background about such conclusions, the Youth Study had data available on high school students living in two orphanages. Another small group of youth lived in families other than their own.

PARENTAL PATTERNS AND YOUTH REACTIONS

Parental patterns in families in the United States display numerous variations. The typical nuclear family of father, mother, and their children is, of course, the predominant arrangement. However, beside this relationship grouping stands the single-parent family head—either a mother and her children or a father and his offspring making up the family constellation. Since remarriage after divorce or death of a spouse is prevalent in this nation, many youngsters live in households with stepparents, and these stepparents may be either fathers or mothers. Still another pattern, but far in the minority, are those parent-substitute situations where no biological parent is available or competent. Foster parents, guardians, and child-care institutions offer concern and attention to the very few, but these family substitutes in child rearing do play an important role. Finally, three-generation families are becoming numerous even in urban society. In these households reside one or more grandparents with their children and their children's children. No one of these arrangements of parental relationship or substitution among high school youth could be ignored.

Mothers and the Family

Parental arrangements in the families of high-school youth were examined in two separate studies. Only youth from the major ethnic group were included in both examinations. No roomers, relatives, or grandparents were in the homes. Age variations within grade levels were controlled. Independent variables included the sex of the respondents, education of own fathers, and the presence or absence of the fathers or stepfathers in the families. Number of brothers and sisters differed in the two samples. The first sample included young persons with two, one, or no siblings. The second analysis consisted of these same groups plus additional ones extending the number of siblings to nine brothers or sisters. The design incorporating three children or less included 324 students. The second study, having a wider range of family size, consisted of 1,440 youth.

Whether the youth lived with both parents, with their mothers only, or with their mothers and stepfathers made no difference for six of the fourteen scales in either study. The arrangement of parents showed no influence on the amount of pessimism in Orientation to Society, Criticism of Education, feelings of personal or social inadequacy, degree of personal adjustment, or concern for problems arising from conformity pressures.

Interpersonal relations within the families revealed strikingly different pictures upon examination of the remaining scale scores in both samples. Responses in relation to attitudes toward Authoritarian Discipline, Family Problems and Tensions, Resentment of Family Life Style, and Resentment of Dependency revealed some marked discrepancies according to the adults available to share parental roles. No distinctions were uncovered for the young persons with two or fewer siblings on Criticism of Youth, Social Isolation, and Financial Problems. However, when families ranged from the largest to the

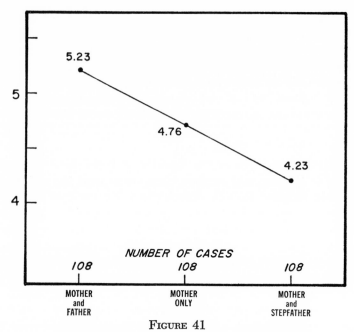

FIGURE 41
Parental Pattern and Authoritarian Discipline

smallest number of children, variations became more apparent for responses on these scales if both parents, mothers only, or mothers and stepfathers were in the homes.

Youth living with both natural parents were substantially more authoritarian in their concepts of discipline than others as revealed in both studies. A slightly more democratic approach was discernible among youngsters living with their mothers alone. Least accepting of traditional authoritarian control of children were those from families with stepfathers.

Young persons apparently can accept the authority of both own parents readily. They carry this into their acceptance of the more traditional ways of child rearing. Mothers may be assumed to be less authoritarian than fathers if high school girls accurately reflect the women who rear them. Girls were more democratic than boys throughout the various analyses of data, it will be recalled. Fathers in the family, it appears safe to assume, modify the more permissive approach of mothers to their children.

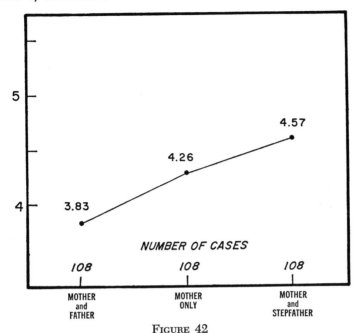

FIGURE 42
Parental Pattern and Family Problems

Stepfathers insert a new element into acceptance of authoritarian relationships by children. Teen-age youth, who lived with their mothers and stepfathers, were the most liberal in their conceptions of parent-child relationships. Their rejection of dictatorial management of children may well be construed as a symbolic exclusion of stepfathers as sources of family discipline.

Mothers who have remarried may be responsible, in part, for such attitudes. Women tend to stand between own fathers and their children by modifying the severity of discipline. This role of mediator might be expected to gain even more emphasis between stepfathers and their stepsons and stepdaughters. Moreover, mothers of these youth probably have had sole control of them over a period of time prior to remarriage. The mothers may be reluctant, therefore, to give up their own pattern of authority which has become accepted by them and their children.

Youth who were living in homes with stepfathers evidenced greater conflict within the family than those living either with their mothers

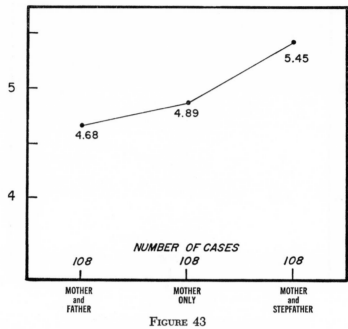

FIGURE 43
Parental Pattern and Family Tension

alone or with both parents. Significantly higher awareness of numerous problems in family relations was indicated. Tensions arising from family interaction were also more acute. Resentment of the way of life at home was more obvious, particularly where one or two siblings were present. Resentment of dependence in these families with stepfathers was also greater.

Stepfathers are considered interlopers by children within the family group, if fiction and hearsay may be taken as evidence. Teen-agers probably consider their presence as distracting the attention of remarried mothers from them and their needs. Reluctance to accept new fathers may also reflect jealousy over replacement of own fathers.

However, even these generalizations must be submitted to closer scrutiny as they reflect the cultural adequacy of families involved. In the larger sample of families having up to ten children, when the father's education was examined in relation to the present parental arrangement in the home, interesting changes in attitudes and concerns were evident. Family tension among these youth was not ap-

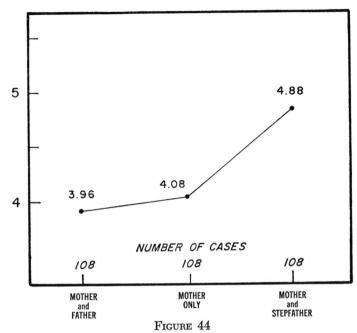

FIGURE 44
Parental Pattern and Resentment of Family Life Style

preciably increased by second marriages of the mothers if their true fathers had attended only grade or high school. Stepfathers in such families evidently contributed enough additional economic security to balance their emotional impact upon youngsters. Youth on these socioeconomic levels were possibly more realistic in recognizing that a father, or father substitute, was a necessity as an added earner of income. Economic competence of the mothers of this group of youngsters is also usually limited in direct relation to their own educational attainment. In acceptance of the harsh facts of life, young persons evidently did not clothe their real fathers with halos of superiority. Inclusion of new adult males in the family circle thus became more readily acceptable.

Sons and daughters whose own fathers were college educated offered vivid contrast. Stepfathers living in middle- and upper-class families significantly increased the family dissonance. These youngsters may well have developed a nostalgic dream of the adequacy of their departed fathers. Their imaginative and real memories of both

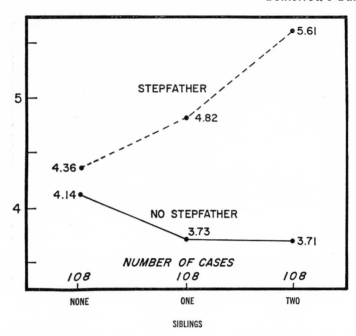

FIGURE 45

Interaction of Parental Pattern and Number of Siblings for Resentment of Family Life Style

economic and emotional aspects of earlier relationships could place their own fathers in a nearly impregnable position.

Somewhat similar results were obtained for Resentment of Family Life Style, or the way family members behaved with each other and the way the household was run. The least resentment was found in families with both true parents where fathers were best educated. Close to this latter group in acceptance of family life style were high school youth in families with mothers as heads, provided their own fathers had been college men. Again, one could hazard the guess that imagination of what home must have been with a highly educated father played a part in the more resentful responses of youth with stepfathers in well educated families.

Resentment of Dependency and Family Problems both followed the same general pattern among youth as did Family Tension and Re-

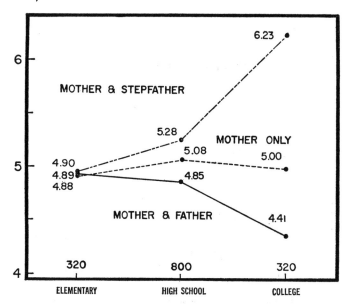

FIGURE 46
Interaction of Parental Pattern and Father's Education for Family Tension

sentment of Family Life Style, testifying further to the significant shift among college-educated families when the original father is replaced by a stepfather.

High school youngsters were least critical of their peers when they lived with their mothers and stepfathers regardless of educational level of their own fathers. Where both parents were in the home or mothers headed the households, their sons and daughters were more critical of others of their own age. Financial Problems were greatest if stepfathers were in their homes. A reminder is in order that the scale on Financial Problems tended to measure an attitude rather than a fact, and this probably accounts for the negative reaction in stepfather families, whether finances were adequate or not.

One further comment should be added from the studies of parental arrangement. In the study involving small families with no more than three children, separate analyses were done on several individual items. Educational level of true father and the arrangement of parents

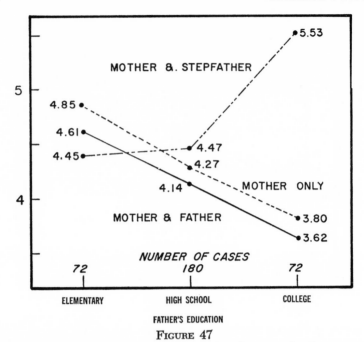

FATHER'S EDUCATION

FIGURE 47

Interaction of Parental Pattern and Father's Education for Resentment of Family Life Style

in the homes were the two main independent variables. Responses to one of the items proved of some significance.

Differences in attitudes toward the working mother were revealed by responses to the statement, "A wife shouldn't have to work to earn part of the family income." Maximum concurrence with this statement occurred when both true parents were family members. Almost as much agreement was expressed by youth with stepfathers. Least agreement was found among youth from families with mothers as family heads. Again, actual experience within the family was probably the telling factor in these responses. It should be recalled that the percentage of all youth in the total sample who agreed with this statement closely paralleled the percentage of mothers who worked.

Because the lone mother as household head is often beset with fears concerning her own ability to fill both parental roles, perhaps it would be well to restate a major finding. Surprisingly little difference was observable in reports of family conflict and concern over

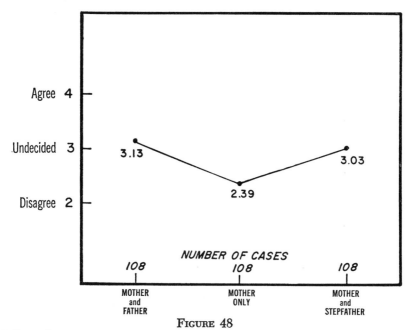

FIGURE 48

Effect of Parental Pattern on Response to Item 30: "A Wife Shouldn't Have To Work To Earn Part of the Family Income"

personal adequacy when both true parents were present or when mothers were the sole parents in families. Difficulties with adolescent children are sometimes assumed to be major when there are no fathers at home. The controlling and steadying influence of a father is indeed valuable during teen-age development, as data in this study reaffirmed. However, homes headed by mothers are evidently not materially damaged when the presence of fathers is impossible. Quality of parenthood as indicated by educational level of parents is, of course, of real importance in both instances as will be highlighted in Chapter XIII.

Fathers and the Family

More attention is usually paid to fatherless homes and those with substitute male parents than those with no mothers or mother replacements. Because data were available, however, it was decided to look at this reversal in parental situations where mothers were missing. A

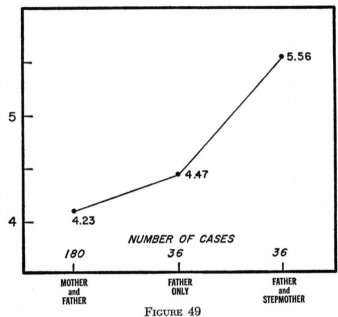

FIGURE 49
Stepmothers Increase Family Problems

refined sample of 252 white students was drawn from three variations
of parental patterns—both parents (180 cases), father only (36 cases),
and father remarried to a stepmother (36 cases)—taking care to
eliminate families with grandparents, relatives, or roomers in the
homes. Other variables used were similar to the previous study except
that the number of brothers and sisters was restricted to three levels—
no brother or sisters, only one sibling, and two siblings. While it
would have been desirable to study larger families, it was impossible
to find adequate numbers of cases with more numerous children to
complete this design.

Parents in the family again proved highly significant in family interaction. Family conflict, including both problems and tensions, revealed
minor distinctions in replies from youth with both parents and those
with fathers as sole parents in families. Lone fathers faced somewhat
more family discord than was found in nuclear families. However,
when stepmothers replaced biological mothers, really significant differences in reported reactions occurred. The introduction of step-

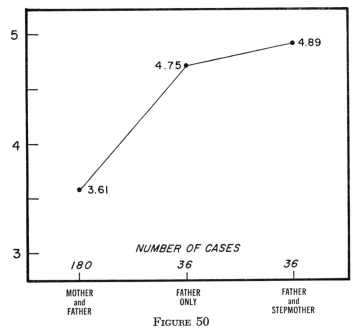

FIGURE 50

Stepmothers Increase Resentment of Family Life Style

mothers, as was the case with stepfathers, produced stress within the family. Family conflicts were distinctly more severe than when fathers had not remarried.

Resentment of Family Life Style was also highest when stepmothers were present. Unlike the earlier situation with mothers alone, the degree of resentment was almost as marked when fathers were sole heads of households as it was when stepmothers were present. It should be remembered that youth indicated that mothers who were lone parents at home impressed them as effective in their roles as home managers and in maintaining the courtesies and niceties between family members. By far the majority of mothers, of course, are more skilled in operation of a household and pay more attention to the amenities of family living than do their husbands. With the loss of their mates, these aspects of family life appear to change less drastically. True mothers, therefore, appear to afford a special essence to the social and emotional climate of the home that is sorely missed by their teen-age children when they are gone.

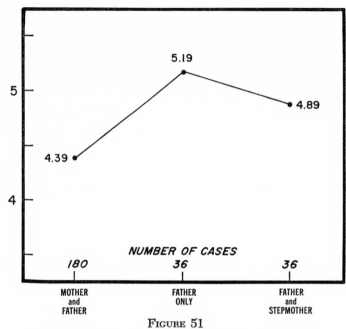

FIGURE 51
Youth with Fathers Only Feel More Financial Problems

Fathers, on the other hand, could be expected not to have the essential skills to keep the household functioning as smoothly nor the concern for family "manners" that their wives possessed. Herein is reflected the relative inexperience and the less adequate education of men as "homemakers" and family managers. Memory of the life of the family in the home with true mothers, therefore, evidently took on retrospective perfection with which fathers could not compete in fact, and which stepmothers could not reach in the minds of their new sons and daughters, no matter what their own competence.

Financial Problems presented another facet of structural influence. Youngsters from families where mothers were missing and fathers were lone parents reported greater concern for financial problems than those from either intact families or from those with stepmothers. Apparently mothers, or mother substitutes, play a mediating role in financial relations between sons or daughters and their fathers. Women are closer to the day-by-day needs of their children or stepchildren. Mothers, real or substitute, appear to be more aware than fathers of financial de-

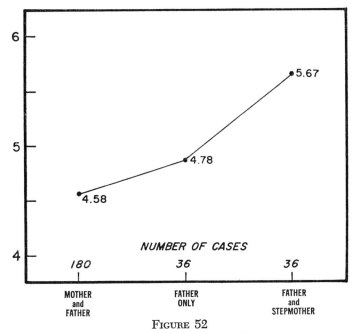

FIGURE 52
Stepmothers Increase Resentment of Dependency

mands placed upon teen-agers. At least these young persons seemed
to sense this.

Dependency relationships are usually somewhat closer between
children and their mothers than children and their fathers. Dependency needs exist at every age. At none, however, are these more sub-
merged by desire for freedom than in adolescent years. When dependency is upon someone not fully accepted in the assigned role, resistance
would be expected to be greater. High school youth expressed more
concern over subordination to parents when fathers were sole family
heads. Fathers obviously do not cushion the emotional impact of their
authoritarian relationships with their children as well as do mothers.
When own mothers were family managers, resentment of their control
was no greater than that expressed by youth with both biological
parents. Stepmothers, as well as stepfathers, engendered displeasure
among youth when they assumed a share of authority. Resentment of
dependence in such cases was greater than existed when fathers were
managing alone.

In summary, it may be stated that, with some minor differences, problems of youthful stress in families increase when either stepfathers or stepmothers assume parental roles. These trends are of a general, low-order nature. Many individual exceptions are readily found. Nonetheless, stepfathers or stepmothers might be intelligently aware that some problems in relationships do arise when teen-age youth are among family members.

Step-Siblings and Half Siblings and Family Conflict

Family Problems and Tensions were found to be more acute when stepparents were members of families of high school youth. How much of this might be attributed to the introduction of step-siblings or the birth of half siblings appeared worthy of exploration. A separate analysis was designed where types of brothers and sisters were systematically varied. All cases were drawn from the larger sample of white youth where mothers had remarried and their current husbands were members of the families. Three types of sibling patterns were distinguished. One group of 110 cases was made up of full brothers and sisters. A second group of 22 cases included only stepbrothers and sisters. A third group of 110 cases was constructed from families with only half brothers and half sisters. Sex of the youth and the fathers' education constituted the other two independent variables for the factorial design. A total of 242 cases was selected to fill the eighteen cells.

Family Problems were reported with only slightly greater frequency among young persons who lived with step-siblings or half siblings. This trend was minimal and not apparent on the more stable scale of family tensions. Nor did type of sibling in the family appear as a significant factor on any of the remaining scales. Conflicts in family interaction as reported among the various parental configurations were evidently not due to the introjection of new brother-sister relationships within the home. Another way of stating this will afford emphasis. Stepbrothers and sisters and half brothers and sisters had relatively little effect upon conflict in family interaction, but substitute parents of either sex did.

DRASTIC DISPLACEMENT OF THE FAMILY

Previous discussions have centered around families where at least one biological parent was present. A small number of youth in the Texas study were living in orphanages. Another minimal group was in

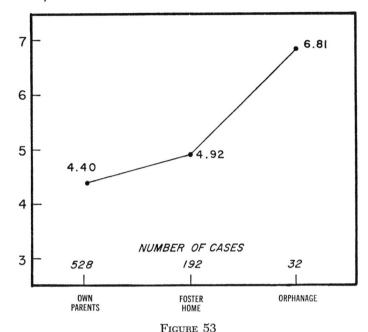

FIGURE 53
Youth in Orphanages Reveal More Family Problems

foster homes or with guardians. When young persons are domiciled in orphanages or foster homes, or with guardians, then drastic displacement from their original families has taken place.

To determine the influence of such radical departures from families of origin, a special study design was constructed. Background factors included sex of youth, fathers' educational level, and patterns of living arrangement. The three family-constellations utilized were youth living with both parents (528 cases), those with adults other than parents (192 cases), and those residing in orphanages (32 cases). A total of 752 cases were drawn from the larger sample to fill the eighteen cells of the factorial design.

Family Problems, Family Tensions, Resentment of Family Life Style, and Resentment of Dependency, exhibited highly significant differences according to family situation. Youth living outside the family setting in institutions displayed major degrees of conflict. Youngsters from intact families revealed the least strain in relationships. Young persons living in simulated family situations fell in between.

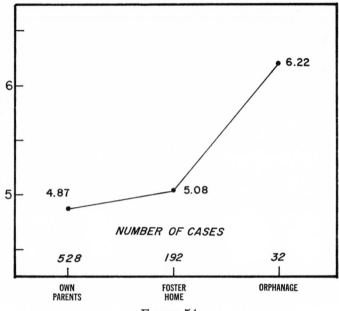

FIGURE 54

Youth in Orphanages Reveal More Family Tension

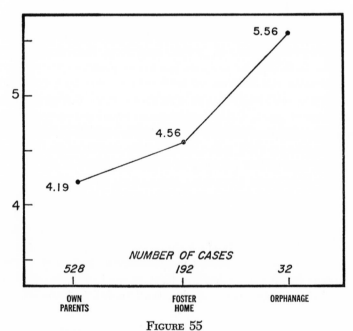

FIGURE 55

Youth in Orphanages Reveal More Resentment of Family Life Style

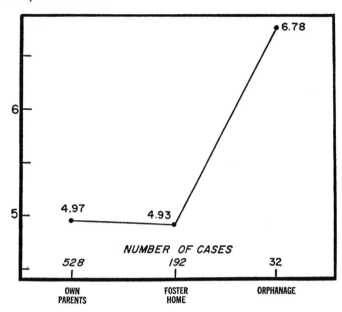

FIGURE 56
Youth in Orphanages Reveal More Resentment of Dependency

Many children living in orphanages have been placed in them because of serious disruptions or displacements in their original families. Moreover, high school youth living in institutions are in daily association with others coming from traditional family settings if they attend public schools. With backgrounds of severe deprivation or death in their original families, stress would be nearly inevitable. When these circumstances are coupled with realization of limitations imposed by their way of life, evidences of conflict would be hard to avoid. Institutions, no matter how well they are managed, could scarcely be expected to serve as adequate replacement for intimate parental relationships. Nor could they be expected to compete with other family arrangements.

Responses revealing personality problems among youth were also more frequent for orphanage residents than for those living in their own homes or the homes of others. They were significantly more concerned over difficulties in personal adjustment. Social isolation was more apparent among them. Youth living in institutions are, in fact,

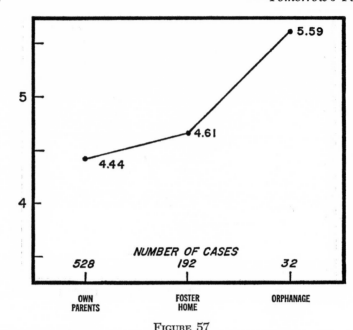

FIGURE 57
Youth in Orphanages Have More Personal Adjustment Problems than Others

more isolated from their peers. Institutional living places certain limitations upon young persons which preclude normal social interaction
as experienced by teen-age youth living in smaller family settings.
Freedom in choices of behavior and even of associates is curtailed by
the size and constitution of the institutional group.

Intensity of problems of adjustment revealed by these young persons
lends itself to conjecture as well. Youth need privacy as well as group
relatedness. Institutional life deprives individuals of essential privacy.
At the same time it forces persons into rigorous group associations
and demands more rigid conformity to adult rules.

Moreover, the fundamental striving for a sense of ego identity, to
use Erik Erikson's concept, would appear to be fraught with difficulties.
Association with meaningful adults in an orphanage is shared with
numerous other children rather than with brothers and sisters as in
normal families. When a warm and intimate relationship with mature
personalities is most needed to assist in the formation of basic attitude

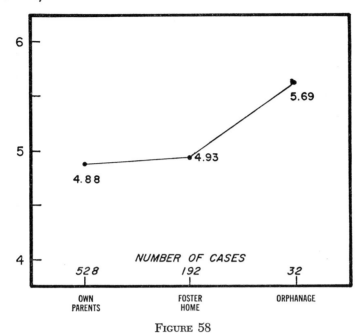

FIGURE 58
Youth in Orphanages Feel Greater Social Isolation than Others

and value patterns, institutions offer the least opportunity for youth-adult interaction.

Concern over conformity pressures among the orphan group was only slightly more obvious than for the two others. In orphanages, girls, rather than boys, indicated slightly intensified critical attitudes toward others of their own age. These girls followed the pattern set by their sex in this research, but with more acute emphasis. Girls in institutions also felt appreciably more isolated than other youth.

Girls living in orphanages and attending public schools apparently were more consciously aware of their unique status than boys living under similar circumstances. This may be accounted for, in part, by their inability to share freely in activities and associations enjoyed by other high school girls. Their opportunity to dress as well as others and to have those accoutrements which high school girls cherish is necessarily limited by their circumstances. In addition, teen-age girls in institutions are often saddled with responsibilities of pseudo-

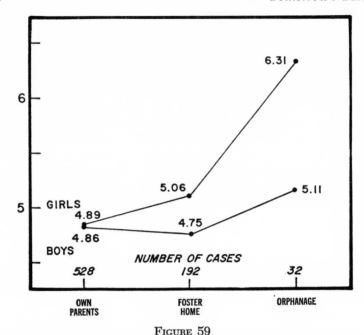

FIGURE 59
Social Isolation Is Greater for Girls Living in Orphanages than for Boys

motherhood for younger children. They are expected to participate in housekeeping chores for the operation of the institution. Their services may be an integral part of the economy of the setting in which they are being reared.

Boys too are expected to perform chores in orphanages. Their roles within the institution, however, tend to be less complicated. They are usually not called upon to carry as fully, or as early, the parental roles assigned to older girls. Moreover, their task assignments are usually not of the same nature as those for girls. The quality of domestic service is lacking. Findings from the Texas study seem to afford additional evidence for the wisdom of breaking down traditional institutional patterns of child care for orphans and substituting new patterns more similar to family living. Foster homes give evidence of superiority when youth reactions are compared.

GRANDPARENTS IN THE FAMILY

Accompanying the rapid increase in number of children in the population since 1940 has been the rise in number of persons in the upper age brackets. Numerous elders in the last half of the twentieth century are caught by the lack of self-sufficiency for later years. Eventually this will be mitigated for many by Social Security and other retirement plans. Responsibility for elders in many current instances rests upon sons and daughters with whom they make their homes. That some of these families would include high-school youngsters was inevitable. Three-generation families, in a highly urbanized society, offered opportunity for investigation of problems of relationship.

Texas youth took grandparents in their homes with comparative ease save in a few circumstances. The presence of grandparents made no significant differences to youth in their replies on eleven of the fourteen scales. Family conflict, as measured by three scales, was significant only if there were two or more grandparents living with the family. A single grandfather or grandmother did not increase or decrease Family Problems, Family Tensions, or Resentment of Family Life Style. Family conflict rose appreciably, however, when there were *two or more* grandparents in the same home with youth and their families. Relationships and problems encountered in three-generation families seemed to be handled satisfactorily as long as there was only a single elder involved. Grandfather or grandmother appeared to be equally acceptable.

When two or more grandparents resided in the same household with their children and their children's children, the number of persons present contributed to strain. Moreover, when elders represented two parental families, the combination produced noticeably greater tension. Two grandparents living with their grown children may represent either the maternal or paternal side of the family. In some instances they may include both. However, three grandparents in a family leaves no doubt that *both* parental families are represented. All of the variations and peculiarities of two separate family backgrounds in attitudes, habits, customs, and personalities become imposed upon still a third set of factors in a younger family.

Teen-age youth very often come under the critical eye of elders. When these eyes belong to two different sets of grandparents plus those of their own fathers and mothers, little wonder tension mounts.

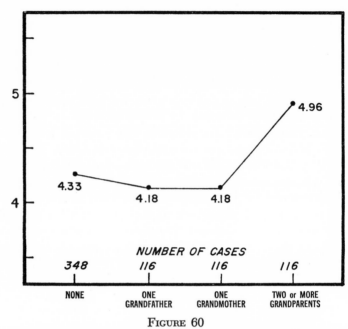

Two or More Grandparents Increase Family Problems

Resentment of Family Life Style is also understandable under these circumstances. Chances are good that "elbow room" is sorely limited in order for the younger family to take care of elders in triplicate or in quadruplicate. Some elders, in addition, have never developed modes of living compatible with those of their more modern sons and daughters. Their high school age grandchildren are at a hyper-sensitive period in their development. They are apt to be peculiarly susceptible to comparative disadvantages in their own way of life. Without added problems, they often become hypercritical of their home and its occupants. The elders, in turn, are no less critical of the young and are frequently equally sensitive.

Families with two or three grandparents alongside youth of high school age are relatively rare. Within itself, such a household in most instances signifies strained socioeconomic resources. Otherwise, these elders would probably be cared for in other settings. With economic strain, social incompatibilities, and space inadequacies, conflict may be nearly inevitable.

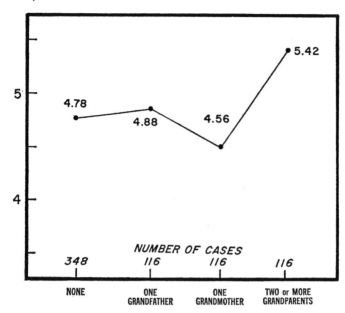

FIGURE 61

Two or More Grandparents Increase Family Tension

These findings were obtained from an especially designed analysis of youth of the majority race. All cases were eliminated where there were relatives or adults other than grandparents in the home. The number of grandparents was varied systematically: no grandparents (348 cases); one grandfather (116 cases); one grandmother (116 cases); and two or more grandparents (116 cases). Sex of the youth and three levels of education of the fathers were included as independent variables. A total of 696 cases was drawn to complete twenty-four cells in the factorial design.

A Look with Precision

To determine more precisely the nature of the influence of grandparents on the problems and attitudes of youth, an additional study was made employing a somewhat different design. Using the same refined sample of white intact families with no roomers or other relatives, the cases were sorted into three classes.

The three groups chosen for this precision design consisted of fami-

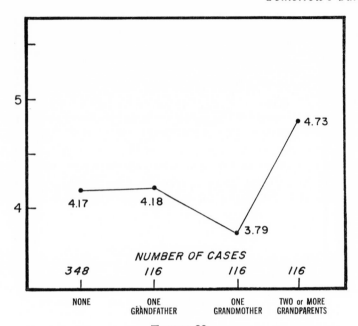

FIGURE 62
Two or More Grandparents Increase Resentment of Dependency

lies with no grandparents; with grandparents from one parental side of the family only; and with grandparents from both sides of the family. A matched design was constructed with forty-six blocks, each block containing one case from each of the three classes of subjects, ranging from no grandparents to three or four.

Youth within a given block were carefully matched on community size, geographic region, sex, and father's education. The analysis was carried out on all fourteen scales and three single items of special interest. This was done to eliminate any possibility of these variables becoming confounded with the main independent variable, the number of grandparents living in the family. Items included were "Children should feel that it is their duty to care for their parents when the parents are old"; "Parents should sacrifice everything for their children"; and "Relatives living in the home always make trouble for the family." Each of these deals specifically with attitudes toward relatives and older persons living within the household.

Family Tension, Problems of Personal Adjustment, Resentment of

Family Life Style, and Resentment of Dependency all rose sharply among youth who lived in families with three or four grandparents. No differences were evidenced between families where there was one grandparent and those where there was no grandparent present. Problems in family relationships evidently do not become acute merely because of the presence of grandparents. Disruption occurs when a family is complicated by the inclusion of a parent or parents of the mother and a parent or parents of the father as well.

Youth displayed no significant variations in their replies to the item dealing with parental sacrifice for their children or for the item concerning relatives living in the home. Highly significant differences were obtained between the three groups on the item which had to do with care of parents when they become old.

Where one grandparent lived with the family of the youth, over half felt it was their duty to care for their parents when they grow old. When three or four grandparents were included in the intimate household from which youth came, 41 per cent of the teen-agers strongly agreed that it was their duty to assume responsibility for elders. Only about one-third of the young persons from families with *no* grandparents in their homes agreed with this statement.

More youth from families who had assumed care of elders in their own homes agreed that responsibility for senior family members should be a part of their own planning. Fewer young persons were found among those with no experience in three-generation living who were sure that this should be a part of their adult obligation. Association with elders in the household evidently became a positive factor in attitude toward their care. Apparently, learning to assume responsibility is superior in this particular facet of family life when intimate living experiences with grandparents is part of the upbringing of young persons. Increase in the number of urban, nuclear families, with their minimal association with grandparents may predict a lessening of acceptance of responsibility for the care of oldsters by their children.

Grandparents—In Summary

No adverse effect upon the problems, concerns, and attitudes of high school youth was revealed because either a grandfather or grandmother lived with the family. Strain upon youth was evidenced by the sharp rise in scores on all of the family-conflict scales in the rather rare situations where three or four grandparents were in the home. However, even here the impact was not entirely adverse. About 41 per cent of these young persons agreed that care of their own parents when they became old was their responsibility. It should be recalled that only family conflict scales were affected even in these unusual circumstances.

Personal and social adjustment scales and measures of social attitudes were generally not modified when members of the older generation were included in families to which youth belonged. Young persons of this era are obviously neither indifferent to, careless of, nor in conflict with their grandparents if the Texas Cooperative Youth Study may be taken as an index.

X: Youth Response to Family Size and Composition

DEMOGRAPHERS have long taken into account family size and its relation to the economy of the country. Economists have also had their say. With few children, the market was doomed. So was the nation, because it would be unable to replace its aging and dying members. Large families, and only large families, could hold the key to continuous prosperity and population growth. All of this, of course, is in sharp contrast to the current alarm about the "population explosion" now considered a world crisis.

Relatively few investigations have been made of the impact of the numbers of children in families on the socialization process. Comparatively little information has been available on the conceptions of youth of their personal adequacy in relation to family size. Their differential responses to patterns of interaction in small, medium, or larger family constellations have had minimal study.

Popular speculation has run the gamut from the presumedly less fortunate lot of the only child to the assumedly salutary effects of being a member of a large family. Many romanticists still extol the virtues of numerous children. Few have been champions of the one-child family.[1]

[1] For an analysis of the advantages of small and large family systems see John H. S. Bossard and Eleanor Stoker Boll, *The Large Family System*, pp. 306–320.

LARGE, SMALL, OR IN BETWEEN

Large families have been surmised to provide the most satisfactory climate for child learning. The more children from whom to learn, the more each child learned. At least speculation has offered this hypothesis for investigation. This premise tends to ignore the major importance attributed to parent-child relationships in the acculturation process. The more children, the more limited must become the association of each child with adults in the family. Older children, by necessity, take on roles in child care and training before they have reached social and emotional maturity.

The affectional relationship between mother and child, considered paramount for emotional security, is progressively diminished as each new child enters the family situation. Demands upon the time of fathers are likewise increased by the weight of numbers who depend upon him for support and response. Youth, for their development of self-sufficiency and independence, require opportunities to go outside the family group into new peer and adult associations. Extrafamilial participation may be appreciably limited for teen-agers where home demands are heavy.

Families with five or six children are social systems quite different from smaller family units, as Talcott Parsons and Robert F. Bales have indicated.[2] Role definitions are distinctive both for parents and older children. Task assignments vary greatly from those encountered by adults or youth in smaller nuclear families.

Large numbers of children are usually correlated with lower educational status of parents. The conditional factors of larger family size in cultural participation of youth suggests a twofold hypothesis. Parents of submarginal educational and occupational status are less well integrated in the dominant cultural system. They are limited in their own adequacy for cultural transmission to their children. Moreover, interpersonal relations between such parents and a particular child are diluted by the demands of their numerous children. Youth, from such families, will thereby be given less intensive and extensive orientation to living in society because of these factors. Evidence from the youth study was available to test these assumptions.

[2] Talcott Parsons and Robert F. Bales, *Family, Socialization and Interaction Process*, p. 18.

At the other extreme, critics of only children describe them as "spoiled." Such single children have been labelled precocious. Domination by and nearly exclusive association with parents has been credited with bringing them to too rapid maturity in some respects while retarding the development of their independence. At the same time, they are often considered lonely from lack of companionship with their own age group. Only children are more closely related to their parents both emotionally and intellectually. The socioeconomic status of the families with one child, or even two or three, offers them open doors to cultural advantage. Whether these are, in fact, assets or liabilities in personality development were given clarification by Texas youth.

What the effects upon youth might be in having been reared to adolescent years in a medium-sized family became an intriguing question. Women in child-bearing years in every status group in the nation recently reported, in a study by Freedman, Whelpton, and Campbell, that they wanted families of three or four children.[3] Families with no children or only one child were considered least desirable by these women. They stressed that they consciously planned for the additions to their families. Their youngsters, they insisted, were desired for their own sakes.

Youth in Texas partially verified the reported desires of mothers studied by Freedman, Whelpton, and Campbell. They indicated that their own personal and social development was more adequate if they were reared in medium- or small-sized families rather than large ones. The nuclear family, compact enough to maintain adequate differentiation of adult and child roles, appeared to be a cultural asset. Where communication and interpersonal response could be maintained in balance between parents and children, the processes of socialization and acculturation were accomplished more satisfactorily.

Numbers of children in the family yielded significant trends in almost every scale of measurement. Invariably the picture was the same. Young persons from the largest families indicated sharp increases in difficulties in personal and social adjustment. Family Problems and Tensions were conceived as more acute. Fundamental attitudes toward society, education, and their peers were more negative. Youth with

[3] Ronald Freedman, Pascal K. Whelpton, and Arthur A. Campbell, *Family Planning Sterility and Population Growth*, pp. 220–226, 402–404.

no more than two or three brothers or sisters offered little or no distinction in their responses. Teen-agers who were only children proved to be no different from those reared in medium-sized families. Family size can, therefore, be assumed to be an important conditional factor for effective growth and development in culture.

Youth Attitudes and Family Characteristics

Responses from 1,440 young persons of the dominant race were utilized to determine the influence of family size upon their attitudes and problems. Age variations within grades were controlled. No adults lived in these households other than parents. Parents in the home were differentiated as own father and mother; mother only; and mother and stepfather. Aside from parental status, independent variables included the sex of the youth, the number of siblings, and the education of their fathers. The latter were considered on three levels: elementary schooling, high school, and some college to professional. The number of siblings varied across five categories as follows: none, one, two, three or four, and five through nine. The resulting four-way factorial design encompassed ninety cells.

This particular design was adopted after completion of a similar study limiting the number of children in the family to one, two, or three. No distinctions in response were discovered among youth in high school whether they were only children, had one brother or sister, or had two siblings. It was then that a more extensive analysis was undertaken using families ranging in size from one child to ten children including the respondent.

Increased personal discontent with people and discouragement about society, as measured by Orientation to Society, was evident as the number of children increased. Little difference was discernible until the number of children in the family reached more than three. Life appeared satisfactory also to youngsters with three or four brothers or sisters, but less so than to those from smaller families.

As previously noted, the largest families in the nation are still found more often in the lower educational, occupational, and income levels. These mothers and fathers, either rural or urban, are heavily burdened to meet the variety of personal and social needs of their children. Both parents may find it necessary to be employed outside the home. Their teen-age children are frequently saddled with the responsibilities of surrogate parenthood. Time for school and for participation with peer

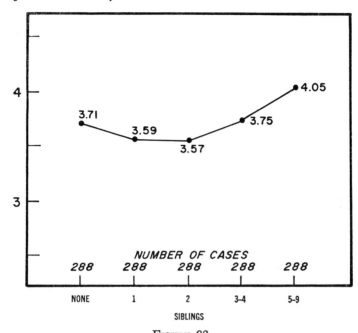

FIGURE 63
Youth from Larger Families More Pessimistic about Society

groups is limited. If these parents had been queried as were their youngsters, they too might have revealed pessimism about the world and what it holds in store for their children.

Perhaps some speculation based upon casual observation and comments by middle-class parents may be voiced here. These men and women of more adequate income and education, who are the parents in large families, probably find themselves under somewhat different environmental pressures. They are well aware of the needs of their children, both in association and in money. However, their ability to offer their numerous offspring opportunities and close association with them equal to that experienced by children in smaller families would appear to be more limited. Furthermore, from their middle-class backgrounds, they have read and heard of the importance of parental companionship with children. If the sheer burden of managing the household with limited outside adult assistance is so great that they cannot provide their children with what they consider important, some par-

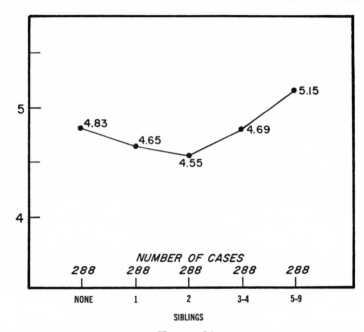

FIGURE 64
Youth from Larger Families Approve Authoritarian Discipline

ents may well become frustrated, and even guilty and less adequate. Others appear to manage large establishments with such skill that they always seem to have time for the needs of each child.

In general, it can be said that the more children in families, the more approving youth were of authoritarian methods in child rearing. However, the exceptions, themselves, are of interest. Teen-agers from families where education of fathers was the least were very much more approving of direct authority when there were more than four children in the family. This was probably because these youth are often burdened with the care of younger brothers and sisters. Youngsters whose fathers were high school educated were more authoritarian if they were only children or if there were more than four siblings. Why only children in these families were so similar to those in the largest families in this group is indeed a puzzler. In families where fathers were best educated—the college men—the sons and daughters were least authoritarian of any of the young persons except

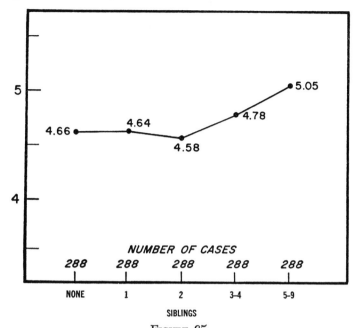

FIGURE 65
Youth from Smaller Families Less Critical of Education

when they were members of families of six or more children. Here they became the most arbitrary toward younger members of their families of any youth included in the study.

Perhaps a few comments are in order as suggested by these findings from youth responses. Ordering and forbidding has an economy all of its own in child rearing. Less time and less sophistication is required for such management. Democratic practices in family life, epitomized by the teaching and reasoning approach in child control, is time consuming. Again, it would seem valid to assume that parents with fewer children have more time for the latter approach. Also, when high school youth share in the responsibility of child management, as they are apt to do in those families with more numerous children, they probably tend to take the short-cut of direct command both because they are less patient and because they may even subconsciously cherish the opportunity to exert direct control over someone in the household, even as they see themselves under the domination of their parents.

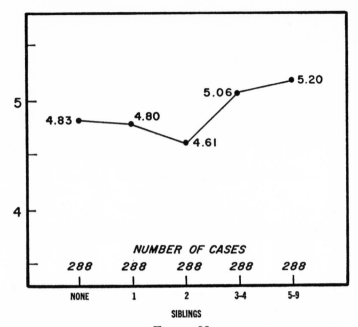

FIGURE 66

Resentment of Dependency Greater in Large Families

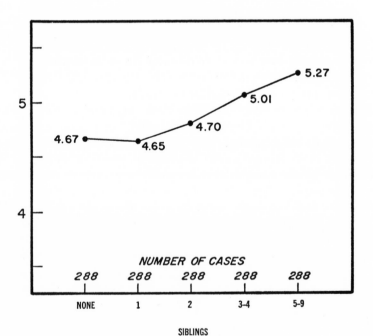

FIGURE 67

Family Tension Greater in Large Families

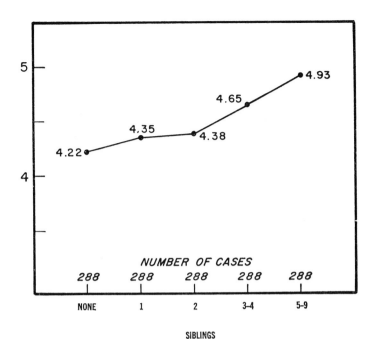

SIBLINGS

FIGURE 68

Family Problems Greater in Large Families

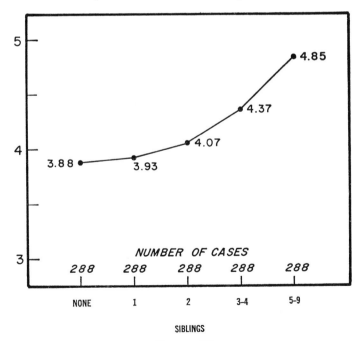

SIBLINGS

FIGURE 69

Resentment of Family Life Style Greater in Large Families

The relationship between size of family and Criticism of Education is similar to that for Orientation to Society, although the differences between only children and those with one or two siblings have disappeared completely. Children from large families tend to be more critical of their teachers and of education in general.

Family Conflict and Family Size

Family conflict, as reflected in the scales on Family Problems, Family Tension, Resentment of Family Life Style and Resentment of Dependency, was more acute in the largest families. As long as family size remained moderate (three children or fewer), similarity in admission of difficulties was evidenced by youth. When the high school student had three or four siblings, tension became more apparent. The sharpest rise in concern over interpersonal relations and family interaction, in general, was indicated by young people from homes with six or more children.

Girls indicated significantly more unrest than boys as family size increased beyond three children. If they lived in households with six children or more, they displayed a real recognition of problems originating in the family. Teen-age boys, regardless of family size, showed no such mounting of interpersonal difficulties at home as the number of children in the family grew.

It may be safely assumed that high school girls play a particularly important role in the families with numerous offspring. In fact, they are quite probably definite assets not only to the economy of such family constellations but to the actual efficiency of the homemaking procedures. Home services to family members would appear to be essential parts of their roles as they help their mothers. They are usually expected to share in the "mothering" of younger children. They help eliminate the need for hired household help. Moreover, girls probably react more acutely to the lack of privacy, which goes with a large family group, than do their brothers. For these reasons, it is not surprising that the level of family tension experienced by teen-age girls in large families was higher than for boys. Where high-school girls were lone children in the home, they reported least family stress. But scores for boys who were only children were only slightly higher than for girls in like family situations. Variations in role expectations and performance within the family, as family size increased, might well be the basis for this sex difference in larger families.

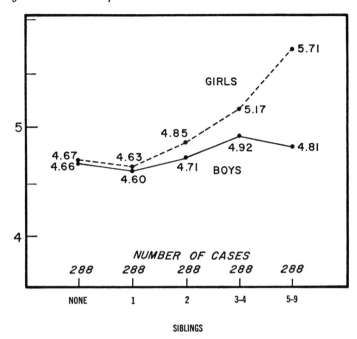

FIGURE 70
Girls in Large Families More Aware of Family Tension than Boys

Not unexpected was the finding that youth from the largest families expressed the greatest resentment for the style of life in their homes. Numerous family members in crowded quarters tend to produce problems in living. Difficulties in management and operation of such households are numerous. Sheer numbers produce confusion of persons and accumulation of things. To bring young friends into such homes, except under unusual circumstances, presents problems for youth, their parents, and even for younger children. An increase in socioeconomic status of the family, as measured by fathers' education, was accompanied by a decrease in resentment of family life style. More space in which to live and greater competency in both relationships and management because of better education, could be expected to make real differences in adequacy of living for large families.

Dissatisfaction over lack of independence from parents was greatest in families with six or more children. This rise in Resentment of Dependency was in direct contrast to smaller families of three children or fewer. The commonly held idea that children reared in larger families are more independent and feel less pressure of parental control is refuted by Texas youth. Lack of independence, real or imagined, is directly related to the perception of the degree of self-determination allowed. Resentment of dependence upon parents may also be an expression of awareness of less freedom in personal life outside the family.

Dependence demanded by parents of larger families is not necessarily related to the desire to hold their youth in check. Authority over them is maintained for what they may contribute to the family economy. Contributions may be additions to family income or to the functioning of the large group in the home. Families of large size cannot afford the luxury of freedom from family responsibilities for their teen-age members. Demands upon these youth, as was indicated in the discussion of Authoritarian Discipline, are apt to be made directly. Little time or effort is available for explanation of why compliance is required or desired. Appreciation for youth services at home often goes unexpressed. Resentment might be an expected corollary where several circumstances combine to hold youth close within the family circle at home.

"Common sense," on the other hand, would dictate that the fewer the children and the more intimate the relationship between parents and youth, the more direct would be the parental control. Resentment of dependence thereby should be higher. To reiterate, this did not prove to be the case. Demand for support from children in small families in money or services is minimal. Intimacy of relationship between generations makes for easy communication. Why certain requirements are made of youth by parents is probably better understood. Conceivably, parents with fewer children also make a concerted effort to move their youth out of the home toward greater independence. Whatever the combination of reasons, youth from the families with few children resent their dependency less than those from larger families.

Social Adequacy and Family Size

Closely related to Family Problems and Tensions are the dilemmas of social adequacy and emotional security. Problems of Personal Adjustment became increasingly apparent to both teen-age boys and girls as family size increased above the medium range, though only

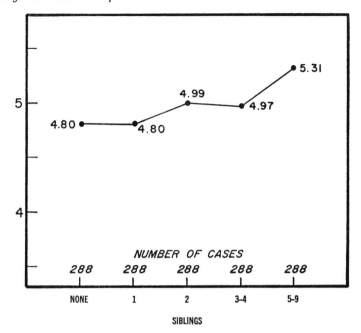

FIGURE 71
Social Inadequacy Greater in Very Large Families

to the .05 level of significance. Therefore, this finding merits only passing mention. Feelings of self-adequacy, surprisingly, were not related to family size.

Expressed feelings of Social Inadequacy were significantly higher among youth as the number of children in the family increased. Young persons from families with three children or fewer were best equipped to meet social demands. Problems in this area became more apparent when four or more children were family members. They were most obvious among families with six or more children.

Social adequacy, as scaled in this study, arises from knowing what to do and how to behave with other persons in a variety of social settings. Being at ease in groups comes from a learned set of behavior patterns. It is understandable that when families are large, less attention can be given to teaching amenities which add to social ease. The price for lack of learning in these areas is reflected in feelings of social incompetence by youth.

Some further speculation may be in order concerning social inadequacy as this relates to family size. Conversational ability and ease in relationships are attributes of the middle class. Knowing how to behave in a variety of situations and having proper clothes are accepted as necessities. Self-assurance at parties and on dates results from early and specific training at home. These are considered stock-in-trade for social acceptance in high school and college. They are considered major assets for adult success.

Youth from different subcultures attending high schools find themselves in daily association with these more sophisticated young persons. Their own inadequacies in these niceties in manners may become painfully apparent. It may be assumed that damaged self-esteem and feelings of social inferiority account for some dropouts. For those with social handicaps, it is apparent their lives could be made happier and more satisfactory. They could be given the opportunity to learn in school those social skills which they would like and need to know. In fact, in one Gulf Coast school exactly such help is being rendered Negro youth through an especially designed course in the homemaking department for both boys and girls.[4]

That young persons from families of six children or more reported more acute feelings of isolation would appear to be contradictory. One might think they lived in social groups large enough to afford adequate companionship and constant associations. However, reported loneliness was found more often among youth from such families. There were no differences among the families with fewer than six children. Again, though this finding was only to the .05 level of significance, it was unusual enough to warrant at least passing attention. Perhaps high-school youth with numerous brothers and sisters suffer from isolation similar to that which is sometimes reported by young mothers. So much time is spent with young children, they contend, that they lose touch with the world outside the home.

Problems with finances, significantly greater for youth from the larger families, were especially intense when there were four or more children. Young persons from these families, even though of average

---

[4] As reported by Mrs. Versa Reece, from a high school in Aldine, Texas, in the summer of 1963. Youth with especially high potential for achievement are given opportunity to take this class. "Practice sessions" are held on trips to restaurants such as that at The Greater Houston Airport and in other situations demanding knowledge of such social amenities.

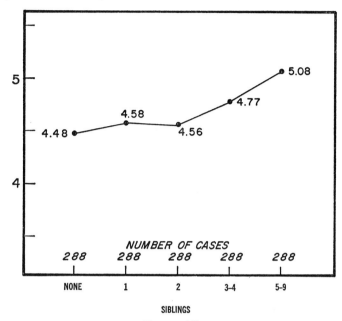

FIGURE 72
More Financial Problems for Youth in Larger Families

or higher incomes, probably received less money to spend than those from smaller family units. Family income has to be extended over a larger number of spenders. These youth may also feel themselves left out when they see the multiplicity of advantages afforded others of their age whose parents have fewer children on whom to spend their income.

It should be stated that numerous high school youth from the largest families are forced to become part-time earners. They must share in producing income for the family or for themselves. Time for activities with their peers is limited by their hours of employment. These factors might very well contribute to the feeling among these teen-agers that they are less a part of adolescent society.

It must be remembered that the results from these various analyses concerning youth and family size which indicate negative aspects of large families are only general trends based on a large representative sample of high school youth. These high school youth, however, have reemphasized the findings of Bossard and Bolls in relation to acute problems in family life where children are numerous.[5] As a parent of five children from the upper middle class stated the problem, "There is the absolute imperative that each child have his share of concern and warmth from each of us. Sometimes it stretches us pretty far." Moreover, perhaps the Cooperative Youth Study is suggestive that careful consideration should be given to the amount and type of responsibility which may be safely assigned to youth.

THE COMPOSITION OF THE FAMILY AND YOUTH REACTIONS

Size of family, as the previous discussion has indicated, plays a very important role in the attitude-value and behavior patterns of young persons. But family size with no discussion of either place among siblings, ordinal position, or the sex composition found within the family seemed to leave something to be desired. Whether it was an advantage or a hazard to be born first, last, or in-between has always caused considerable speculation in families. Here was an opportunity to gather evidence to paint a realistic picture. Moreover, whether it was an advantage to be reared a sister among brothers or a brother among sisters also has been a matter of conjecture among parents. Again, here was the place to check responses of youth who had grown up in families dominated by one or the other sex.

The Ordinal Position of Youth in Families

One special study was designed to attempt to discover the relationship of the ordinal position of youth in families to family and personal problems. Unusual restrictions were placed upon the sample in order to insure that confounding variables were completely eliminated. The sample was composed of white intact families. None was included with grandparents, roomers, or other relatives living in the home. No half brothers or sisters or stepbrothers or sisters were included. Only youth from families having three children were selected. This restriction was imposed to make possible an intensive analysis of the impingement of sex of brothers or sisters upon the respondent, as well as the effect of his place in the birth order in the family.

Independent variables which were systematically analyzed in this particular design were sex of the youth who was the respondent; sex of the two siblings—both male, both female, or mixed; and the ordinal

---

[5] Bossard and Boll, *Op. cit.*

position of the high school youth in relation to the age of the other two children in the family. All possible combinations of these three factors resulted in a basic factorial design having eighteen cells. A total of 1,020 cases was selected to insure an adequate number for conclusive results. Because of the unusual nature of this analysis and its relevance to much current speculation on the importance of sibling order, all of the higher order interaction patterns as well as the main effects were extracted and tested for significance.

Ordinal position of a high school youth among other children in the family made no difference in his reactions to family conflicts or on scales measuring personal effectiveness. His position made him neither more nor less critical of society or of other people. His response to his educational experiences was in no way influenced by the place to which he was born in his family. He was neither more nor less authoritarian because he came into the world as the first, middle, or third child in his family. Criticism of the behavior of his peers was not influenced by his place among his siblings.

Sympathy is often expressed for the unfortunate middle child. However, his family problems and tensions, his personal adjustment, his feelings of self and social adequacy, the extent to which he may feel isolated from his peers, the conformity pressures from schoolmates of which he is aware—none of these showed variation in intensity whether the youth was number one, two, or three in his family. Resentment of family life style and resentment of dependency were neither more nor less because of ordinal position. Even financial problems showed no influence if there was an older or younger sibling or if the respondent was first, middle, or last born.

The sex of siblings in the family apparently was also of no significance. The lack of interaction between the sex of respondents and ordinal position among siblings is most striking. That the sex of other children was not significant is worthy of repetition. The myth of the disadvantaged middle child is laid to rest. So is the myth that it is important for both children and their families that the first born should be a boy.

The Impact of Sex of Siblings on Youth Response

Since the above analysis was restricted to families with only three children, no generalizations could be made without further study as to the importance of the sex of siblings in determining the adequacy

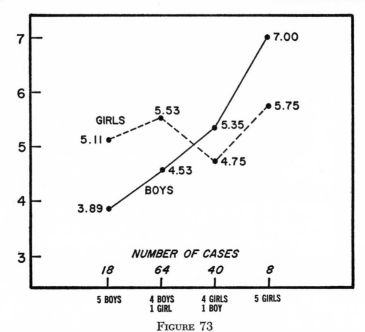

FIGURE 73
Relation of Financial Problems to Sex and Sex of Siblings

of youth in larger families. Investigation of this question was undertaken more systematically for the largest family groups. A new factorial design was constructed consisting of white intact families who had six children, including the respondent. The two independent variables of this special design consisted of sex of the high school youth and four variations of sex among his siblings: (a) five brothers; (b) four brothers and one sister; (c) four sisters and one brother; and (d) five sisters. A total of 130 cases was drawn from the refined sample for this analysis.

Little or no difference was discovered in three of the four sibling patterns for the thirteen scales measuring attitudes and problems of youth. When there were five brothers, four brothers and a sister or four sisters and a brother, no significant variations in response were revealed save on Financial Problems.

Financial troubles for boys were more evident as the number of sisters increased from none to five. With more sisters in the family, less money was probably available for boys to meet their own special

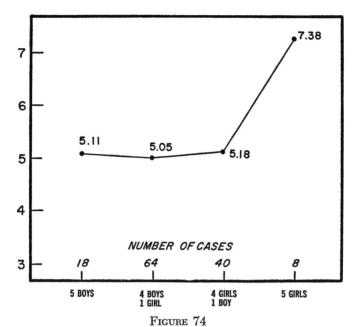

FIGURE 74

Presence of Five Sisters Increases Negative Orientation to Society

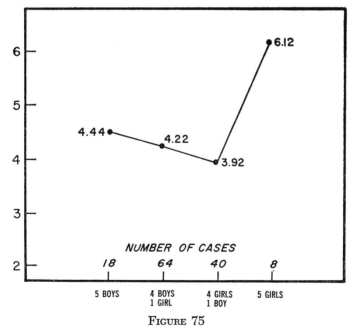

FIGURE 75

Presence of Five Sisters Increases Criticism of Education

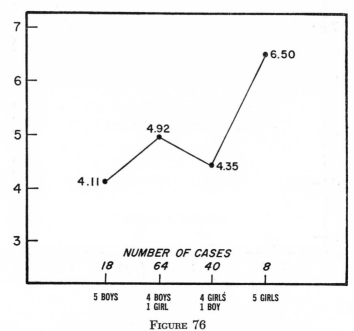

Figure 76
Presence of Five Sisters Increases Family Problems

needs. When there were five sisters, there was no difference in the responses of the high school girls, regardless of the distribution of siblings, except in slightly higher scores on Financial Problems. Again, the more girls in a family, the greater was the probable drain upon financial resources. Less money apparently was available for teen-age girls as well as teen-age boys.

Both boys and girls with five sisters had significantly higher mean scores than the other three groups on seven scales: Criticism of Education, Orientation to Society, Family Problems, Resentment of Dependency, Resentment of Family Life Style, Social Isolation, and Personal Adjustment. These youth who were surrounded by sisters were significantly less sure of themselves and were more openly critical than those who had at least one brother with whom to share problems.

A single youthful male in a household with five sisters and a mother would indeed find himself overwhelmed by femininity. In all probability he would frequently feel himself under pressure to conform to predominantly feminine standards of behavior. Open criticism by his

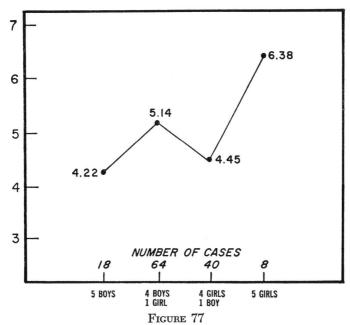

FIGURE 77

Presence of Five Sisters Increases Resentment of Dependency

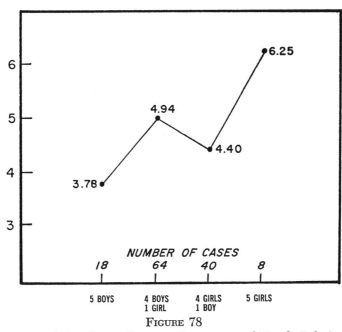

FIGURE 78

Presence of Five Sisters Increases Resentment of Family Life Style

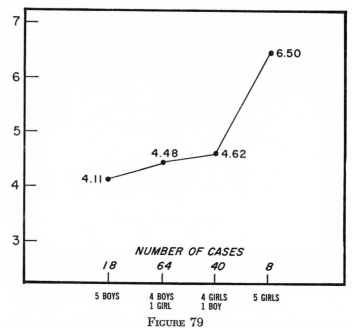

FIGURE 79

Presence of Five Sisters Related to More Problems of Personal Adjustment

sisters or condescending tolerance of the lone young man would not be conducive to feelings of adequate personal or social adjustment. Resentment of Family Life Style has no mystery in its origin when a teen-age boy lives in a household that is woman-centered to this degree. Six women, including his mother, in one household is a goodly number. Indeed, the father in such a household has a very special role defined for him in relation to his son and his son's need for masculine identity.

A completely masculine household, save for the mother, produced no such responses either from the sixth son or from a single sister. Indeed, this finding would appear to undergird the popular contention that women are reared to place emphasis on minutiae and to turn critical eyes upon these either in physical setting or behavior. If this be true, stress for either high school boys or girls would be less in their day-by-day living at home were the sex ratio reversed in favor of the male. Of course this is a speculative comment, but the fact remains

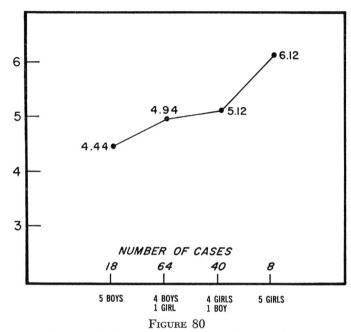

FIGURE 80

Presence of Five Sisters Increases Social Isolation

that either a sister or a brother in teen-age years found life considerably less demanding if other siblings were all brothers.

Interestingly enough, the high-school girl in the family with five sisters found herself in fully as difficult a situation as a boy in like circumstances. The leavening influence of even a supporting brother is absent. The role of a father for six daughters spreads the masculine influence very thin indeed. Moreover, any high school girl in a family group is an obvious and visible family member. She is beginning to have dates. She has an increased desire for associations outside the family. She looks at her own family life with the critical eyes of young and relatively unsophisticated maturity. She would indeed feel that she lived at home in a strange world of all women when she was one of seven of a single sex, counting her mother. Her father could not prevent her comprehension of such complications.

These comments are generalized in relation to an unusual study of an unusual situation. It should also be emphasized that they are based on only eight cases where all five siblings are girls. The results are sufficiently dramatic, however, to justify comment. When there is the more normal distribution of sexes in a family, it appears that greater ease in living results. Even though parents might wish it otherwise, they cannot control the sex distribution among their children. However, they can be aware of the hazard for high school youth who must live in a family where there is unusual multiplication of the female sex in the family structure.

XI: The Married High School Student

MARRIAGE is presumed to mark the attainment of adult status. Marriage usually heralds the departure from the family of orientation by movement into the new family of procreation. Parental roles and relationships change. No longer are fathers and mothers of the newly married responsible for the processes of socialization and acculturation which they assumed with the birth of their children. Their task of preparing their young for adult participation in culture is supposedly concluded.

The young married couple is expected to be ready to pick up with their own offspring the tasks just completed by their parents. How effective their tutelage for their new roles has been depends, in large measure, upon the subcultural group to which their families belonged. Their capacity for adult adequacy in acculturation of their young also rests, in part, on the educational level which they, themselves, have achieved. Family background and schooling will be reflected in their ability to transmit richness, poverty, or mediocrity in cultural heritage to their children. Cumulative evidence to substantiate these conclusions has already been submitted in the discussions of family structure and will be enlarged upon in the chapter on parental education and youth responses.

Age at marriage is directly related to adequacy of preparation for adult roles. Hardly any phenomenon in the last decade has created more comment than high school marriages, in spite of the fact that teen-age marriages have been a part of the culture of the nation throughout its history. But until fairly recently the large proportion of early marriages has been confined to the working class. Marriage, as a youth problem, became a matter for discussion when more high school boys and girls from middle-income families began to marry while still in school.

As of 1958, one-fourth of all eighteen-year-old girls in the United States were married. This is the typical age for the senior year in high school. One-sixth of all seventeen-year-old girls and one-sixteenth of all sixteen-year-old girls in the population were also married that year.[1] No such phenomenal percentage of teen-age boys had married. But there had been an increase among them as well. Rhea I. Keeler reported that in 1940 some 0.6 per cent of married men were eighteen years of age or under. The number had increased to 3.0 per cent by 1950; in 1957, it had reached 4.3 per cent.[2]

All of this would suggest that there has been a major rise in percentage of teen-agers who have married. This is not the case. A decade ago 1.1 million young persons in teen years, or 9 per cent of the total youth of these ages, had married. In 1958, 1.5 million were married. This was a decrease of 1 per cent of the total youth in the teen-age brackets, though it was an increase in actual numbers.[3] Attention has evidently become centered on high school marriages as they have become more prevalent in higher socioeconomic groups in the nation.

Marriage for youth in the working class is expected soon after they have either quit or finished high school. Being a wife in this particular cultural group is the usual transition from girlhood to womanhood. Girls in families with more limited incomes and education have less concern for themselves as individuals. Their central roles are those of wife and mother.[4] They do not conceive of these roles as requiring other than a high school education if this much. Their involvement

[1] Daniel Seligman and Lawrence A. Mayer, "The Future Population 'Mix'," in *Fortune*, LIX (February, 1959), 94 ff.

[2] Rhea I. Keeler, "Early Marriage Trend," in *The Delta Kappa Gamma Bulletin*, Vol. 28 (Spring, 1962), p. 42.

[3] Eleanor H. Bernert, "Demographic Trends," in *The Family and Social Change*, p. 48.

[4] Lee Rainwater, Richard P. Coleman, and Gerald Handel, *Workingman's Wife*, p. 68.

in culture is peripheral. They accept it as such, as did their mothers before them.

Traditionally, women in the upper classes marry later than women in the blue-collar subculture. The former have been reared with the conception that they have roles both as individuals and as married women. Their parents expect them to complete high school, and are hopeful that they will attend junior college. A substantial number of such families are now expecting senior-college graduation for their daughters. These parents anticipate that their daughters will participate actively in the dominant culture of their nation and community, though not to the same degree as their sons. They desire an education for their girls which will make them relatively self-sufficient and yet acceptable as marriage partners. While the difference in age of marriage between girls in these diverse groups has been decreasing since World War II, the gap remains. Age of marriage for men in the working class is also lower than that of young men who finish high school and attend college. Here again, however, there has been some shift. An increase of marriages by younger men while still in high school or attending college has been noticeable.

Paul C. Glick and Hugh Carter have pointed out that persons who have left high school before graduation get married at a younger age than do others. For men who drop out of high school, the median age of marriage is 22.8 years; for women who drop out, the median age of marriage is 19.1 years. College graduates are the oldest, on the average, when they marry. The median age for men is 26.0 and for women, 23.8 years. Circumstances which hold persons in high school or college, and postpone marriage past teen years, also appear to discourage divorce and contribute to more stable marriages.

On the other hand, persons who discontinue their education before completion of high school tend to have lower incomes and higher divorce and separation rates. More children are born to these families. The cumulative effect of low income and high birth rate is associated with poor health and small living quarters. Limited resources among the parent generation make assistance to the newlyweds nearly impossible. Earlier marriages tend to halt education. Opportunity for future employment in occupations requiring skill is materially hampered.[5]

[5] Paul C. Glick and Hugh Carter, "Marriage Patterns and Educational Level," in *American Sociological Review*, XXIII (June, 1958), 294–300.

Kingsley Davis has pointed out that early marriage also tends to discourage technical and professional education in an era when unskilled labor is needed least. More years in school are required for semi-skilled, skilled, and professional jobs. This is where the demand for workers lies. Moreover, he believes that younger marriages discourage creativity and scientific advancement among both men and women. Freedom from heavy responsibilities is necessary for such achievement, he insists. Indeed, he considers teen-age marriage a "waste of talent." [6]

Perhaps it would not be amiss to mention a series of comments from youth themselves. Discussions by high school students in some 299 schools were held under the direction of the Texas Youth Participation Committee for the 1960 White House Conference on Children and Youth. Over 60 per cent of these schools chose high school marriages as an important topic for consideration. Young persons in their reports to the state committee added weight to the findings from the youth study to be reported shortly. The majority did not approve of early marriage.

Several of their comments bear repeating. One group wrote, "Before a teenager can be a good husband or wife, mother or father, he has to be mature, responsible, dependable and honest. The students need more guidance at home, at school, and in the community on marriage problems." Causes of early marriage included in their listing were, "insecurity, unhappiness, poor guidance, little or no responsibility assumed at school or at home, emotional and mental immaturity and a search for attention."

These conditions arose, according to the discussion findings, because, "They [the high school students] drift into an emotional state they cannot handle from too early dating, too late hours, and lack of supervision." "Most of the girls can't boil water, and have no idea what it costs to run a home." Certain recommendations were advanced to meet this problem. Education for marriage and parenthood was advocated: "Most instruction should come from the parents but the schools could: (1) have courses on marriage and parenthood, (2) offer pamphlets on the subject, (3) encourage teen-agers to read these articles, and, last, (4) encourage them to seek advice from higher authorities."

[6] Kingsley Davis, "The Early Marriage Trend," in *What's New*, No. 207 (Fall, 1958), pp. 2–6.

High school students continued their recommendations by saying, "The youth should receive some experience at home concerning housework. Teach marriage responsibilities and home economics. Teach youth to marry someone they respect, with whom they have a common interest." They continued, "Perhaps a special course in high school should be offered which presents all sides of married life. Thus, more youth having all the facts, would be discouraged from marriage, realizing their immaturity, bringing divorce rates down, and making happier young lives." [7]

As a whole, young persons in the Cooperative Youth Study were not overly enthusiastic about early marriage when they participated in the study. They were asked to respond to the item, "I would like to get married as soon as possible." As indicated in Table 31, three-fourths of them replied that this statement was false or did not apply to them. Approximately 14 per cent felt that this statement was true and was of much or great concern to them. The remainder expressed little or no concern for the problem, although they agreed they wanted

TABLE 31: *Responses of Youth to Items Related to High School Marriages*

	Percentage who marked:				
	False		True		
Item	Does not Apply	No Concern	Little Concern	Much Concern	Great Concern
I would like to get married as soon as possible.	74	4	7	5	9

	Percentage who:				
Items	Strongly Agree	Agree	Are Undecided or Uncertain	Disagree	Strongly Disagree
High school marriages can only lead to trouble.	7	12	28	35	18
Whenever a girl marries, she should drop out of high school.	7	11	14	35	32

[7] Texas Education Agency, *Texas Youth Participation for the White House Conference on Children and Youth*, pp. 27–32.

to marry as soon as possible. The majority of students were not willing to agree that, "High school marriages can only lead to trouble." A little over half disagreed with this concept of youthful marriage. About one-fourth were undecided. Less than 20 per cent thought this was a true statement. Still another facet of this current social problem was brought out by the statement, "Whenever a girl marries, she should drop out of high school." This was held to be false by two-thirds. Fewer than a fifth of the youth believed that marriage should end the high school career of girls.

MARRIED AND UNMARRIED STUDENTS—A COMPARISON

The greater majority of high school students remain unmarried until they drop out or graduate from the secondary schools. The exact number of married students attending high schools in Texas is not known. No record has been kept by the Texas Education Agency. However, it would be safe to assume that the number ranges from a tiny handful in certain communities to many more in high schools in different subcultural and social-class areas of larger cities.

The 1.1 per cent of married students in the study sample permitted sufficient cases for a special investigation of the attitudes and problems of this somewhat controversial group. Background factors studied systematically in the analytical design included: (a) sex of student; (b) marital status (married versus single); and (c) fathers' education on three levels—elementary, high school, and college. A total of four hundred cases was drawn to fill the twelve cells of the factorial design.[8] Only white students were included.

Attitudes of Married Students

The lack of any significant differences between married and unmarried high school students in several areas that were investigated is particularly interesting. These findings are important because they run counter to popular assumption.

Lack of interest in school is often given as a reason for early marriage, and this is no doubt true for the many young people who drop out of high school before its completion. These youth were, of course,

---

[8] This does not mean that 400 married students were included since the total number in the sample was not quite 150. Instruments from married and unmarried students were used in order to make comparisons.

inaccessible for this particular study. However, those who were married and *remained in school* in spite of marriage are indeed both unusual and worthy of consideration. Young men and women, who had married and who were continuing their high school studies, were not unhappy with their educational experiences nor were they falling below grade requirements in spite of their new responsibilities. The scale on Criticism of Education indicated both circumstances.

Problems of Personal Adjustment were no greater in general for the married than the unmarried youth. Obviously, young persons included in this study who were married did not marry because of acute feelings of personal maladjustment, as high school youth had assumed in their discussions for the White House Conference. This is a most important finding in that very often not only unmarried youth, but adults attribute early marriage to problems of personal adjustment. Also, these data run counter to the findings of two recent studies of the young married—one of men [9] and one of high school girls.[10] Of course the same instruments were not used in these three studies, but the distinctions in their conclusions are worth consideration.

Moreover, popular literature often assumes that if these youngsters were not maladjusted, they would not marry at an early age. This particular study indicates that further investigation is warranted before it is argued that all teen-age youth who marry while still attending high school are suffering from emotional problems of one sort or another. Granted that married youth still in high school are a select group, they do represent a growing segment of our population which it is especially important to understand.[11]

Married students showed significantly better attitudes toward society and the world as a whole than did unmarried students. They were more cheerful about their prospects in light of the current world situation. This optimism was in the face of very real problems concomitant with marital responsibilities complicated by the attempt to finish a

[9] Floyd M. Martinson, "Ego Deficiency as a Factor in Marriage: A Male Sample," in *Marriage and Family Living*, XXI (February, 1959), 48–52.

[10] J. Joel Moss and Ruby Gingles, "The Relationship of Personality to the Incidence of Early Marriage," in *Marriage and Family Living*, XXI (November, 1959), 373–377.

[11] See Lee G. Burchinal, "Research on Young Marriage: Implications for Family-Life Education," in *Family Life Coordinator*, Vol. 9 (September–December, 1960), pp. 6–24.

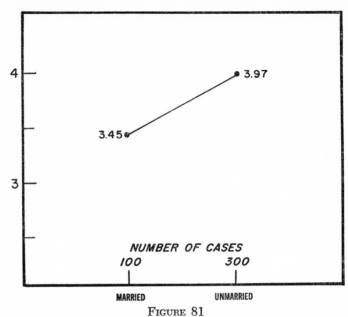

FIGURE 81

Married Students Better Oriented to Society than Unmarried Students

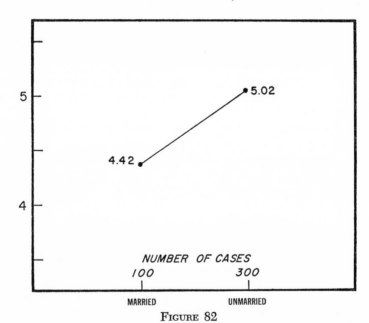

FIGURE 82

Married Students Less Accepting of Authoritarian Discipline than Unmarried Students

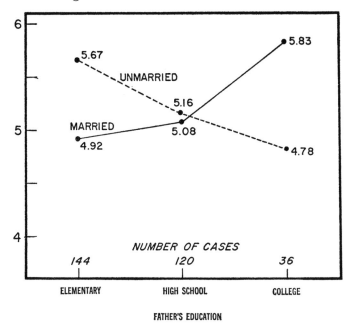

FIGURE 83
Relation of Criticism of Youth to Marital Status and Father's Education

formal education. From these data, marriage, even at high school age, would appear to represent a stabilizing element in conception of the world and its problems.

Authoritarian Discipline in child rearing was less accepted by married high school students than by those who were unmarried. For both young men and women, their concept of discipline was more democratic as their fathers' education improved. As was noted in the discussion of grade level in high school in Chapter VI, the more mature youth became, the less authoritarian were their responses. High school students who had married and assumed adult roles in their teen-age years reflected increasing maturation in their attitudes toward children. Married young persons still in high school had already surpassed the educational level of their parents in many instances. Democratic relationships and sharing in family life are more prevalent among the better educated.

Married high school girls were more critical of their peers than were married boys, just as all girls in the study were more critical than the boys. Unmarried youth of both sexes were more critical of other youth when the education of male parents was limited. Married students reversed this finding. If educational opportunities for the fathers had included college, then their married sons and daughters were more unhappy about the behavior of their peers. This may be evidence of growing responsibility and assumption of adult attitudes by these youngsters because of their marriages. Whether these young persons were aware of it or not, they obviously had come to look upon behavior of unmarried peers from the status of young adults.

Family Problems were reported as slightly fewer among the married than the unmarried high school students. This was probably a reflection of their move into a new family relationship in their own family which they found satisfying. A word of caution is in order, however, since it is impossible to tell how much these youth were responding to this scale in terms of the family which they had recently created instead of the family from which they came.

Attitudes reported by married as compared to unmarried students in high school suggest that married youth, either boys or girls who have the courage and motivation to continue their education, are more mature individuals than typical unmarried youngsters. Married students, however, might possibly be very conscious of their special status. Some of them may have made a deliberate attempt to deny negative attitudes and problems of adjustment in order to defend their early marriages.

Married Students and Family Conflict

Differences in response between married and unmarried students were particularly striking concerning Family Tension and Resentment of Dependency. The Family Tension scale, it should be recalled, is a comprehensive series of items indicating conflict between parents and youth. The more limited Family Problem scale, previously discussed in its relation to married youth, has to do with attitudes toward family relationships in general. Resentment of Dependency is the scale of statements which reveals resistance to parental control.

Married students, both boys and girls, generally displayed less Family Tension than unmarried. They also indicated less resentment over dependence upon parents. However, when sociocultural group mem-

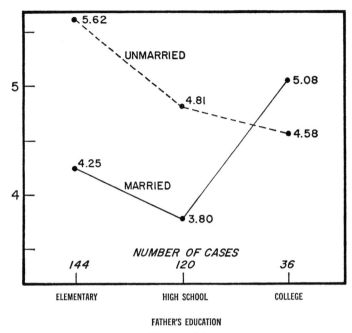

FIGURE 84

Relation of Family Tension to Marital Status and Father's Education

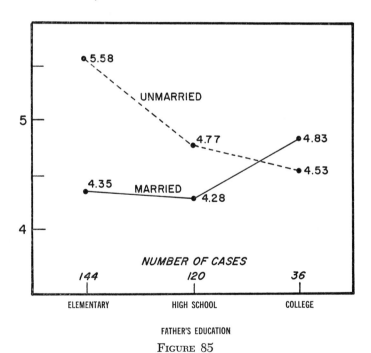

FIGURE 85

Relation of Resentment of Dependency to Marital Status and Father's Education

bership was taken into account, this generalization did not hold. Married youth sensed greater stress than did non-married in their relations with their parents when they had college-educated fathers. These same youth were more resentful of continuing dependence when their fathers were college men. High school youth who were married got along best with their parents if their fathers had attended elementary or secondary school only.[12]

Expectations by parents may account, at least in part, for these distinctions in reaction between the married and unmarried youth. Families where fathers' education was no more than twelve years apparently found it easier to grant adult status and relative freedom to their married teen-age children. They had probably not counted on delayed marriage. College education was not necessarily a status symbol, either for themselves or for their children. Acceptance of lesser achievement by, and more limited ambitions for, their children apparently reduced the pressure by parents upon their young when they married.

Marriage is neither expected nor desired for high school youth of either sex by upper–middle-class families. Radical readjustment of aspirations of parents is called for when their offspring defy parental ambitions and marry young. This is especially true for sons. Dreams of college graduation, with enhanced social and occupational status above that achieved by fathers and mothers, have to be revised downward in the light of reality. However, if their daughters by chance marry the "right boys," trauma for their parents is not as great. After all, they have anticipated marriage as the desired career, in the long run, for their girls.

Children of college-educated parents more often expect parental aid after marriage, or these parents are forced by their own ambition or sense of duty to share in financial support of the new family. They want their sons to graduate at least from high school. Control by parents, in many instances, goes hand-in-hand with financial backing of the new marriage. Dependence upon parents after marriage is, no doubt, galling to many middle-class young males. Results from both of these situations evidently tend to bring overt unhappiness and conflict.

Resentment of Family Life Style, the third of the scales which indicates family conflict, followed patterns similar to those of Family Ten-

[12] Lee G. Burchinal, "Adolescent Role Deprivation and High School Age Marriage," in *Marriage and Family Living*, XXI (November, 1959), 378–384. Especially note the summary on p. 384.

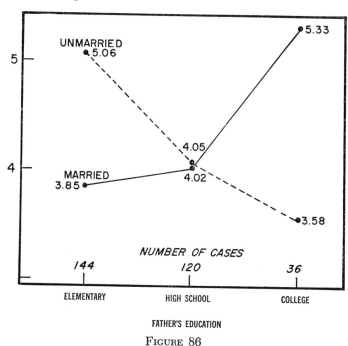

FIGURE 86

Relation of Resentment of Family Life Style to Marital Status and Father's Education

sion and Resentment of Dependency. Resentment of how the family was living rose steadily for married students by social status. It was least among youth with uneducated fathers and highest for those from middle- and upper-class homes. Exactly the opposite was revealed for unmarried students. Resentment of Family Life Style was highest for those from families of lower educational level. It was least for those with college-educated parents. Young persons who had been reared in homes of adequacy were obviously reflecting the radical shift in living standards which had come because of their marriages. Young people of middle and upper classes have been accused of wanting to begin at the level of living which their parents have achieved by the time of the marriage of their children. This study gave indication of the validity of this observation.

High school youth by necessity of their age have been married only a short time. Middle- and upper-class girls usually are ineffective and inefficient in their household management when compared to their mothers. Shock at the cost of maintaining a home is often a reality. Disappointment that their new homes cannot meet the standards to which they were accustomed, or of which they had dreamed, found expression in resentment of their way of life for these young married persons.

On the other hand, when young married students had come from lower-class homes, they showed the least resentment of the style of life in which they were living. Probably here was indication of the release of tension from overcrowding if they were in new homes by themselves. Also, these particular young persons had already achieved high school status. They were probably putting into practice somewhat higher standards of home living than were customary in their parental families when their fathers had completed only the eighth grade or less.

Problems of Social Inadequacy, Conformity and Isolation

Married high school students revealed three other noteworthy differences from unmarried students in their expressed concerns as measured by the scales for Social Conformity, Social Isolation, and Social Inadequacy. Concerns over peer-group conformity were encountered more often by married boys than by young wives. On the other hand, it was the unmarried girl in school who experienced greater stress to conform to her own age group.

Boys who marry early might be expected to chafe under the curtailment of their independent activities. Though they make their own choice to skip "the adolescent moratorium," as Erik Erikson describes this period of freedom, they evidently resent its loss. Freedom to participate in the male peer-group culture is denied them by the step they have taken. At the same time, their unmarried friends, themselves feeling pressures for social conformity, and having been the associates of the married boys for years, no doubt exert pressure upon them, either overtly or covertly, to remain a part of their group life. Married girls, as has been indicated, revealed no such severity of pressures to remain within adolescent culture.

Married high school boys and girls, as a whole, responded that they suffered less from feelings of Social Isolation and Social Inadequacy than their unmarried counterparts. Evidently their companionship compensated for whatever limitations were imposed upon them by

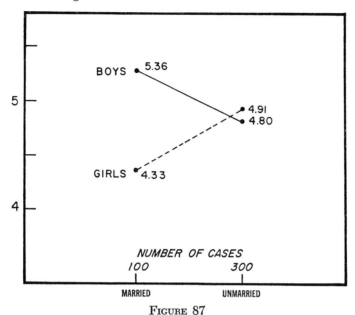

FIGURE 87
Effect of Marriage on Concerns about Social Conformity Is Different among Boys and Girls

their schools or their unmarried classmates in social activities. It can be assumed that many early marriages take place to avoid a feeling of being "left out" by agemates.

IN SUMMARY

Marriage for high school students serves to condition their participation in culture from two points of view. It may seriously limit preparation for adult roles, economic and social, in middle income-bracket families. Participation in adolescent culture is definitely impeded by the early assumption of marital status.

Marriage in high school represents a serious break with family aspirations and mores among youth whose parents are college educated. This was reflected in responses to the scales indicating family conflict. Youth at this socioeconomic level evidenced greater stress in their relationships with their families of origin. They were more aware of Family Tension. Resentment of Dependency was higher among them. Resentment of Family Life Style was more apparent. Among single students, on the other hand, it was members of this same sub-cultural group who displayed the least conflict.

Married students of college-educated fathers were more critical of other youth and expressed greater concern over their inadequacy. In their haste to become adult, they tended to become hypercritical of other teen-agers. At the same time, they felt themselves less accepted among their own age group. The assumption of married status without necessary socioeconomic competency created resentment of dependence upon parents. These married high school youngsters from college-educated families were indeed marginal in their place in culture. They were unprepared for the responsibilities of adult participation. They were limited, if not barred, from their age-group society.

The large majority of teen-agers who marry drop out of school. These youth, usually from blue-collar families, take up full-time roles as homemakers and earners. Consequently the analysis in this chapter is restricted to a very special group of youth who were either motivated enough by their own ambitions or by their parents' pressure to remain in school.

Married students, as an over-all generalization, indicated by their responses to attitude and problem scales that they make surprisingly good adjustment to their new status. Or, these youth may be less inclined to admit having problems and conflicts because of their marriages.

Further investigation definitely is indicated in relation to married high school youth. Blanket conclusions cannot be reached concerning the impact of marriage in teen years because the findings on all scales were not universally negative. No unequivocal observation is possible from this study. Social-class membership places radically different requirements upon youth for cultural participation. Divergent definitions of sex roles and of ages of maturation arise within the socioeconomic groups from which these youth come. That high school marriages are all bad, all good, or in between is not a valid assumption from the analyses of data from the Texas Cooperative Youth Study. Judgment concerning this phenomenon of the mid-twentieth century should be withheld.

XII: Youth Present a Case for Education tor Homemaking and Family Life

〜〜〜〜〜〜〜〜〜〜〜〜〜〜〜〜〜〜〜〜〜〜〜〜〜〜〜〜〜〜〜〜〜〜〜〜〜

YOUTH WERE UNAWARE that they would submit irrefutable evidence about their attitudes and concerns in personal and family living which would build the case for educated parents. They were equally unsuspecting of the documentation they would provide in support of specialized educational opportunities toward competence and effectiveness in personal and family living. This they accomplished through replies to an interest inventory, the third instrument utilized in the Texas Cooperative Youth Study.

Moreover, they were entirely unacquainted with the theoretical position of Talcott Parsons and Robert F. Bales. These social scientists have noted the "professionalization" of the mother role in the socialization of the child and the wife-homemaker role in marriage. They have stressed the importance of the expressive and subjective contributions women make to their families, but they also indicated the importance to child development, marriage, and family living of the "values of rationality." [1] Home economics, the action science, has its basis in the physical, life, and behavioral sciences in combination with aesthetics. Relevant information from all of these is blended for utilization of homemakers and parents as they perform their complex functions within the family. In fact, homemaking as well as home

---

[1] Talcott Parsons and Robert F. Bales, *Family, Socialization and Interaction Process*, pp. 25–26.

economics has acquired many of the attributes of applied science.

Neither had these young persons who participated in the study heard of the conceptualization of Cloward and Ohlin in *Delinquency and Opportunity,* where they have stressed that many problems of youth deviation arise from inadequate opportunities for socialization in the family and the community. Nor could they have known of accumulating evidence that fruitful attack upon major problems of deficiency in socialization and personality development may be accomplished through a revolution in environmental adequacy.[2]

Again, these students added the weight of their own evidence to the findings of a recent survey of adult homemakers. Clubwomen in the nation pointed toward the need for formalized educational experiences for the "vocation" or the "profession" of homemaker-parent and marriage partner not only among subcultures in the nation which were less adequate, but also in their own varied strata in society. These women agreed that mothers are not training their daughters sufficiently for their adult roles as mothers and homemakers. Their silence concerning their sons was indeed telling. They did indicate the imperative for more adequate knowledge concerning attitudes toward homemaking as a vocation or profession. Skills essential for taking care of the nutritional and clothing needs of the family rated below the areas of family living already indicated.[3]

High school students not only expressed interest in various aspects of their own development and family life as areas for study, but they added the weight of their attitudes toward the necessity for adequate preparation for home and family living. Over three-fourths of them believed that high school girls should "spend a lot of time in high school" learning to take care of the home and family. Agreement was also high that boys should spend some time in high school homemaking classes "in order to help learn to manage a home." Youth who were seniors were most emphatic concerning the necessity for education for home and family life for both sexes.

Over half of these teen-agers agreed that "discussion of problems of personal and family life should take place in classes made up of both boys and girls." Again, it was the more mature youth who were most sure of their position. Well above three-fourths of the young

[2] Richard A. Cloward and Lloyd E. Ohlin, *Delinquency and Opportunity.*

[3] "Findings of General Federation of Women's Clubs Home Life Survey," in *The Journal of Home Economics,* LIV (June, 1962), 435–436.

persons desired an opportunity to understand physical, emotional, and social changes as these related to their own personal development.

Youth apparently are coming to recognize the need for study in this emerging field of professionalization and in the sciences applicable to human relations in the family and to homemaking. How intensive should be the formal education in these fields would again be related to the cultural adequacy of the homes from which youngsters come. For some, those whose families were minimal in cultural, social, and economic opportunities, the school would bear the major burden for teaching toward basic improvement in home living, family interaction, and child rearing. The schools would, of necessity, assume the role of motivator toward a more rewarding home life and more satisfying relationships in the family. For others, the schools could well take the course of transmitting the ever increasing volume of new knowledge available in these fields. They could also share in upgrading competence in use of knowledge in home and family living, partially gained at home, but made incisive through systematized and organized instruction at school. Again, sex differences would modify time requirements and subject matter offered for their information.

Teen-agers have thus suggested, through expression of their attitudes and concerns in personal and family living and through an inventory of their interests, that education may be a major predicate for the stability of families of the future. They have expressed a definite desire for opportunity to study in school toward improved parenthood, happier marriages, and better homes. The specific evidence they offered appears in the following analysis of information gleaned from an inventory of their interests and will show the order of importance in which they ranked need for learning in various aspects of personal and family life.

A Study of Youth Interests

Statements utilized in the instrument, Interests in Personal and Family Living (Form III), were, in the main, in the words of youth themselves. This was also the origin of most items for the other two measurements used. Some few additions were submitted for this last instrument by members of the research team in order that all curriculum categories of homemaking education in public-school courses might be covered. These categories were designated as The House and Its Furnishings; Managing Time and Energy and Work; Feeding the Family; Clothing the Family; Development of Family Members; Personal, Family, and Community Relationships; Personal and Family Health; and Relation of Homemaking to Vocation. A composite picture of responses of youth from the study has already been written into a state curriculum guide for home- and family-life education in Texas.[4]

Young people readily indicated the intensity of their interest in some one hundred statements on a three-point continuum ranging from "strongly interested," or "mildly interested," to "not interested." As would be expected, their concern was widespread and the percentage of youth who were mildly or strongly interested ran high in almost every category. However, item analysis of the interest statements, plus some twenty-one topics from the instruments pertaining to attitudes and concerns, revealed some variation by sex and grade level. Finally, a comparison was made between the replies of 11,168 white students and those of some 672 high school teachers representing a cross-section of subject areas taught. Data were not available on a larger sample of teachers, nor were enough teacher instruments obtained to make a comparison between Negro youth and their teachers.

The items of highest priority of interest to youth were determined by computing the combined percentage of respondents who checked strongly or mildly interested. An arbitrary cut-off point of 80 per cent was chosen since it clearly represented a sentiment expressed by an overwhelming majority. Items considered of highest priority by youth as these related to their social selves reveal their conception of significant issues in their lives. A presentation of these items, beginning with those of greatest interest and ranked downward, offer implications not only for curriculum planning but for counselors in high schools as well.

Note should be taken that these statements range from the most complicated facets in human interaction such as, "How to get along with other people," to the simpler elements of social etiquette as implied in "How to order food in a restaurant." They have to do with everything from problems of emotional understanding as revealed by concern with "Controlling one's temper" and handling "Jealousy as a personality problem" to the desire to understand "people of other nations and other races."

[4] Texas Education Agency, *A Working Guide for Developing Homemaking Education Curriculum in Local Communities.*

TABLE 32: *Items of Highest Priority Concerning Self*

LISTED IN RANK ORDER

How to get along with other people.
How to meet people and feel at ease with them.
Expressing one's self well.
What is acceptable behavior on dates.
The effects of the place one lives on personality.
How to organize work to save time and energy.
Understanding my behavior and that of others.
Selecting appropriate clothes which will best suit my build and personality.
Controlling one's temper.
Authoritative and correct information about sex.
What personality characteristics make for popularity.
All kinds of information on the etiquette of dating.
Planning for use of one's leisure time.
How to handle fears.
How shyness happens and how to overcome it.
Understanding people of other nations and other races.
Why one person's personality differs from another.
Jealousy as a personality problem.
How to order food in a restaurant.

Situational aspects of daily living, as represented by "The effects of the place one lives on personality," were indicated as of relevance. So was such a highly personalized matter as the desire for "Authoritative and correct information about sex." Perhaps as significant as the degree of interest in certain aspects of the self and the self-in-relation-to-others, was the relatively wide span of concern with the multiplicity of factors involved in problems of social interaction. Again, these statements are of real relevance to counselors as well as teachers.

Interpersonal relations within the family and the operational aspects of the home made up a second category of interest among high school youth. First priority was given by them to various relationships between family members. High school youth, at least in theory, accept the necessity for joint planning, sharing in work and responsibilities related to family life. Moreover, they expressed concern for information related to activities in which all family members could participate. Family problems, they indicated, required understanding if they were to be dealt with intelligently. All of these, of course, are closely related to their interest in the home as a source of citizenship training and as the center for learning democratic principles of human relationships.

TABLE 33: *Items of Highest Priority Concerning the Family and the Home*

LISTED IN RANK ORDER

To learn how the family can plan together, share work and responsibilities.
How to get along with and do things for elderly people.
Well planned activities that everyone in the family can participate in.
How to understand and deal with problems families usually have.
How to develop citizenship through home and family living.
Learning democratic family practices.
What is involved in setting up and maintaining a home.
Each family member having a place for his things.
How to have a place of my own for my clothes and my other belongings.
Getting a meal ready to serve so that all food will be ready at the same time.
Planning nutritious meals.
Cooking different foods to get variety in family meals.
Rearranging dark and unattractive rooms to make them more usable.
How to plan a house to fit our family needs.

That learning to care for elders was of second highest priority in this list of items was somewhat unexpected. However, this was foreshadowed by agreement that young persons should care for their parents when they become elders. This, it will be remembered, was previously reported as having been adhered to by some three-fourths of the youngsters.

Immediately following these concerns with family interaction were a series of items related to the environment of the home and its operation as a part of the matrix of family life. That a real desire existed to learn what it took to establish and maintain a home is significant. More to be expected was concern evidenced for development of certain skills relating to nutrition and family meals.

TABLE 34: *Items of Major Concern about Marriage and Parenthood*

LISTED IN RANK ORDER

What is to be considered in choosing a marriage partner.
Planning for marriage.
Child care in emergency situations.
Understanding prenatal care and how children are born.
How children grow and develop.
How to take care of and entertain sick children.

Not only were youth logical in the arrangement of items by relative importance but also in sequence in those pertaining to marriage and parenthood. What to consider in choosing a marriage partner was given precedence over planning for marriage. The only item which was out of sequence in their listing by interest had to do with care of children in emergency situations. This, no doubt, is a direct reflection of the uncertainty of the times and of the emphasis on Civil Defense and disaster training in the public schools. Also it may arise from the services many teen-agers render as baby-sitters.

TABLE 35: *Items of High Priority in Personal and Family Health*

LISTED IN RANK ORDER

What health problems a family is likely to face.
Keeping mentally and physically fit.
First aid in a disaster or an emergency.
Making the home safe from accidents.
What to do when somebody in the family gets sick.
When it is important to seek help from a doctor.
Dangers from self-doctoring.
What health and protective services are available for families.
What to do to get rid of body odor.

As each category of interests has been discussed, evidence mounts that youth are concerned for others as well as for themselves. In no listing of interests was this more evident than among those items directly related to family health. Family problems in health topped the list. "Keeping mentally and physically fit," though stated as if it were related only to self, could well be construed as including both self and family members. This interpretation would probably be equally correct for other items which seem related only to youth but which probably carry the connotation for them that they apply equally well to others in the family group. The final item on personal hygiene is, of course, an exception.

Preparation for personal employment took top billing, and "How to prepare one's self for a part-time job" also carried priority. Young persons obviously look to school for assistance in getting ready for their earning roles, both in personal and vocational qualifications. Consumer problems ranging all the way from how to buy intelligently to how to invest savings offer clues to learning experiences desired by youth in the field of finance and money management. The economics of family life also came in for its share of consideration. Whether to

TABLE 36: *Items of Highest Interest Concerning Personal Employment and Family Finance*

LISTED IN RANK ORDER

How to apply for a job—manners, grooming, clothing.
Judging advertising intelligently and buying wisely from it.
Where to go and things to do which will cost little or no money.
How to prepare one's self for a part-time job.
Investing the money one saves.
What kinds of insurance a family needs.
How to judge what is a good buy by reading labels on cans, clothes, and appliances.
How to buy and take care of appliances for the home.
What sort of house and furnishings we could have on our income.
What to look for when buying or building a house.
Social Security and how it applies to us.
How one gets a good credit rating.
Advantages of renting or owning a house.
How to cut down the cost of clothes and yet keep them good looking.
Knowing my share of the family clothing money.
What to look for when you buy furniture.

---

buy or rent a home rated not far below the desire to know what sort of a house and furnishings could be achieved at certain income levels. Again, concern with problems related to "the family of origin" of these young persons was evidenced through their ranking of such items as "Knowing my share of the family clothing money," and "How to cut down the cost of clothes and yet keep them good looking."

The remainder of the some one hundred items included in the inventory of interests fell below this top 20 per cent. However, the fact that these were not considered of major importance by youth in no way detracts from their relevance to education for effective and efficient home and family living or as leads to where personal and group counseling may be indicated. In fact, the lesser concern of youth for some items may indicate real need for stimulation of interest and the development of a feeling of responsibility to learn more about them.

Agreements and Disagreements by Sex

Rather than carrying out statistical analyses for the entire sample of 12,892 youth, studies of variations by sex and grade level were made of special samples drawn to represent major stratification categories in the over-all design. These categories were of special interest to curriculum planning. Those utilized are listed below:[5]

TABLE 37: *Stratification Categories Used for Analysis of Sex and Grade-Level Differences in Interest Items**

Geographic Region	Size of Community	Size of Sample
East Texas	Medium	275
Gulf Coast	Medium	163
Central Texas	Medium	652
West Texas	Medium	359
South Texas	Small	216
West Texas	Small	1,118
Gulf Coast	Metropolitan	1,034

* White youth only.

Tests for significant differences for sex and grade level were made for every item in the inventory, one sample at a time. Where no sex variations were present in all save one or two of the seven samples, it was assumed that the general trend was sufficiently over-riding to justify an interpretation regardless of sex. Where significant sex differences did occur, they were listed separately and are discussed prior to the more general trends applicable to all youth. While no systematic tests for regional variations in interests were made, if responses varied widely they were not included in the following presentation.

Interests of boys in learning about various aspects of home and family living did differ from those of girls in high school but not as widely as might have been anticipated. They expressed greater concern for statements more generally accepted as interwoven in the masculine role. "Social Security and how it applies to us" was given higher priority by boys than by girls. "How to 'do-it-yourself' or 'build-it-yourself'" was not quite universally accepted as of greater male interest, but it was usually considered so. "How one gets a good credit rating" also was usually more imperative to boys than to girls.

Statements in which girls were more interested than boys lend strength to the assertion that there remains a sphere of work in the home which is delegated to woman. Moreover, these concerns still have to do with home management, family interaction, and mother-

---

[5] Chi Square was used for testing the significance of differences. A difference was considered significant only if the Chi Square was significant beyond the .01 level.

hood. At least, the listing of items as described in Table 38 bears this out.

TABLE 38: *Items of Major Concern to White Girls* *

THE HOUSE AND ITS EQUIPMENT

How to beautify the house and its grounds.
What sort of house and furnishings we could have on our income.
Rearranging dark and unattractive rooms to make them more usable.

MANAGING TIME AND ENERGY AND WORK

How to understand and deal with problems families usually have.

FEEDING THE FAMILY

Getting a meal ready to serve so that all food will be ready at the same time.
How to order food in a restaurant.
Cooking different foods to get variety in family meals.
Planning nutritious meals.
Preparing quick family meals.
Feeding small children and the rest of the family.
Buying foods which will give us the most for our money.
How to get family members to eat what they ought to.
How to deal with special food problems of family members.
How to select, prepare and serve food for various occasions.

CLOTHING THE FAMILY

Selecting appropriate clothes which will best suit my build and personality.
How to have a place of my own for clothes and my other belongings.
How to cut down the cost of clothes and yet keep them good looking.
When it is cheaper to buy clothes and when it is best to make them.
How to launder, press, and make simple repairs on clothes.
Skills which give the ability to construct and make clothes fit.
How to glamorize "hand-me-downs" and "made-overs."
How to assemble clothing babies need.

DEVELOPMENT OF FAMILY MEMBERS

How children grow and develop.
Understanding prenatal care and how children are born.
How to get little children to behave.
Why little children behave as they do.
Why children suck fingers, bite fingernails, stammer, and show other signs of
   problems.
Games, puzzles and story telling for young children.

---

* Items are arranged by rank order of interest and by areas of Homemaking Education.

TABLE 38: *Items of Major Concern to White Girls—Continued*

PERSONAL, FAMILY, AND COMMUNITY RELATIONSHIPS

Planning for marriage.
How to tell younger children there is to be a new baby.

PERSONAL AND FAMILY HEALTH

Child care in emergency situations.
How to take care of and entertain sick children.
Gaining or losing weight and how to maintain normal weight.

Even more impressive than sex differences in interest in home and family living were the likenesses evidenced among white youth in varied sized communities ranging from the smaller in South and West Texas, through the medium in other regions, to the metropolitan in the Gulf Coast area. While there was not yet unanimity in all community sizes, in five or more types there was agreement of the following mutuality of concern.

TABLE 39: *Items of Common Interest to White Boys and Girls* *

THE HOUSE AND ITS EQUIPMENT

How to buy and take care of appliances for the home.
What to look for when buying or building a house.
Advantages of renting or owning a home.

MANAGING TIME AND ENERGY AND WORK

How to organize work to save time and energy.
Getting the most from our family money.
Judging advertising intelligently and buying wisely from it.
Where to go and things to do which will cost little or no money.
Investing the money one saves.
Planning for use of one's leisure time.
What kinds of insurance a family needs.
What and how to buy on "lay away," "time payment," "installment plan."

DEVELOPMENT OF FAMILY MEMBERS

Authoritative and correct information about sex.
How to handle fears.
Making toys and play equipment for children.

* Items are arranged by rank order of interest and by areas of Homemaking Education.

TABLE 39: *Items of Common Interest to White Boys and Girls—Continued*

PERSONAL, FAMILY, AND COMMUNITY RELATIONSHIPS

How to develop citizenship through home and family living.
Understanding people of other nations and other races.
Learning democratic family practices.
Information about divorce and its effects on the family.
Information about community services available for families.

PERSONAL AND FAMILY HEALTH

Keeping mentally and physically fit.
What health problems a family is likely to face.
First aid in a disaster or an emergency.
Making the home safe from accidents.
Dangers from self-doctoring.
What health and protective services are available for families.
What to do to get rid of body odor.

RELATION OF HOMEMAKING TO VOCATION

How to apply for a job—manners, grooming, clothing.
How to prepare one's self for a part-time job.

Other items were of common interest to boys and girls in from one
to five of the community sizes which were included in this analysis.
From these, as grouped in Table 40, was indicated the increasing overlap of mutual regard by men and women for their joint responsibilities
in the home and with their families. Many statements in this table still
would be considered as in the prerogative of women in more traditional settings. However, in an increasing range of communities,
regardless of size, there is evidence as Henry A. Bowman states it, that
"Man is no longer a guest in his own home." He is rapidly becoming a
participant in his household in many more of its operational aspects
as well as in its patterns of family relationships.

In other words, while there still remains some real division of labor
between the sexes within the home, the areas of sharing and overlap
are becoming ever wider. That this is well on its way was revealed by
this analysis of interests of high school youth. Evidence is mounting
that there is rapidity in development of the concept of supplementary
and complementary roles of men and women in modern family life,
rather than a clear-cut dichotomy of interests and functions between
the sexes.

TABLE 40: *Items Indicating Development of Mutuality of Interests between Boys and Girls* *

THE HOUSE AND ITS EQUIPMENT

The effects of the place one lives on personality.
Each family member having a place for his things.
What to look for when you buy furniture.
How to plan a house to fit our family needs.

MANAGING TIME AND ENERGY AND WORK

To learn how the family can plan together, share work and responsibilities.
Well planned activities that everyone in the family can participate in.
What is involved in setting up and maintaining a home.
How to judge what is a good buy by reading labels on cans, clothes, and appliances.

FEEDING THE FAMILY

Danger of following food fads.
Planning for food buying.

CLOTHING THE FAMILY

Learning to buy clothes for the whole family.

DEVELOPMENT OF FAMILY MEMBERS

Understanding my behavior and that of others.
Controlling one's temper.
How to get along with and do things for elderly people.
Why one person's personality differs from another.
Jealousy as a personality problem.
How children form acceptable habits.
More about children in order to be able to earn money baby sitting.

PERSONAL, FAMILY, AND COMMUNITY RELATIONSHIPS

How to get along with other people.
How to appreciate and enjoy all family members.
Expressing one's self well.
How to meet people and feel at ease with them.
What is acceptable behavior on dates.
To learn how to handle disagreements in the family.
All kinds of information on the etiquette of dating.
What personality characteristics make for popularity.
What is to be considered in choosing a marriage partner.
How shyness happens and how to overcome it.

---

* Items are arranged by rank order of interest and by areas of Homemaking Education.

TABLE 40: *Items Indicating Development of Mutuality of Interests between Boys and Girls—Continued*

PERSONAL AND FAMILY HEALTH

What to do when somebody in the family gets sick.
When it is important to seek help from a doctor.
How to get rid of pimples and have a clear complexion.
Taking care of the mother and an infant.

RELATION OF HOMEMAKING TO VOCATION

Exploring job opportunities using homemaking training.

Grade-Level Variations

Levels of interest in certain categories of home and family education served to further reveal the processes of maturation which are accomplished during the four years of high school. However, as there were common interests between the sexes in many items listed, so were there also areas of overlapping between concerns of youth in the first two and last two years of secondary school. As would be expected, evidence accumulated that young persons completing high school were moving rapidly into young adulthood when the establishment of their own homes and families was of increasing relevance.

Perhaps it would be well to examine first the areas of common concern to all grade levels in high school. Some of these were found in all seven categories of items. Interests in family economics were numerous, ranging from various credit plans to consumer guidance for effective purchasing of material goods. In addition, how to use leisure time proved to be a universal. General information pertaining to various aspects of feeding the family and clothing family members showed no differential by age.

Of major concern to youth, no matter what grade in school, was the development of family members and of self. Here was found the desire by all high school youth to learn of human behavior and mental health. Controlling temper, handling fears, jealousy as a personal problem, and behavior which gave warning of emotional maladjustment in children were indicated as of serious concern to all ages. Developmental aspects of children were surprisingly universal in their appeal. Relationships between persons, within the family, and in the larger community demanded attention of all youth. Specifics in child and family health were listed. The breakdown in items is to be found in Table 41.

TABLE 41: *No Variation in Interest by Grade Levels*

THE HOUSE AND ITS EQUIPMENT

How to "do-it-yourself" or "build-it-yourself" to make home more comfortable, convenient, and in good repair.
Each family member having a place for his things.

MANAGING TIME AND ENERGY AND WORK

What and how to buy on "lay away," "time payment," "installment plan."
Where to go and things to do which will cost little or no money.
Planning for use of one's leisure time.
Social Security and how it applies to us.
How to judge what is a good buy by reading labels on cans, clothes, and appliances.

FEEDING THE FAMILY

Preparing quick family meals.
Planning nutritious meals.
Getting a meal ready to serve so that all food will be ready at the same time.
Cooking different foods to get variety in family meals.
How to deal with special food problems of family members.
Planning for food buying.

CLOTHING THE FAMILY

Learning to buy clothes for the whole family.
How to launder, press, and make simple repairs on clothes.
Skills which give the ability to construct and make clothes fit.
Selecting appropriate clothes which will best suit my build and personality.
Knowing my share of the family clothing money.
How to cut down the cost of clothes and yet keep them good looking.

DEVELOPMENT OF FAMILY MEMBERS

Why children suck fingers, bite fingernails, stammer and show other signs of problems.
Controlling one's temper.
How to handle fears.
Games, puzzles and story telling for young children.
Why one person's personality differs from another.
How children grow and develop.
Understanding prenatal care and how children are born.
How children form acceptable habits.

TABLE 41: *No Variation in Interest by Grade Levels—Continued*

Jealousy as a personality problem.
How to get little children to behave.
How to get along with and do things for elderly people.

PERSONAL, FAMILY, AND COMMUNITY RELATIONSHIPS

How to get along with other people.
How to appreciate and enjoy all family members.
Information about community services available for families.
To learn how to handle disagreements in the family.
Understanding people of other nations and other races.
How to develop citizenship through home and family living.
What personality characteristics make for popularity.

PERSONAL AND FAMILY HEALTH

Child care in emergency situations.
Taking care of the mother and an infant.
Making the home safe from accidents.
Dangers from self-doctoring.

Youth in mid-adolescence in the ninth and tenth grades gave priority to only eleven items of special concern to them. These were related to themselves as persons save in one category. Young children and their care was of importance to this age level. Other areas ranged from interest in job opportunities, to dating information, to the need for "a place of one's own," on to the danger of food fads. As might have been expected, care of complexion proved to be a major issue at this age. Table 42 presents this picture.

TABLE 42: *Items of Major Interest in Ninth and Tenth Grades*

FEEDING THE FAMILY

How to select, prepare and serve food for various occasions.
Danger of following food fads.

CLOTHING THE FAMILY

How to have a place of my own for clothes and my other belongings.
How to glamorize "hand-me-downs" and "made-overs."

DEVELOPMENT OF FAMILY MEMBERS

More about children in order to be able to earn money baby sitting.
Making toys and play equipment for children.

TABLE 42: *Items of Major Interest in Ninth and Tenth Grades—Continued*

PERSONAL, FAMILY, AND COMMUNITY RELATIONSHIPS

What is acceptable behavior on dates.
All kinds of information on the etiquette of dating.

PERSONAL AND FAMILY HEALTH

How to take care of and entertain sick children.
How to get rid of pimples and have a clear complexion.

RELATION OF HOMEMAKING TO VOCATION

Exploring job opportunities using homemaking training.

Developmental tasks of young adults came to the fore as revealed in Table 43 when items of major interest to eleventh- and twelfth-grade students were listed. In almost every category, the emphasis was upon family life. The establishment of the home loomed large. Family finances were emphasized as of importance. Planning for marriage, learning democratic family practices, how to meet others with ease and to express one's self well were listed. In other words, here lies a wide area of need for specific preparation in class room and counseling for the assumption of new roles in family and community, and a need for guidance in the movement toward the broader independent life of the adult. It is true that many will have the intervening years of college preparation. However, in all probability the last years in high school will offer the sole opportunity for acquisition of specific knowledge in the field of marriage and the family, even for the college bound.

TABLE 43: *Items of Major Interest in the Eleventh and Twelfth Grades*

THE HOUSE AND ITS EQUIPMENT

The effects of the place one lives on personality.
What sort of house and furnishings we could have on our income.
What to look for when you buy furniture.
What to look for when buying or building a house.
How to buy and take care of appliances for the home.
How to plan a house to fit our family needs.
Advantages of renting or owning a home.

Table 43: *Items of Major Interest in the Eleventh and Twelfth Grades— Continued*

MANAGING TIME AND ENERGY AND WORK

Getting the most from our family money.
What is involved in setting up and maintaining a home.
How to organize work to save time and energy.
How to understand and deal with problems families usually have.
To learn how the family can plan together, share work and responsibilities.
Investing the money one saves.
What kinds of insurance a family needs.
How one gets a good credit rating.

FEEDING THE FAMILY

Feeding small children and the rest of the family.
Buying foods which will give us the most for our money.
How to get the family members to eat what they ought to.

PERSONAL, FAMILY, AND COMMUNITY RELATIONSHIPS

Expressing one's self well.
Information about divorce and its effect on the family.
Planning for marriage.
Learning democratic family practices.
What is to be considered in choosing a marriage partner.
How to meet people and feel at ease with them.

PERSONAL AND FAMILY HEALTH

What health problems a family is likely to face.
Keeping mentally and physically fit.

Certain items from the instrument on attitudes and the one on concerns of youth were included in this particular item analysis when these were directly related to attitudes or problems relevant to curriculum planning in home and family-life education. Indirect implications, of course, are woven throughout the findings on attitudes and concerns of youth.[6]

No difference in grade level was found among those who agreed that their homes were too cluttered to be comfortable and among those

---

[6] It is hoped that a future analysis of these data will be built around their implications for curriculum planning in high school in Homemaking Education and in college in Home Economics. However, this task is beyond the competence of the present authors.

who were hesitant to bring friends into their homes because the houses were unattractive.

Youngsters in the earlier grades of high school exhibited impatience with extended tasks and with planning their finances. They expressed this in response to the items, with which they agreed more than their older classmates: "It takes so long to make things that I don't like them when I finish them." And, "Planning ahead how to spend my money is a waste of time"; "There is no sense in keeping track of money spent." Additional knowledge, and years, would seem to be needed to bring the relevance of these items into focus. The push for time was also indicated by these same youngsters agreeing that, "Most of the time I'm so busy I can't get through a meal fast enough."

Agreement was also indicated by the younger high school students with the statement that "Clothes I like always seem to cost more than I can afford to pay." They also manifested the belief that, "The kind of clothes you wear has no effect on your personality."

That boys need some high school homemaking so that they can learn to help manage a home was agreed to more strongly by freshmen and seniors among the youth. Students in the intervening years were less sure. Moreover, it was the freshmen in high school who expressed the idea that they saw "no reason for every boy and girl to understand the physical changes which occur during adolescence." Here may be evidence of basic unsureness of self and of the timidity so often encountered in these years of rapid growth and development.

Among the very small percentage of youth agreeing that eating breakfast was more trouble than it was worth, there were no distinctions between grades. The same prevailed for those who admitted they disliked cooking—a surprisingly small 16 per cent. While 82 per cent stated that "It is as important for girls to learn how to make clothes as how to buy them," this agreement was neither greater nor less for the first and last two years of secondary school. The meagre 7 per cent who felt that studying about health practices in class was a waste of time was distributed throughout grade levels.

A single problem was included in this item count, and it had to do with religion. Some 50 per cent of the young people agreed that they did not feel they lived up to their religious teachings as well as others. If this was their response, it ranged across grade levels and showed no evidence of difference between early or later years in high school.

INTERESTS OF HIGH SCHOOL TEACHERS

High school teachers, some 672 of them in white high schools and representing all subject areas including homemaking, were generally more concerned with every item in the Interest Inventory than were the youngsters whom they taught.

Men teachers were not as universally interested in items listed as were women. However, they were more impressed than women teachers, save those in homemaking, with such statements as "Advantages of renting or owning a home"; "How one gets a good credit rating"; "Making toys and play equipment for children"; "How to get little children to behave"; "How to tell younger children there is to be a new baby"; and "Taking care of the mother and an infant." Homemaking teachers joined the men in their greater concern for the last four items listed.

Homemaking teachers also were more concerned than other teachers, both men and women, in such areas as: "The effects of the place one lives on personality" and how to "do-it-yourself"; what is involved in various credit plans; where to go to have a good time with less expenditure of money. As would be expected, they wanted to know more about "How to get the family members to eat what they ought to." They were interested in personality differences, in problems revealed in child-behavior such as thumb sucking, stammering, and nail biting. Young children—including prenatal and infant care—were high in priority for these teachers, as was their desire to have information on how to entertain small children.

No doubt homemaking teachers were thinking of the youth whom they taught when they indicated the importance they attributed to such items as "What is acceptable behavior on dates"; "All kinds of information on the etiquette of dating"; "What is to be considered in choosing a marriage partner"; "Planning for marriage"; "Information about community services available for families"; "Information about divorce and its effects on the family"; and "How to take care of and entertain sick children." They also took special note of interest in "How shyness happens and how to overcome it."

Homemaking teachers in high school would not have been true to their profession had they not thought that "Girls ought to spend a lot of their time in high school learning about taking care of the home and family." They also believed that "Discussion of personal adjustment and family life should take place in classes having both boys and girls." These women were joined by all other teachers of their sex in stating that "Boys need some high school homemaking so they can learn to help manage a home."

All women who taught, regardless of whether homemaking, English, history, or any other discipline, were interested in home furnishings and how to buy these intelligently. Making dark rooms attractive and the beautification of home and grounds was universally appealing. They were interested in consumer buying and learning to use good judgment in their purchases. They joined in their emphasis upon the desirability of knowing how to prepare quick family meals, how to feed small children with the rest of the family, how to plan and serve meals efficiently, how to give variety to family menus, how to manage special food problems of family members, how to purchase food wisely. Also, they wanted to protect themselves against food fads. These women, who held professional responsibilities and were evidently homemakers as well, were concerned with every aspect of clothing for the family as listed in the interest inventory.

Understanding the behavior of others, controlling temper and handling fears were considered important by women teachers of high school youth. Elders attracted their attention. Expressing one's self well, getting along with people, and development of democratic family practices were indicated of real significance. That men who teach youth were not equally impressed by the paramount meaning of these items for effective home and family living is an important revelation in itself.

Personal appearance, including complexion care and weight management, were not unexpected items of concern for women who teach. "What to do when somebody in the family gets sick" again indicated the area of responsibility of many of these women in their dual roles of professional workers and homemakers. Finally, they, with homemaking teachers, were interested in exploring job opportunities using homemaking training.

HIGH SCHOOL YOUTH AND THEIR TEACHERS

High school youth, while less concerned than their teachers in the majority of items listed, revealed more interest in a number of areas than the adults who taught them, men or women, homemaking teachers or others.

In feeding the family, these youth gave more emphasis to small children and the rest of the family than did their elders. Getting a meal ready to serve, *in toto,* was significant to them as was the selection and preparation of foods for a variety of occasions. "How to order food in a restaurant" is taken for granted by adults, but for the teen-ager, it is an area where they obviously felt they needed help.

Concerns over clothing, which were more important to youth than adults, included learning how to launder, press, and make simple repairs. Skills for construction of clothing, and fitting them, appeared desirable. When it was cheaper to buy than to make clothes caught the attention of youth. They were concerned with having a place of their own for their clothes and other belongings. Glamorizing hand-me-downs was of interest as was the selection of clothes to enhance personality. Having a good idea about their share in the family clothing budget made sense to students. And there was some interest, above their elders, in preparing clothes for the infant.

"Authoritative and correct information about sex" was an expected item of priority for teen-agers. So was the need for knowledge for better earning opportunities afforded by baby sitting. How to care for sick children and taking care of the mother and infant were areas of need expressed more by youth than adults. Also they considered how to tell younger children of the arrival of a new baby something they wished and needed to know. Certainly to be expected was their paramount attention, over that of their teachers, to learning how to apply for a job—including manners, grooming, and clothing—as well as to exploring job opportunities using homemaking training. Preparation for part-time jobs fits in nicely with time available to students for earning. Here again is indication of a counseling as well as a teaching need.

In interpersonal relations, the developmental stages of these youth were evidenced by their interest in what is acceptable behavior on dates, the etiquette of dating, planning for marriage, and choosing a marriage partner. All of these items were related to current imperatives in the lives of high school youth and, of course, were of lesser concern among teachers. Closely allied to these interests was the desire of students to know "What personality characteristics make for popularity."

Some attitudes youth held, different from those of their teachers, displayed their less mature judgement. They agreed that eating breakfast was more trouble than it was worth—an indication of the national problem of malnutrition far too prevalent among high school youth. Youngsters also expressed the feeling that, "Most of the time I'm so busy I can't get through a meal fast enough."

Cost of clothing was more of a problem to youth than to their teachers, and youngsters believed that girls should learn how to make clothes as well as how to buy them.

Youth, more often than those who instruct them, felt that studying health practices in class was a waste of time. Also, about a fourth of the sample saw no reason why boys and girls should understand physical changes which occur during adolescence.

Contrast in what was considered more important by teachers and by youth offers indication that both the knowledge and the wisdom of the former needs to be imparted to the young in many aspects of family life. On the other hand, youth have pointed up to those who instruct them that they have areas of concern which teachers may be either minimizing or even ignoring. Each of these age groups, youth and adults, revealed to each other information for consideration.

A PHILOSOPHICAL NOTE

While this presentation of data has been a listing of interests of youth and of their teachers in various categories of home and family living, it covers ground strikingly similar to evidences presented of "a new cultural adjustment" noted as arising in the United States. These were itemized in an article honoring John Dewey's 100th birthday in the *Saturday Review*.[7] Both the presentation of youth interests in this study and the evidences of improvement of the quality of culture in the nation are directly related to the educational needs of man. Notable among the testimony of accruing cultural assets offered by the American scholars honoring John Dewey were "A preoccupation with the character of family life" and with "the character of our neighborhood settings." Included, as well, was indication of a greater and more widespread interest in "the design and decor of our homes." Concern for "the general area of our manners and deportment" was linked closely with "the movement away from the 'greasy spoon' eatery."

[7] A manifesto signed by Joe Burnett, Hobert W. Burns, Nathaniel L. Champlin, Otto Krash, Frederick C. Neff, and Francis T. Villemain, "Education in Society," Section 1 of "Dewey and Creative Education," in *Saturday Review*, November 21, 1959, p. 20.

Advance was pointed out in "skills of interior, architectural, and industrial design." "New clothing and attention to grooming" were listed. In addition, note was taken of a growing market in books, magazines, art films, reproductions of paintings and sculptures. Nearly all of these were also either included among, or closely related to, those of interest to youth in home and family life as furnished by them for the study. "Qualitative excellence" as needed in these important facets of human experience appears to be gaining pervasive acceptance among scholars and students alike.

XIII: The Case for the Educated Parent

CULTURAL PARTICIPATION has its being in communication. Resources in culture are doomed to remain hidden and unattainable unless people possess the capacity to perceive, to learn, and to transmit what is available. The more complex the society, the greater the need for proficiency in communication and for depth of perception.

The ability to see, to know, and to understand opens the gateway to sharing in the richness and variety of the creations of man. How far the gate is ajar for any individual is determined, in large measure, by the opportunities he has had to acquire the knowledge, beliefs, and values by which men deal with the world as well as the skills to utilize the "artifacts" of this technological culture. Socialization in the family, education in the schools, and participation in community life are major channels for effective human interaction.

The imperative for parents is the quality of children they will bear and rear. The openness to experience which they achieve for their young determines the degree to which the potentialities of the child may be developed. The breadth of learning of culture and the depth of its meaning available to children largely foreshadow adult adequacy. The paramount contribution offered by educated parents to their children is the capacity for a participating share in society.

Closed doors to cultural variety and richness, and closed minds are intimately related. Education does not guarantee openness in personality, but it does furnish man opportunity to become free. He develops the capability to be a receptor of his culture. He may share in its creation and its modification. He becomes an essential force in its on-going nature and its change. He is involved. From his involvement, he derives his own capacity to grow and to function.

Persons deprived in communicative ability are woefully limited. Circumstances beyond their comprehension or control may force them to skim the periphery of all that society has to offer. They remain unaware of either the depth or breadth of the cultural complex even of their own nation—let alone of the world. They are incapable of taking from its vast stores or of contributing to its creative strength.[1]

The case for education is made most often in relation to scientific and technological need. Education is even more essential for the advancement and survival of the United States because of what it affords in quality of personalities. Persons are the nation. Democracy is the most sophisticated form of organized society. Men govern themselves through sharing in decision-making and in the creation of the very values by which they live. Education affords the tools and the insights to gain from life and to give to it. Both processes are required for the enhancement of man and for the survival of society.

THE EDUCATION OF PARENTS—AN INFLUENTIAL FACTOR

The definite impact of the education of parents upon their offspring has been documented by the Texas Cooperative Youth Study. Young persons from families where mothers and fathers have enjoyed added years in school have revealed, in general, their superior qualifications for effective relationships and sharing in culture. Their responses to measures of personal and family competence furnished the evidence.

The particular courses of study pursued by parents of these Texas youth are not known. Approximate years in school for them were reported by their sons and daughters. Errors of a year or so may have crept into these data. Young persons might tend to overestimate school attendance by their parents because of its link to social status.

The case for the educated parent here presented is not the case for one or another specific type of education. What courses of study would best prepare for parenthood have not been determined. The

[1] Gordon W. Allport, "The Psychology of Participation," *Personality and Social Encounter,* chapter 12, pp. 181–198.

focus is upon the differential responses of youth from homes of various levels of educational attainment.

The Education of Fathers

Membership in sociocultural groups in this nation is largely determined by the educational level of the fathers, closely followed by the school achievement of mothers. Occupational status is correlated with education. In fact, these two determinants are interwoven to the point where education of fathers would suffice for status identification, at least when dealing with general trends.

Problem areas in certain segments of the population are intertwined with minimal schooling and submarginal access to the varied traits of the culture. Employment in substandard occupations, both in income and consistency of jobs, goes with elementary education or less. Demands for unskilled labor are decreasing rapidly, and drastic curtailment is expected by 1970.

The educationally and occupationally deprived are slowly decreasing in number, but among them are still to be found the majority of school dropouts. The highest rates of delinquency and truancy come from such families. Family disorganization as displayed by divorce, desertion, and separation is prevalent among this submarginal group. The accumulation of deprivation which arises from insufficient income and inadequate schooling is reflected in personal insecurity and family stress as reported by high school youth.

Strikingly illustrative of this point was a fact sheet released in September, 1960, by the Texas Social Welfare Association pertaining to Aid to Dependent Children. At that time, 68,869 children from 19,135 families were receiving aid from the state. Heads of households of 10 per cent of these families showed no formal education. The remaining 90 per cent had not attended school beyond junior high. By far the majority had no skills which were marketable in either city or country. White families numbered 60 per cent of the group; 40 per cent were nonwhite. These persons were described as the most severely disadvantaged group in the state's population. Major problems for children and youth accrue from inferior education and low earnings.

Youth in the Texas study verified these conclusions. The level of fathers' education usually proved to be a good measure of socioeconomic status and of accessibility and availability of cultural resources.

Significant trends across three levels of fathers' education were obtained from most of the scale scores on attitudes, concerns, and problems of youth in several factorial designs. A consistent decrease in negative social attitudes in most of the scales reflecting both personal-social problems and family conflict occurred as the education of fathers moved from elementary school to some college training. Differences between youngsters from families of different educational levels can be generalized regardless of community size, sex, number of brothers and sisters, or grade levels. The more years in school fathers had completed, the less indication of sociocultural problems and tensions among their children.

The Education of Both Parents

The educational level of mothers and fathers was combined in an analysis of variance, together with the sex of respondents, in order to determine where differences were discernible in impact of the educational attainments of mothers and fathers upon their teen-age sons and daughters. A refined sample was drawn consisting of youth from intact white families. No relatives or unrelated roomers were living in the homes. In addition to sex of respondent, five levels of education were distinguished for both mothers and fathers: grades 0–8; grades 9–11; completion of high school; some college; and two or more years of college. By examining the three independent variables in all possible combinations, a total of fifty cells was obtained for the factorial design. Replications of the basic design yielded a total of 650 cases.

Parallel findings as related to the education of both fathers and mothers were revealed in relation to several attitudes scales, to measures of family conflict, and to concepts of youth in relation to their own adequacy. The influence of fathers' education on their sons and daughters has been noted in several previous analyses. As the educational level of both parents increased, so was the Orientation to Society of their children more positive. So also did their Criticism of Education decrease. Attitudes toward Authoritarian Discipline for children were modified toward more democratic relationships among youth of better-educated parents. Family Tensions and Problems were reported less often by boys and girls from parents with more years of formal schooling. Resentment concerning family life style was modified. In addition, young persons with the more highly educated fathers and mothers felt more secure in social relationships. Under these same circumstances, they also indicated fewer financial problems.

Middle- and upper-class status can be equated with high school graduation or even higher educational attainment. If this criterion for these status positions can be accepted, then the Texas Cooperative Youth Study indicates quite clearly that middle- and upper-class youngsters do not suffer from being reared under the demands of such parents or the value system of middle- and upper-class culture, as some appear to assume. While some academicians and some nonacademicians have speculated that the pressures upon such youngsters may carry real hazards for their social-emotional development, youth in this study indicate that generally speaking, middle-class parents are not only desirable but also helpful. Their positive assistance is evidenced in youth acceptance of the attitude-value complex predominantly held in the nation. Moreover, the sons and daughters of such parents presented fewer problems and concerns as they grew toward adulthood.

Those who have tended to doubt the child rearing practices on these socioeconomic levels, and also those who have found the middle-class "design for living" acceptable and desirable will both find these data of importance. Again, and perhaps even more imperative, these findings lend credence to the real possibility of ameliorating both the cultural and economic disabilities of the 11 million children whose parents are the functionally illiterate, by holding them *in* school *through* high school.[2]

The Education of Mothers

When the education of mothers of high school youth was examined separately, several interactions with the sex of their children were significant. As the years of schooling of mothers increased, as already noted, the attitudes of their youngsters toward the world and toward people improved. This was true for both boys and girls. However, as previously reported, girls were appreciably more optimistic in their Orientation to Society than boys. In one instance, and why would be hard to discover, girls whose mothers were college women but had had less than two years of college were the most satisfied of all with the future of society and with their relationships with people in general.

---

[2] Michael Harrington, *The Other America,* p. 187.

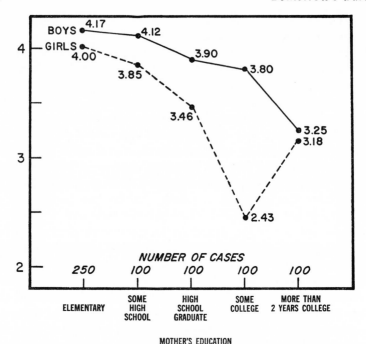

FIGURE 88
Relation of Orientation to Society to Sex and Mother's Education

The downward trend in distrust of fellowmen and of the future for boys was significant in that it proved to be a variation on some other scores measuring family conflict and personal competence.

Sex differences, in fact, were relatively unimportant in measures of family conflict and personal competence when mothers had attended elementary school, junior high, or high school. Marked discrepancies became evident, however, when mothers had attended college but had remained for less than two years. Sons of these women were more aware of Family Problems and Tensions. They judged themselves as less adequate, both personally and socially. They sensed more difficulties in Personal Adjustment. Resentment of the way of life at home was equalled only by boys whose mothers had not finished high school. In passing, they felt they encountered greater financial difficulties as well.

Explanation of the origin of the concerns of high school boys whose mothers had been to college but had not remained for two years more

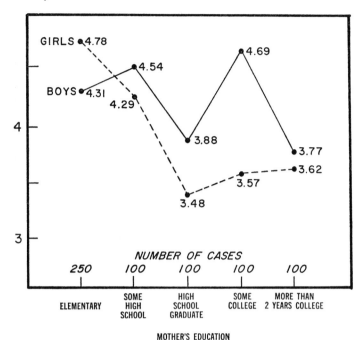

FIGURE 89

Relation of Resentment of Family Life Style to Sex and Mother's Education

is not easy. Perhaps some speculation will be acceptable. Women on this educational level may be moving up the social ladder with their husbands, or they may be desirous of a transition from one social status group to another. Consequently these women are probably not at ease either in their present status or about the position they hope to attain. Numbers of them may have married men with more education than they. As they attempted to measure up to what they conceived as the requirements of their husbands, their own stresses were apparently intensified. Inadequacy, which they felt, could have been transmitted to their teen-age sons. Perhaps, in addition, they placed too great an emphasis upon achievement at school and in peer groups for their boys. Moreover, one could guess that these women would tend to over-emphasize "things" in their homes, housekeeping details, and niceties in behavior which would be difficult for teen-age boys to accept or appreciate. On the other hand, perhaps some displayed relative in-

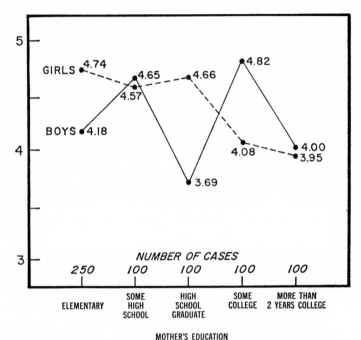

FIGURE 90
Relation of Personal Adjustment to Sex and Mother's Education

ability to operate their homes with ease and efficiency. This would be in direct contrast with their ambitions, and to this, their sons might react negatively.

Whatever the true explanation, Resentment of Family Life Style was greatest for high school boys whose mothers had attended college but not as much as two years. The only exception was girls whose mothers had had only elementary education. Women, it should be remarked, may marry social position. Men are usually forced to earn socioeconomic success. Youth study evidence indicates that these mothers did exert greater pressure upon their sons than upon their daughters.

Adolescent boys are often at variance with society in definition of acceptable behavior. Rebellious acts are not uncommon at any socioeconomic level. Flaunting of adult mores is sometimes accepted by middle-class mothers with tacit approval as a part of transition rites to adult manhood, as Talcott Parsons indicated in a previously quoted article. Often such behavior is abetted, though not openly or even consciously, by women who see their sons' actions as expressions of growing masculinity. Ambivalence on the part of mothers for achievement by their sons and for their participation in the adolescent moratorium, at one and the same time, could not help but create confusion and insecurity. In addition, emphasis upon school accomplishment and social success by ambitious mothers may be unremitting. Their sons may despair of pleasing. From the responses of these young males, feelings of inadequacy and of lack of personal adjustment were coupled with recognition of greater stress in family relations.

High school boys reared by mothers who had two or more years of higher education seemed to live in a more relaxed atmosphere as did those who were sons of women who completed high school but went no further.

Tensions are not all bad. Healthy anxiety of a mild degree is an essential part of motivation for self-development. These are accepted facts in mental health. Perhaps mothers who have completed two years or more of college or who have settled down with some sense of security through having completed high school have come upon the proper balance between stress for motivation and support for self-confidence. Less secure and less well-informed mothers, either because they tried to get a college education but dropped out after barely beginning or because of insufficient schooling for their current social roles, may lack the capacity to provide resources for frustration tolerance, which is an important facet of maturity. "Divine discontent," which in essence is ambition, is different from tension for which there appears no release. At any rate, boys with mothers who completed high school or had more than two years of college were aware of fewer problems and less tension, and described themselves as feeling more adequate both personally and socially.

High school girls exhibited somewhat different patterns of response than boys. Greater stress was encountered on nearly all fronts by girls when their mothers had only elementary schooling. Family Problems and Tensions were more acute. Girls were more keenly aware of their own personal limitations. They recognized their inability to function with ease in social situations. They were beset with problems of Personal Adjustment as noticeable as those encountered by boys whose mothers had gone to college less than two years. Their financial problems were strikingly evident. Resentment of home living was

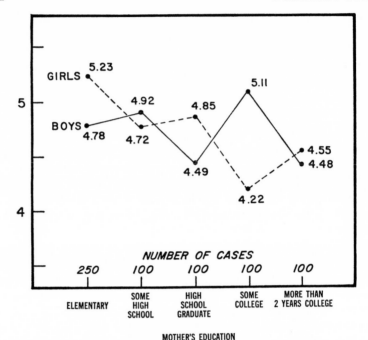

Relation of Family Tension to Sex and Mother's Education

high. Fewest pressures upon girls were apparent among those whose mothers had finished some college but not two years or more. This finding is diametrically opposite to that obtained for male youth.

Young girls, whose mothers had gone only to elementary school, have already surpassed them in education as indicated by their presence in high school classes. Many of their problems may have had their origin in that they were already better informed than their own parents. Many of them would be aware of differences in the way of life of their families and those for youth from other types of homes. Aspirations and goals for themselves had probably already outstripped any opportunity for easy realization.

Release from deprivation in family life for many of these girls rests upon the possibility of marriage with men on another subcultural level. To attract such men, these young women may strive to achieve behavior they imagine is prevalent in middle-class groups. Their definitions of "lady" may become more rigid and conventional than for those who belong to the middle classes. When these girls, or their families, cannot measure up to what they wish to attain, their sense of self and social adequacy may be materially threatened.

Girls exhibited a steady decline in family stress and in self doubt as the education of their mothers increased through college. No significant variations in this trend were observed except in Family Problems and Tensions and in feelings of self adequacy. Mothers who had had less than two years of college produced daughters who were least troubled by family pressures and feelings of inadequacy. When mothers had completed two or more years of college, their daughters indicated slightly more discomfort with their families and somewhat less self-confidence. Their mothers apparently made demands upon their daughters which were not always easy for the youngsters to achieve or to accept.

Girls mature more rapidly than do boys, both physically and socially. Their relationships with their mothers are more intimate. In middle-income families, they are expected to be attractive, well groomed, and to "behave like ladies." Aggressive behavior is not expected or tolerated as it is sometimes from their brothers. They probably incorporate the aspirations of their mothers into their own lives with relative ease. They usually receive more attention, get more praise, and encounter less blame than their brothers. However, it is worthy of note that best-educated mothers had sons and daughters who were quite comparable in their reporting of minimal family problems and tensions.

PARENTS AND THEIR OCCUPATIONS

Occupations and their relationship to cultural adequacy offer another interesting evidence of the tangential nature of employment and education. A nine-point scale of occupational levels for fathers was collapsed into seven categories:

(a) Unskilled workers
(b) Semi-skilled manual workers
(c) Skilled manual workers
(d) Farm owners and managers
(e) White collar workers
(f) Small businessmen
(g) Professional and large businessmen

Work status for mothers was encompassed in two categories: home-makers and employment outside the home. Consideration of all possible combinations of sex, mothers' work status, and fathers' occupation yielded twenty-eight cells in the basic factorial design. A refined sample consisting of intact white families, with no roomers or relatives living in the home, was used. Fourteen replications of the basic design yielded a total of 420 students.

TABLE 44: *Mean Scores for Father's Occupation and Five Significant Scales*

Father's Occupation	Orienta-tion to Society	Criticism of Education	Resentment of Family Life Style	Social Inade-quacy	Financial Problems
Unskilled Worker	4.40	4.82	4.77	5.27	4.90
Semi-skilled Manual Worker	4.10	5.13	4.55	5.70	4.95
Skilled Manual Worker	3.37	4.63	4.03	4.92	4.97
Farm Owner and Manager..	3.75	5.23	4.43	5.05	4.83
White Collar Worker	3.75	4.72	3.87	4.70	4.68
Small Businessman	3.50	4.73	3.53	5.00	4.38
Professional and Large Businessman	2.97	4.10	3.43	4.60	4.27

The educational level of fathers increased with their occupational status. Types of employment proved to be of considerable significance with respect to the responses of youth on several scale scores. Children of unskilled workers, rural or urban, were much more negatively oriented to society than young persons from other occupational groups. A consistent advance toward a more positive outlook on life was apparent as fathers moved up the scale toward professional and management positions. Similar results were obtained for Resentment of Family Life Style, Social Inadequacy, and Financial Troubles. This is telling evidence of easier access to and availability of cultural assets to middle- and upper-income families.

Youth from families with fathers who were farm owners or managers were the most severely critical of education. Least negativistic about school were young persons whose fathers were engaged in the professions or large business enterprises.

More important for consideration were rural youth from the lowest economic and educational levels, farm laborers and tenants. They were less critical of school and teachers than children of the owners or managers for whom their fathers worked. Perhaps they recognized education as their only opportunity for escape from the fates of their fathers. Young people whose fathers were farm laborers and tenants evidently understood the limitations of their parents' socioeconomic position. Accumulation of capital by laborers or tenants to become farm owners is recognized as of the past. Cost of farm land and equipment makes this transition prohibitive. Improved living conditions through more adequate income may be appraised as the only way out of stark poverty. Education becomes desirable to these deprived youth, though it may be little understood for its value by their parents.

Why youth from families of farm owners and managers were most critical of school is a bit difficult to discern. Agriculture production does not hold the status nor command the income it once did. However, perhaps the owners or managers of land still feel that they "have it made." Because their children are economic assets such parents seldom encourage school attendance after the sixteenth year when compulsory attendance ends. Resistance to education by these youth may reflect a culture lag in their fathers. These men may sincerely believe, even in this era of technological advance, that an agrarian way of life is feasible even when it is built on minimal education and family labor. While these fathers may not overtly discourage their children about school, they probably do not offer much encouragement either.

Another line of speculation may be worth pursuing briefly. The higher scores on Criticism of Education by young persons from families of farm owners and managers may arise from their discontent with the kind of curriculum available to them in their high schools. Perhaps they feel that it is not functional for their lives. For many it may not be, in truth, if it is geared to college preparatory work. Be these comments as they may, the contrast between youth in the upper and lower strata of farm economy is of interest.

Positive attitudes toward education were encountered among youth whose fathers were skilled or white-collar workers, and operators of small businesses. Sons and daughters of urban unskilled laborers were more resistant to school, but not to the same degree as children of farm owners. The importance of education to the great middle class, lower and upper, is evidenced in the responses of high school youth, even as it is in parent-teacher organizations.

Social Inadequacy was most apparent among youngsters from unskilled-worker families both in the country and in town. These youngsters also expressed the greatest resentment over their ways of life at home. They were in high school, it should be remembered, while their parents probably never completed elementary grades. They had learned of better ways of living. They had glimpsed a more rewarding way of life. No wonder they were aware of their own Social Inadequacies and of the insufficiences of their own homes.

Working Mothers and Their Children

Whether mothers were full-time homemakers or were employed outside the home made no significant difference in the attitudes of their sons and daughters. High school students whose mothers were working for pay were no more nor less optimistic about society and people than those whose mothers were at home. They were no different in their conceptions of proper discipline for children. Attitudes toward school and their academic competence appeared to be approximately the same. Neither Family Problems nor Family Tensions were more acute among them.

Youth from homes of working mothers were aware of no more problems of Personal Adjustment nor did they feel any less adequate in social situations than children of women whose major concern was homemaking. No variations were exhibited by peer-group behavior in either isolation from their peers or pressures for conformity. Their Resentment of Dependency was not implicated with the working status of their mothers. Employment of mothers, rather than being a major defect in modern family life, appeared not to be a determining factor in the over-all effectiveness of their teen-age children.

Exceptions to this generalization should be noted on three measurements employed in the youth study, all involving higher order interactions of mother's occupation and other background variables. Because of its relative insignificance, only slight mention should be made of the minimal difference in recognized financial problems. Boys, whose mothers were employed for wages, admitted slightly less concern over money than did those whose mothers were housewives. No difference between girls was discovered.

Responses to the scale indicating feelings of Self Inadequacy were very much alike for youth whose mothers were employees or homemakers. However, some minor interaction was discovered between these groups when occupation of fathers was taken into consideration.

Youth who expressed feelings of greater self inadequacy among those whose mothers were employed were from families where the

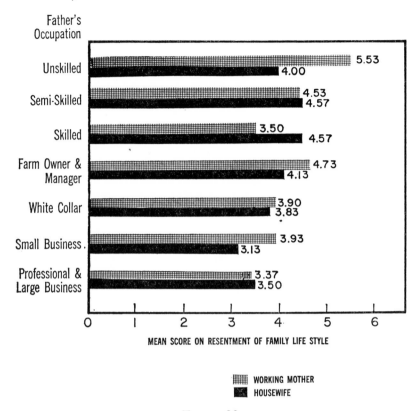

Father's
Occupation

MEAN SCORE ON RESENTMENT OF FAMILY LIFE STYLE

WORKING MOTHER
HOUSEWIFE

FIGURE 92
Relation of Resentment of Family Life Style to Mother's Work Status and
Father's Occupation

fathers were unskilled, semi-skilled, or white-collar workers. Women,
whose husbands were working on such jobs, were probably employed
on like levels of skill. Limited education and occupational competency
more than likely placed these parents in the lower income brackets
for services rendered. Earnings from both parents may be necessary
to hold the family at even a subsistence level of living. Many jobs
classified as white-collar come under the category of minimal in demand for education and in pay. Feelings of personal inadequacy
among youth from such families could not be attributed alone to the
employment of their mothers. A combination of causes including in-

ferior cultural advantages and educational and economic capacities of both fathers and mothers must be taken into account.

Young persons from homes where their mothers were full-time homemakers displayed more Self Inadequacy if their fathers were skilled manual laborers. These young persons lived in families with incomes often equivalent to or above some white-collar, small business, and even professional persons. However, their patterns of behavior and their value structures are distinct from these other groups.[3] Awareness of these differences may account for less confidence in self.

Resentment of Family Life Style displayed variations with fathers' occupations between youngsters whose mothers were employed and those with homemaker mothers. Students whose fathers were farm laborers, unskilled workers, or farm owners or managers displayed more critical attitudes if their mothers were employed. Rural home life, when mothers held jobs, evidently left something to be desired.

Youth from homes where mothers did not earn an income were most critical of their home life if their fathers were in the skilled-labor category. These youngsters in high school possibly had developed ambitions which would eventually move them out of the socioeconomic class of their parents. Their mothers' services at home evidently could not compensate for the discontent engendered by their ambitions. Their parents probably even encouraged them in their aspirations.

Least critical of family living were students whose mothers remained at home and whose fathers were in small business. Women in these homes have evidently accepted homemaking as a professional career. From this, they gain their basic satisfaction. They apparently transmitted contentment to their families as well. In passing, it is worthy of note that among these women are found large numbers who combine professionalized homemaking with the stimulation of volunteer services. This is likewise true of numerous women whose husbands are professionals or business executives.

A final striking finding demands report. Youngsters, whose mothers were employed and whose status level was indicated by the professional or managerial roles of their fathers, expressed least concern

[3] Lee Rainwater, Richard P. Coleman, and Gerald Handel, *Workingman's Wife*. And Patricia Cayo Sexton, "Speaking for the Working-Class Wife," *Harper's Magazine*, CCXXV (October, 1962), 129–133.

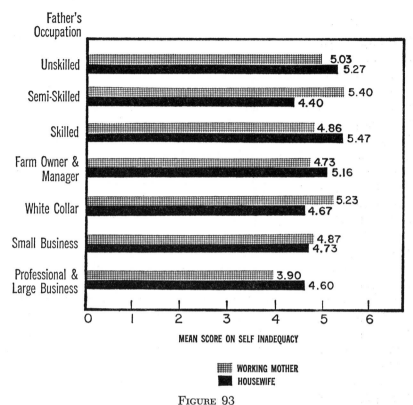

Father's
Occupation

FIGURE 93
Relation of Self Inadequacy to Mother's Work Status and Father's Occupation

over their personal adequacy. Among youth with working mothers they were also the least resentful of family life style. Apparently they were more adequate and self-assured than youth from the same socioeconomic group whose mothers were full-time homemakers.[4]

[4] The meaning of mothers' occupational status from a statistical point of view may need some interpretation. Whether or not mothers work outside their homes has little relationship with the main socioeconomic variables: from the factor analysis summarized in Table A-4 in Appendix A it is apparent that mothers tended to be housewives if they had large families. They tended to be employed outside their homes if families were smaller. Whether or not mother worked outside the home and the total number living in the home were both defining variables for Factor V.

Family Income and Youth Contributors

Earnings by youth for contribution to family income should be included in any discussion of cultural adequacy of families. When young persons attending high school worked to help support the family, family size and socioeconomic status were correlated. Financial participation was also correlated with lower occupational and educational levels of parents. These youngsters were likewise from larger families. Large families of the undereducated and untrained require all available earners to maintain a subsistence living.

Working and going to high school were significantly related to negative attitudes toward society. Feelings of Social and Self Inadequacy were greater among employed youth still in school. Awareness of Social Isolation was apparent. The contention is made that work for pay helps build character. When teen-agers must earn to contribute to family support, it also is apt to produce personal and social problems. Early dropout from school may well be predicted for many of these young persons.

Employment, itself, is obviously not the important criterion for youth adequacy. Necessity for financial assistance by youth in school indicates family deprivation and poverty. It implies minimum conditions within the home to assure adequate background for accomplishment of the developmental tasks which are a part of growth toward adult maturity. Exceptions can be found to this generalization, but problems of youth more often than not have their origin in family limitations. Correction and mediation of difficulties and tensions among these youth no doubt lie in modification and improvement of the family matrix in its community setting rather than in therapy for individuals.[5] Improvement in the ability of family members to participate in culture and better access to cultural experiences and opportunities would seem to offer major promise.

"Elbow Room" and Family Adequacy

"Elbow room" is the ratio of the number of rooms in the house to the number of persons living in the home. This ratio is still another

[5] Richard A. Cloward and Lloyd E. Ohlin, *Delinquency and Opportunity*. From a different point of view, this same problem has been attacked by James B. Conant, *Slums and Suburbs*.

symbol of conditional participation in culture. The small house with numerous occupants usually indicates deprivation. Crowded homes are associated with limited education and occupations low in remuneration. Luxury of space, or adequacy of room, goes with better education and higher income. When socioeconomic level of the family was held constant, the number of persons in families appeared to be unrelated to the number of rooms in the home. Other than at the upper levels, families tended to live in what they could afford rather than in what family size required.

A refined sample consisting of intact white families with no relatives or roomers in the home served as the source from which the analysis of "elbow room" was made. Included in the factorial design were three independent variables: sex, "elbow room," and fathers' education. For purposes of analysis as an independent variable, "elbow room," the index of living space per family member, was divided into seven levels expressed in stanine scores: 1 + 2; 3, 4, 5, 6, 7, and 8 + 9. The higher the score, the greater the amount of "elbow room." Fathers' education was broken into five groups: grades 0–4; grades 5–8; grades 9–11; grade 12, and college education. All possible combinations of these three variables resulted in a sixty-cell factorial design. A total of 560 cases was drawn from the refined sample for the analysis.

Youth who were least hopeful about the future and were distrustful of their fellowmen came from homes where the ratio of space per person was least. That Family Tension was highest among this same group was not unexpected. That resentment over the way of living was also maximum was predictable. Large families cooped up in houses which afforded minimal "elbow room" for family members could scarcely be expected to avoid disorganized housekeeping and interpersonal conflict. That young persons from such homes also experienced more financial problems could almost be left unsaid.

More space for each person coupled with more years in formal education for fathers, produced the greatest satisfaction with family life among high school youth. However, "elbow room" alone was not enough to produce these desirable results. Boys and girls whose fathers attended four grades of elementary school or less and lived in spacious quarters were approximately as critical of their homes as were those who resided under circumstances of minimal adequacy. More "elbow room" per person does not always afford better living arrangements for the family. Many spacious houses in rural communities and in inter-stitial areas in cities are in sad states of deterioration. Living in them may be as near mere existence as living with real poverty in space.

Poverty in space pushed to its maximum the tension level within families. Youngsters from homes where "elbow room" was least, were distressingly aware of family conflict. Even a minimum improvement in space per person brought significant modification of stress.

Higher status and adequacy in life space at home are synonymous. Perhaps youngsters who lived in homes affording a middle range of "elbow room" wanted and needed more personal living space than they could have. In any event, Family Tension was minimal among youth whose homes afforded the greater ratio of space per family member. Another observation may be in order. Families who live in largest houses and have more adequate incomes may sometimes suffer from social rather than physical distance. Family Tension and social distance are probably correlates, no matter what the living space for each person. What may be indicated is that there is, in fact, an optimum in "social elbow room"—neither too small in space nor too large in social distance.

One single highly significant interaction between sex of the respond-ents and "elbow room" was revealed. Social Inadequacy was reported as significantly higher for girls than for boys, except under one or two special circumstances. Social adjustment for girls was much more difficult than for boys when "elbow room" was at a premium. Not until stanine scores reached five or above was there noticeable improvement in their feelings of social adequacy.[6]

Boys, by contrast, found more severe problems in social relationships when they came from houses of mid-range in the ratio of rooms per persons living in them. Boys tended to react more acutely to the way of life in the home. Their greater Resentment of Family Life Style indicated this. Girls were more influenced by the amount of space available to them as reflected in their relationships with others. Privacy and aloneness would appear to be more important to girls. Orderliness in the home and behavior of family members with one another seemed to hold greater meaning for boys.

---

[6] A stanine score of 5 or above is equivalent to an "elbow room" index of 1.285 or greater. The number 1.285 is the index obtained when a family of seven lives in a nine-room house.

AN EDITORIAL COMMENT

Education of parents has emerged from data presented in numerous analyses from the Texas Cooperative Youth Study as a major conditioning factor in making available to youth resources and opportunities for adequate participation in culture. Education of mothers and fathers is the source of and the reason for the development of youth toward maximum competence in school, in interpersonal relations within the family, in the conceptions of their own personal adequacy.[7] The level of cultural participation of parents is, from this evidence, an imperative determinant in what children will gain from and eventually give to society.

Education in today's schools has among its major responsibilities the promotion of quality of parenthood to assure the quality of persons in this nation. No other aims for education can be attained without sound personalities through which to proceed toward other goals and ideals. No fact has become more obvious from this research than that young persons must remain in school and become well educated in order to perform the paramount obligations of their adult lives—the rearing of children in competent families residing in adequate homes.

Totalitarian countries may wish to explore institutional rearing of children. Democratic society, if the Texas study is reliable, can afford nothing less for the survival of its way of life than well-educated parents, establishing and maintaining satisfying family living at home and for their children.

[7] The research of Fred Stroedbeck and his associates at the University of Chicago with culturally deprived nursery-age children is of major relevance to this statement. Also see Edward J. Ryan, "Personal Identity in an Urban Slum," in *The Urban Condition*, edited by Leonard J. Duhl, pp. 135–150. Most important also is a second essay in this same volume: Thomas Gladwin, "Strategies in Delinquency Prevention," especially pp. 269–274. For a dramatic statement of the devastating impact of poverty, both economic and cultural, see Harrington, *The Other America*.

APPENDIXES

APPENDIX A: METHODS OF ANALYSIS

Several methods of analysis were employed in the Texas Cooperative Youth Study. Because of the extensive nature of the data, the analytical methods are primarily statistical in nature. In the sample of nearly 13,000 cases which were scored, coded, and punched on IBM cards for analysis, several minor biases were present in spite of the precautions taken in defining the population and setting up strata throughout the state of Texas for sampling from high schools. The biases resulted because of too many cases in some strata and not quite enough in others. While such biases as were found are insignificant for many types of analyses, it is important to correct for them if one is interested in saying something specific about the general high school population in Texas.

A sample of one thousand cases was carefully selected from the total 1956 sample in such a manner that each of the five geographic regions, four community types and two racial groups contributed students in exact proportion to population figures obtained from the 1950 census. This sample of one thousand cases can be considered truly representative of high school youth in the grades nine through twelve throughout the state of Texas during the spring of 1956.

The statistical analyses undertaken can be divided into two general types. The first was descriptive statistics such as means, standard deviations, frequency distributions, and intercorrelations where pertinent for variables obtained on both the face sheet and the questionnaire scales.[1] The second was rigorously controlled analyses of variance in order to test hypotheses about the relationships between personal-background characteristics of the youth and his attitudes and personality characteristics as measured by the

[1] For some of the variables having skewed distributions, both means and medians have been computed. In some cases a variable is so sharply skewed that only the median represents an appropriate measure of central tendency. Computation of standard deviations as measures of the degree of variability has been limited to variables that are not badly skewed, with the exception of Items 168 and 192 from Form II.

scales in Forms I and II. For the first type of analysis, the sample of one thousand cases provides an excellent, stable set of data from which one can generalize about the characteristics of youth in general in Texas high schools. For the second type of statistical analysis, special samples were drawn carefully from the entire pool of data in such a way that certain major variables were held constant or systematically varied as independent variables in the design. In each case the dependent variables[2] or scores used in these analyses consisted of all fourteen scaled scores plus occasional selected items that had been stored on the master IBM card (Card A).

CHARACTERISTICS OF TEXAS YOUTH: A DESCRIPTIVE ANALYSIS OF ONE THOUSAND CASES

Qualitative Variables

The variables for analysis can be classed into four different types according to the nature of the variable. A considerable amount of the data, especially student characteristics coded from the information sheet, are qualitative in nature. Variables such as geographic area, community and school type, sex, race, marital status, and religious preference represent qualitative characteristics of the population as contrasted to quantitative traits such as age or score on the Family Tension scale.[3] The most meaningful type of analysis for many such variables, descriptively speaking, is merely to present the frequency distributions of the different categories within the variables. Frequency distributions can be easily converted into percentages or proportions by proper placement of the decimal point since there are one thousand cases in the sample. For example, a frequency count of the variable *sex* reveals that there are 481 boys and 519 girls in the corrected sample of one thousand cases. These figures can be easily translated into proportions of .481 and .519 or into percentages of 48.1% and 51.9%. Similar frequency distributions are given for a number of such qualitative variables in Table A-1.

[2] Such variables are often referred to as *dependent* variables as contrasted to the factual characteristics such as age and sex which are referred to as *independent* variables. This custom arises from frequent practice of stating that response variables *depend upon* both the situational or stimulus variables and the organismic or personal variables. Since the situational variables have been held reasonably constant throughout this study by standardized directions and instructions for filling out the inventory materials, most of the variation in response from one student to the next can be attributed to personality differences and person-oriented background variables such as sex, family structure, and ethnic group.

[3] Some variables that are essentially qualitative in nature can be roughly scaled so that quantitative analysis can be carried out. Occupational level is one such variable.

TABLE A-1: *Distributions of Variables Not Included in Correlation Matrix*

IBM Col.	Variable	Coded Frequency Distribution * (N = 1,000)											
		R	X	0	1	2	3	4	5	6	7	8	9
1	Geographic Area				132	240	41	418	169				
2	Community Type			345	141	149	157	55	25	12	14	102	
5	School Type			707	124	169							
6	School Size			24	152	160	122	59	27	52	129	120	155
10	School Grade			276	242	246	236						
11	Sex			481	519								
12	Race			876	124								
14	Guessed Height	32	26	4	4	12	64	160	186	175	141	105	91
15	Guessed Weight	12	27		8	38	194	242	193	162	79	34	11
16	Community Size			152	125	142	109	82	11	120	259		
17	Residence		19	270	711								
18	Birthplace	3	28	513	83	44	19	143	61	44	14	52	16
19	Marital Status		23	966	11								
20	Homemaking												
	Males		144	303	7	9	2	2		14			
	Females		22	45	51	159	119	63	12	48			

* Consult Coding Key in Appendix E to interpret coded data in terms of original values.

TABLE A-1: *Distributions of Variables Not Included in Correlation Matrix—Continued*

IBM Col.	Variable	R	X	Coded Frequency Distribution (N = 1,000)									
				0	1	2	3	4	5	6	7	8	9
21	Parents' Marital Status	:	21	774	19	108	28	49	1	:	:	:	:
22	Older Brothers	:	52	593	177	99	45	24	8	:	1	:	1
23	Older Sisters	:	49	582	221	74	47	18	8	1	:	:	1
24	Younger Brothers	:	49	517	261	111	42	15	5	:	:	:	:
25	Younger Sisters	:	48	550	245	105	34	13	3	:	:	1	1
27	Parents	:	16	768	78	12	1	1	2	59	22	35	6
28	Grandparents	:	11	16	59	20	1	1	4	:	2	886	:
29	Family Structure	:	8	899	11	42	5	35	:	:	:	:	:
30	Household Membership	:	10	917	55	15	3	:	:	:	:	:	:
36	Work at Home	:	40	263	329	178	103	43	23	15	2	2	2
37	Work on Job	:	66	537	134	96	37	43	29	19	10	11	18
40	Sleeping Quarters	:	8	575	293	83	26	10	1	3	:	:	1
41	Family Car	:	6	719	178	33	11	:	:	4	49	:	:
42	Religion	91	73	18	413	166	29	115	10	1	56	28	:
43	School Bus	331	75	309	295	109	109	46	5	43	3	3	3

Quantitative Variables

A second kind of variable differs from the first only in its possession of quantitative properties rather than qualitative ones. For such characteristics as age, number of members in the family, or father's education, the difference from one category to the next is one of degree rather than of kind. For such variables it is possible to compute statistics that summarize conveniently the frequency distributions. Of course one can also examine the frequency distributions themselves in the same manner as for the qualitative variables. For many such quantitative variables, means, standard deviations and intercorrelations can be computed and such computations provide powerful tools for summarizing descriptively the characteristics of Texas youth in general. The means and standard deviations, as well as frequency distributions, are summarized in Table A-2 for quantitative variables derived from the personal-background information obtained from the face sheet.

Dependent Variables

The third class of variables consists of the fourteen scaled scores obtained from Forms I and II, the attitude and problem inventories. Since these scaled scores had been standardized in the pilot study, their distributions tend to be normal in shape with the exception of the four short scales at the end of Form II. Unlike the quantitative variables derived from the factual information about each student, these scores reflect the attitudes of the respondent about himself, his family, his friends, and the world around him.

Means, standard deviations, and intercorrelations can be computed for these scaled scores in the same manner as for the quantitative background variables with which they may be related. Means, standard deviations, and frequency distributions for these scaled scores are presented in Table A-2.

TABLE A-2: *Means and Standard Deviations of Thirty-Eight Selected Variables*

IBM Col.	Variable	Mean	Standard Deviation	Coded Frequency Distribution (N = 1,000)											
				R	X	0	1	2	3	4	5	6	7	8	9
13	Age	3.16*	1.36	..	2	7	98	242	260	213	136	37	5	0	..
26	Total Siblings	2.74	2.28	..	52	121	219	208	115	87	66	50	38	17	27
31	Total in Home	4.86	1.77	..	37		1	25	188	276	211	98	56	42	66
32	Father's Education	3.15*	1.58	7	43	19	83	266	236	208	61	9	68		
33	Mother's Education	3.35*	1.46	15	38	22	35	206	273	280	58	13	60		
34	Father's Occupation	4.37*	2.08	10	139	37	78	8	134	220	112	109	102	46	5
35	Mother's Occupation ⎱ No Mean or S.D. obtained since			593	45	5	23	0	102	43	3	139	12	34	1
38	Help Support Family ⎰ these variables are dichotomized				62	120	818	..							
39	Rooms in House	6.48	1.54	..	15		2	2	15	71	178	247	216	125	129
44	Orientation to Society	4.09†	1.90		3		88	168	107	260	110	149	78	31	6
45	Authoritarian Discipline	5.09	1.90		2		19	77	81	215	256	119	89	94	48
46	Criticism of Education	5.01	2.01		1		22	98	126	172	180	173	100	72	56
47	Criticism of Youth	5.19	1.66				20	52	92	108	332	146	186	55	9
48	Family Problems	4.51	2.00		2		56	105	186	188	149	113	122	59	20
49	Self Inadequacy	5.05	1.75		1		15	56	149	112	314	117	158	54	24
50	Family Tensions	4.99	1.82		1		32	31	135	250	172	157	121	73	28
51	Personal Adjustment	4.55	1.91		1		54	105	146	169	238	126	84	56	21
52	Social Inadequacy	5.14	1.81		1			116	50	181	264	145	128	88	27
53	Resentment of Family Life Style	4.36	2.18				126	96	170	100	212	131	69	65	31
54	Social Conformity	4.85	1.68						312	151	220	111	123	68	15
55	Social Isolation	4.96	1.38		2					572	181	61	104	61	19
56	Financial Troubles	4.69	1.44						291	174	240	183	76	31	5
57	Resentment of Dependency	5.00	1.71		1				265	177	199	139	118	76	25

Sociological Variables (rows 13–39)

Problem and Attitude Scales (rows 44–57)

* Consult Coding Key in Appendix E to interpret the coded mean and S.D., e.g., the mean for Father's Education at 3.15 indicates the average educational level of the fathers is slightly above the tenth grade.

† All Scale Scores were converted into stanines on the basis of the 1955 pilot samples.

TABLE A-2: *Means and Standard Deviations of Thirty-Eight Selected Variables—Continued*

IBM Col.	Variable	Mean	Standard Deviation	Coded Frequency Distribution (N = 1,000)											
				R	X	0	1	2	3	4	5	6	7	8	9
58	Item 12	2.02	1.08	..	..	..	397	330	161	78	34	..	..	..	..
59	Item 16	3.45	1.13	..	1	..	73	118	279	346	183	..	..	..	..
60	Item 21	3.93	1.02	..	2	..	32	80	120	455	311	..	..	..	..
61	Item 29	3.07	1.10	..	1	..	105	186	320	311	77	..	..	..	..
62	Item 30	2.89	1.21	..	2	..	151	250	243	267	87	..	..	..	..
63	Item 33	3.73	1.22	..	1	..	74	108	145	355	317	..	..	..	..
64	Item 47	1.97	0.95	..	2	..	334	470	105	69	20	..	..	..	..
65	Item 53	4.23	1.07	..	2	..	38	57	84	281	538	..	..	..	..
66	Item 58	3.90	1.19	..	1	..	56	111	90	362	380	..	..	..	..
67	Item 62	4.09	1.09	..	1	..	44	66	95	347	447	..	..	..	..
68	Item 72	3.55	1.18	..	2	..	76	124	192	384	222	..	..	..	..
69	Item 85	2.60	1.26	..	1	..	236	302	159	233	69	..	..	..	..
70	Item 100	2.01	1.15	..	3	..	441	288	120	115	33	..	..	..	..
71	Item 168	1.71	1.33	..	6	..	740	41	69	51	93	..	..	..	..
72	Item 192	2.23	1.38	..	4	..	473	124	175	142	82	..	..	..	..

Problem and Attitude Items (items 12 through 192)

Item Variables

A fourth class of variables consists of the individual items within the two inventories, Form I and Form II. In Form I, thirteen items were singled out for special study and in Form II, two items—Items 168 and 192—were analyzed separately. Although it might have been desirable to include additional items beyond these fifteen, the analysis as planned was already very time consuming and expensive. Consequently, only the fifteen most interesting items were treated independently of the scaled scores. Most of these items were not represented in any of the scales and were of special importance in their own right. Since each item had a five-point response continuum with increasing weights ranging from 0 to 4 assigned to each category, means and standard deviations as well as product-moment correlation coefficients could be appropriately computed. The frequency distributions, means, and standard deviations for these fifteen items are presented in Table A-2.

CORRELATIONAL AND FACTOR ANALYSIS OF QUANTITATIVE VARIABLES

Correlations and Their Matrices

Correlations among all possible pairs of thirty-eight different variables were computed in order to determine the relationships both between the background and the response variables and within each set of measures. Product-moment correlation coefficients were computed for thirty-six of the variables because two variables were dichotomous in nature, mother's occupation and whether or not the student helped to support the family. A different kind of correlation coefficient was used whenever either of these two variables entered into the correlation matrix. Biserial correlation coefficients were employed when either of these variables was correlated with the other more continuous measures, and a tetrachoric correlation coefficient was computed to obtain the correlation between these two dichotomous variables. The complete intercorrelation matrix is presented in Table A-3.

TABLE A-3: *Correlation Matrix of Thirty-Eight Selected Variables from Student Information Sheet and Forms I and II* *
(Most r's are based on an N of 983; the lowest N for an r is 802.)

Variable	IBM Col.	13	26	31	32	33	34	35	38	39	44	45	46	47	48*	49	50	51	52	53	54	55	56	57	58	59	60	61	62	63	64	65	66	67	68	69	70	71
Age	13																																					
Total Siblings	26	06																																				
Total in Home	31	00	62																																			
Father's Education	32	-12	-29	-22																																		
Mother's Education	33	-13	-33	-24	61																																	
Father's Occupation	34	-04	-27	-19	48	39																																
Mother's Occupation	†35	04	18	25	-19	-20	07																															
Support Family	†38	10	32	28	-25	-23	-16	39																														
Rooms in House	39	-10	-15	-03	32	35	38	05	-21																													
Orientation	44	-02	20	16	-18	-20	-20	-04	-20	-19																												
Discipline	45	-05	22	17	-16	-17	-12	-03	26	-15	45																											
Criticism of Education	46	-05	12	09	-15	-15	-13	-07	23	-10	48	29																										
Criticism of Youth	47	-04	09	06	-10	-13	-09	00	08	-10	34	40	22																									
Family	48	-03	14	08	-13	-13	-09	-02	14	-10	26	22	04	09																								
Self	49	-02	16	06	-13	-17	-09	-03	13	-16	39	22	37	26	37																							
Tensions	50	-04	19	15	-15	-16	-11	-09	13	-14	25	15	20	19	46	34																						
Personal	51	-05	09	02	-08	-11	-01	-10	00	-09	22	09	20	24	19	25	41																					
Social	52	-06	11	08	-15	-17	-08	-07	06	-12	23	16	18	23	20	20	42	58																				
Life-Style	53	00	20	12	-18	-18	-14	-11	12	-18	27	11	18	16	23	42	20	72	65																			
Conformity	54	-03	15	05	-07	-11	-02	-06	17	-08	20	12	16	17	14	32	16	22	49	39																		
Isolation	55	-03	09	05	-06	-10	-07	-06	16	-13	21	06	13	13	19	22	17	11	54	44	45																	
Financial	56	03	16	07	-13	-18	-08	04	08	-10	15	12	20	15	28	29	13	06	44	50	34	35																
Dependency	57	-09	09	09	-15	-11	-09	-02	06	-07	24	12	20	15	41	28	15	20	42	56	37	42	41															
Item 12	58	00	-07	-04	11	09	09	00	-17	09	-20	-28	-09	-17	11	-07	01	-02	-07	00	-06	-06	00	-02														
Item 16	59	07	-06	-18	03	01	01	-01	-07	-02	-22	-27	-13	-13	-01	-14	03	03	-09	02	-04	-04	03	05	15													
Item 21	60	-04	-18	-14	15	16	16	-02	-33	16	-33	-24	-31	-14	-15	-13	-13	-15	-06	-12	-11	-11	-07	-09	14	15												
Item 29	61	-03	-14	-11	14	16	16	-03	-16	08	-24	-14	-19	-14	-18	-19	-14	-07	-14	-07	-11	-10	-15	-15	-04	08	10											
Item 30	62	07	-07	-04	-03	00	39	-12	-02	-01	-12	-07	-12	-08	-06	-05	-02	-02	-02	-04	-02	-04	07	-05	06	06	07	14										
Item 33	63	-03	-23	-15	18	18	18	01	-19	11	-27	-20	-22	-15	-06	-04	-11	-02	-08	-06	-08	-08	-03	-03	08	19	22	20	06									
Item 47	64	00	-06	00	08	01	01	03	-04	05	00	-09	08	-08	10	01	-03	-04	-10	-06	-09	-02	-05	-05	12	-03	02	-03	00	-02								
Item 53	65	00	-14	-09	07	11	11	10	-21	10	-24	-27	-16	-12	-04	-17	-04	-10	-09	-06	-08	-09	-02	-04	16	16	22	01	02	17	01							
Item 58	66	00	00	05	-02	05	01	05	-03	09	-14	02	-09	02	-17	-04	-04	02	-01	-02	-01	-17	-02	-17	-09	-07	03	-03	03	-02	-05	-03						
Item 62	67	-02	-10	-04	04	07	08	-02	-18	09	-26	-19	-26	-14	-14	-14	-08	-03	-08	-06	-07	-10	00	-09	11	07	16	05	06	17	-06	17	02					
Item 72	68	-10	-13	-12	09	04	04	-03	-14	-07	-05	-17	-02	-13	-10	-09	-08	-08	-08	-05	-07	-10	-06	-09	01	16	16	06	06	08	05	04	-06	02				
Item 85	69	01	-05	-05	-02	-03	00	00	-06	02	-16	-24	-02	-11	-11	-08	-02	-32	-08	-16	-11	-27	07	-04	08	08	09	01	-01	08	08	05	02	02	01			
Item 100	70	03	03	00	-16	-17	-12	13	-02	-12	09	-07	16	-03	16	14	07	02	02	10	00	02	07	09	03	10	-08	-09	-04	-11	04	-06	-13	-06	-04	-02		
Item 168	71	11	08	-02	-09	-12	-04	-04	00	07	05	03	00	00	00	07	00	22	11	24	15	14	18	19	18	-04	-04	-09	-09	-05	-08	-01	-05	-03	-05	-03	16	
Item 192	72	-03	01	-03	-11	-12	-12	-13	07	-10	10	12	08	09	09	24	07	35	18	26	16	16	20	21	-03	-03	-08	-08	-06	-03	-04	-01	-09	-03	-04	-01	06	19

* Decimal points are omitted.

† This is a dichotomized variable and all correlations with it are biserials; 35 versus 38 is a tetrachoric coefficient.

It is convenient to think of this large matrix in terms of smaller inter-correlation matrices such as the interrelationships among the nine background or sociological variables, intercorrelations among the fourteen problem and attitude scales, and intercorrelations among the fifteen individual items. These triangular matrices are represented along the diagonal section of the larger matrix. If one is interested in interrelationships between different sets of variables, the three rectangular matrices remaining in the off-diagonal sections of the larger matrix are convenient for this purpose.

Stability of Individual Correlations

Because of the large number of cases used to compute this intercorrelation matrix, the individual correlation coefficients are highly stable. Even a rather low and trivial relationship, such as a correlation of .09, is statistically significant from zero although of little interpretive significance. The amount of variation in one variable that can be accounted for by variation in another variable is given by the square of the correlation coefficient between the two measures. For example, the correlation between father's educational level and father's occupational level is .48. Squaring this number gives .23, or 23%, as the amount of variance common to both measures. Thus one can see that a correlation as low as .10 is really rather trivial in spite of statistically significant departure from zero. The square of .10 yields an estimate of common variance of only one per cent, leaving 99% of the variation in Y unexplained by its correlation with X.

Economy of Factor Analysis

While each of the many correlations in this matrix can be interpreted in its own right, the number of such correlations when treated singly is very large, 703 different correlation coefficients for a matrix of thirty-eight variables. A convenient and powerful method for analyzing such a correlation matrix is the method of factor analysis.[4] The purpose of such analysis is to determine a small number of factors which, when appropriately combined, will reproduce nearly all of the common variance represented by the inter-correlations among the original variables.

A Mathematical Description

Quite often it is possible to reduce a large correlation matrix to a much smaller factor matrix in which factor loadings for each of the original variables are given. Such factor loadings can be considered equivalent to correlation coefficients between the original variable and the hypothetical

---

[4] For a good discussion of factor analysis see B. Fruchter, *Introduction to Factor Analysis*. A more advanced discussion of many of the problems in factor analysis is given in L. L. Thurstone, *Multiple-Factor Analysis*.

factor. The sum of the squares of such factor loadings for a given variable is called the communality of the variable and represents that proportion of the total variance in the original measure which is common to the other variables in the correlation matrix. Just as for a single correlation coefficient where the square of the correlation represents the proportion of variance common to two variables, the communality of a variable represents the proportion of variance shared by the variable in question with all other variables in the matrix. By subtracting the communality from 1.00, one can obtain the proportion of variance in a variable which is unexplained by the interrelationships of that variable and all others in the correlation matrix. Part of this unexplained variance can be attributed to errors of measurement due to unreliability of the variable in question. Part of this unexplained variance also can be attributed to unique factors independent of the common factors shared with other variables in the correlation matrix.

Factor Analyses and the Youth Study

Several factor analyses were carried out on the intercorrelations among these thirty-eight variables. The first analysis employed Thurstone's centroid method of factoring, using the entire matrix of thirty-eight variables.[5] Seven factors were needed to explain 99 per cent of the estimated common variance among the thirty-eight variables. The centroid factor matrix was rotated graphically in an attempt to achieve simple structure.[6] The rotated factor loadings, together with the estimated communality for each of the variables, are presented in Table A-4. In examining these factor loadings it must be remembered that there are three classes of variables represented in the analysis—nine variables taken from information about the student and his background; fourteen variables that represent the fourteen scaled scores, six from Form I and eight from Form II; and fifteen variables that represent individual items from Forms I and II.

[5] Thurstone, *Op. cit.*

[6] A factor matrix is said to have simple structure when the number of zero (or near zero) loadings is maximized. Since there is an infinite number of possible solutions to the problem of rotating the obtained factor matrix into a final frame of reference, simple structure provides a reasonably unique and parsimonious criterion. By maximizing the number of near zero loadings, the problem of interpretation is usually simplified considerably.

TABLE A-4: *Rotated Centroid Factor Loadings for Thirty-Eight Variables*

Variable	I	II	III	IV	V	VI	VII	h^2
				Factor*				
Age	−08	−13	−04	−02	08	10	23	09
Total Siblings	10	−42	10	−02	60	−18	06	59
Total in Home	05	−29	06	−06	60	−17	−02	49
Father's Education	05	73	02	−06	−07	−18	−10	59
Mother's Education	03	71	03	−09	−17	−20	−17	61
Father's Occupation	−01	68	13	−08	10	14	14	54
Mother's Occupation	−14	−12	−10	00	39	17	−07	23
Support Family	−02	−29	23	11	21	−26	21	31
Rooms in House	−01	48	−05	−10	13	00	−14	28
Orientation	11	−28	32	54	00	−15	−08	51
Discipline	−10	−27	54	22	07	−16	−16	47
Criticism of Education	13	−17	17	55	−01	−13	00	39
Criticism of Youth	03	−18	55	16	01	21	−27	48
Family	42	−08	−07	46	15	08	−10	43
Self	28	−13	24	51	08	16	11	46
Tensions	79	−20	21	09	09	04	−05	73
Personal	74	−11	30	05	−07	12	20	71
Social	51	−13	47	15	−01	21	11	58
Life-Style	74	−25	18	14	00	08	−05	67
Conformity	44	−12	41	−03	02	−06	14	40
Isolation	48	−10	42	09	00	05	17	46
Financial	56	−19	14	06	10	17	07	41
Dependency	68	−17	15	12	00	00	−08	53
Item 12	−15	−21	32	−01	−08	−21	−01	22
Item 16	−17	00	28	24	09	−11	−17	21
Item 21	01	−30	16	33	08	−26	12	31
Item 29	12	−18	04	24	17	04	−09	14
Item 30	09	−19	−07	12	01	−24	−26	19
Item 33	−07	−22	10	35	21	−07	02	24
Item 47	01	−14	16	−20	−04	−04	00	09
Item 53	−03	−15	24	21	03	−23	10	19
Item 58	35	02	−06	19	−13	07	03	19
Item 62	00	−10	10	30	03	−23	10	17
Item 72	01	−08	17	05	20	02	03	08
Item 85	−02	−01	51	04	02	19	−15	32
Item 100	10	−17	−17	25	02	15	13	17
Item 168	32	−15	−06	04	−05	00	19	17
Item 192	30	−20	08	02	−16	−02	02	17
% Total Variance	10.3	7.8	6.0	5.0	3.2	2.3	1.7	(36.3)
% Common Variance	28.4	21.5	16.5	13.8	8.2	6.3	4.7	

* Decimals Omitted.

A second more rigorous factor analysis was carried out for a smaller number of variables using the IBM 650 electronic computer then at The University of Texas. A special correlation matrix was made up consisting of twenty-one variables—the fourteen scaled scores and seven of the nine background variables. Because of the dichotomous nature of two background variables, Mother's Occupation and Help Support Family, these two variables were left out of the second factor analysis.

Principal Component Method Applied

A principal component method of factor analysis was employed for this smaller matrix in order to get a more exact solution to the question of how many factors to extract.[7] This method is particularly appropriate where one wishes to explain a maximum amount of common variance among intercorrelations with a minimum number of factors. One can determine more

[7] The principal-component method of factor analysis is extremely laborious unless carried out on a high speed computer. Consequently, this analysis was not feasible in this study until eighteen months after completion of the first centroid analysis. As a first approximation to estimates of the communality for entry in the diagonal cells of the correlation matrix, the highest correlation in a given column was employed. All twenty-one of the latent roots were extracted using a program for the IBM 650 computer developed by Howell and Hall. The latent roots were arranged according to their magnitude and plotted with the rank order of the root on the abscissa and the magnitude of the root on the ordinate. Since negative roots produce imaginary factors, the number of factors to be extracted should certainly not exceed the number of positive latent roots. By assuming that the negative latent roots represented various kinds of insignificant error and by assuming that the same amount of error exists above the zero value as well as below it, one can estimate the number of important factors to extract by drawing a line above the abscissa, equivalent in magnitude to the asymptote of the line below the abscissa. In this particular instance, nine factors were estimated as necessary to account for all the important common variance in the twenty-one-variable matrix. New estimates of communalities based upon these nine factors were inserted in the diagonal values of the twenty-one-variable matrix and the principal components analysis was carried out all over once again. Convergence of the new communalities obtained from nine factors in the second analysis upon the estimated communalities from the first analysis proved to be sufficiently good to terminate the analysis. All of the final communalities agreed within one per cent with the estimates inserted at the beginning of the second principal-component analysis. A normalized varimax program proposed by Henry Kaiser (see H. F. Kaiser, "Computer Program for Varimax Rotation in Factor Analysis," in *Educational and Psychological Measurement*, Vol. 19 (1959), pp. 413–420) was employed as a machine approximation to simple structure for rapid rotation of the principal component factor matrix. The varimax solution proved to be fairly close to simple structure and was chosen as a final solution without any additional rotation in spite of the fact that it could have been improved slightly.

precisely when to stop extracting factors by using the mathematically more exact principal component method than one can by using the centroid method. The results of this factor analysis are presented in Table A-5. A total of nine factors was extracted and rotated using the normalized varimax method, a completely objective procedure for rotating the matrix to a final solution.

TABLE A-5: *Normalized Varimax Rotation of Principal Component Factor Matrix for Twenty-One Variables*

Variable	I	II	III	IV	V	VI	VII	VIII	IX	h²
Age	−04	−11	−05	01	−02	−02	00	31	−02	12
Total Siblings	10	−20	12	76	06	04	00	13	−07	68
Total in Home	03	−14	08	75	03	02	01	−07	05	61
Father's Education	−07	76	−08	−14	−09	−01	−01	−07	−07	63
Mother's Education	−12	70	−09	−18	−03	−06	−05	−21	−11	61
Father's Occupation	−01	59	−05	−14	−04	−09	04	04	32	49
Rooms in House	−10	44	−15	03	−04	00	−06	−16	36	39
Orientation	14	−14	56	09	18	39	01	−01	−08	55
Discipline	08	−10	67	13	−03	06	−06	−03	−02	50
Criticism of Education	09	−10	34	04	24	51	08	−07	01	47
Criticism of Youth	18	−04	56	02	01	−01	10	−06	00	37
Family	23	−09	05	05	61	18	08	−02	−02	47
Self	33	−08	28	04	24	30	40	−01	−04	51
Tensions	72	−07	10	12	45	−07	−05	−06	−04	77
Personal	80	−01	08	−02	10	06	18	−03	02	70
Social	73	−10	12	02	−02	09	27	−11	−02	66
Life-Style	66	−10	05	10	41	06	−08	05	−14	67
Conformity	62	−01	20	05	−05	02	−11	02	03	44
Isolation	67	−04	10	00	−03	12	03	−07	−07	49
Financial	57	−07	02	07	24	03	07	16	03	43
Dependency	59	−10	08	12	41	02	−12	−21	05	59
% Total Variance	18.6	8.5	6.8	6.1	5.5	2.8	1.6	1.4	1.4 (55.7)	
% Common Variance	35.2	16.1	12.9	11.6	10.4	5.3	3.1	2.7	2.7	

As indicated by the percentage of common variance explained, Factor I is by far the most important. The last three factors are so small that they can be considered residual and ignored for all practical purposes. Of the six major factors, four are concerned with the attitude and problem scales, while two deal with background characteristics of the students. The results of the two factor analyses are sufficiently similar to justify using the more rigorous, objective principal component analysis for further interpretation.

Factor I—Personal-Social Adjustment. The principal factor has loadings ranging from .57 to .80 on the eight scales in the problem inventory. In addition, low loadings are obtained for the two problem scales in the attitude inventory, Family Problems and Self Inadequacy. All other loadings are near zero. All ten of these scales reflect variations of the same general theme: admission of feelings of inadequacy in making a good person-social adjustment.[8]

Factor II—Educational Level of Parents. The second most important factor in this analysis of intercorrelations among the seven background variables and the fourteen scaled scores is clearly educational level of the parents. Factor II is defined, primarily, by father's education and mother's education with loadings of .76 and .70, respectively. Two other variables show appreciable loadings on Factor II—father's occupational level and number of rooms in the home (loadings of .59 and .44). It is interesting to note that none of the fourteen scaled scores shows appreciable loadings on this socioeconomic factor. As would be expected, number of children in the family has a low negative loading on Factor II, indicating a light tendency for the more educated parents to have smaller families.

Factor III—Negative Social Attitudes. Factor III is comprised chiefly of variables in Form I which reflect negative social attitudes such as acceptance of Authoritarian Discipline, Negative Orientation to Society, Criticism of Youth, and Criticism of Education. The only variable in Form I which has no loading on Factor IV is Family Problems.

Factor IV—Size of Family. Factor IV is a rather specific factor defined entirely by size of the family (loadings of .75 and .76 on total in the home and total number of siblings, respectively). This doublet factor arises primarily from the fact that the two variables defining it are inevitably correlated to a very high degree. The factor itself is of minor importance since it has no other significant loadings.

Factor V—Conflict within the Family. The fifth largest factor has loadings scattered across both Forms I and II. The highest loading for Factor V is .61 on Family Problems, followed by .45 on Family Tensions, .41 on Resentment of Family Life Style, and .41 on Resentment of Dependency. All four of these scales deal with problems of conflict within the family, and especially between the student and his parents. Since these four scales are the

[8] Another slightly different way of looking at Factor I is to consider this pattern of loadings as evidence of a general tendency either to check the various items in Form II as False or to check them as True. Such tendencies are often referred to as response sets. Some individuals are more likely than others to check almost anything as False, regardless of the content of the item. This type of response set is much more characteristic of individuals who do not understand the content of items which they are reading than of well educated, intelligent subjects. The very structure of Form II is conducive to a high degree of agreement among different scales. It seems quite plausible to assume that an individual who admits concern with a variety of problems in his family or social life would be more likely to check a wide range of items as contrasted to the person who believes he has no problems, or at least is unwilling to admit having any.

only ones in the set of fourteen which deal directly with family conflicts, Factor II is clearly a family conflict factor. It is interesting to note that low loadings are also obtained for Criticism of Education, Self Inadequacy, and Financial Trouble. In other words, there is some tendency for individuals who admit of family conflict to be critical of their teachers and of educational practices in their school.[9]

Factor VI—Negativism. The sixth factor is defined by Orientation to Society and Criticism of Education, the two most negativistic scales in the entire set. Since this factor is independent of the more general social attitude factor (III), it can be interpreted as dealing specifically with negativism.

Remaining Factors. The three remaining factors are much less significant, accounting for only 9 per cent of the total common variance in the intercorrelations matrix. Factor VII is defined primarily by two variables, Self Inadequacy and Social Inadequacy, suggesting that there is some significant residual variance in these two scores in addition to the variance due to the main factors. Factor VIII is defined primarily by age of the respondent and can be considered of little importance. Factor IX is a low order residual factor with significant loadings on two socioeconomic variables, father's occupation and number of rooms in the house.

The results of these two factor analyses—the first on a large matrix of thirty-eight variables and the second on a submatrix of twenty-one variables—are quite clear in their meanings. Most of the significant common variance among the many variables in this study can be adequately explained in terms of a relatively small number of factors. Five factors are needed to account for the intercorrelations of the fourteen scaled scores. Four additional factors are necessary to account for individual differences in the most important background variables.[10]

[9] Another way of looking at Factor V is to consider it as a factor reflecting that proportion of family conflict variance after extraction of all the variance in Form II which can be accounted for as due to either general problems or to a response set tendency to check True or False, regardless of the specific nature of the problem indicated (Factor I).

[10] In a related study utilizing Forms I and II of the Cooperative Youth Study together with a large number of other variables obtained from the entire freshman class at Southwest Texas State College in 1956, similar results were obtained. A factor analysis of an intercorrelation matrix for thirty variables yielded eight factors, five of which were significantly loaded on scales from the Cooperative Youth Study. Factor I was defined primarily by the Mooney Problem Checklist. A significant loading was also obtained for Personal Adjustment from Form II, indicating a general agreement between the Mooney and the CYS instruments. Factor II was defined primarily by scholastic aptitude and performance scores. A significant high loading was obtained on Criticism of Education (−.48), with a somewhat lower but still significant loading on Orientation to Society (−.28),

MINIMAL SCORES FOR MAXIMAL DIFFERENCES

If one were compelled to select a small number of scores by which to represent most of the individual differences reflected by the fourteen scaled scores, probably three scores would be adequate: (1) a general scale comprised of Personal Adjustment, Social Inadequacy, Social Conformity, Social Isolation, and Financial Troubles in Form II; (2) a general scale of negative social attitudes comprised chiefly of the first four scales in Form I; and (3) a family problem scale comprised of items in Family Tension, Resentment of Family Life Style, Resentment of Dependency, and Family Problems. The chief difficulty of course in collapsing the fourteen scales into only three more general scales is that a number of these scales have unique variance over and above the variation common to other variables in the study. In spite of the fact that there is a generally high degree of intercorrelation among all of the variables in Form II, a fact which accounts for most of the variance in Form II appearing in Factor I, there is still some significant nonerror variance unique to the individual scales. In Form I where one is dealing with social attitudes, the amount of significant unique variance is even greater, as evidenced by the lower values for estimated communalities (ranging from .37 to .55 in the principal component analysis). It is primarily for this reason and the fact that each of the fourteen scales has a relatively high degree of internal consistency and was carefully established on an a priori basis, that all fourteen scaled scores were retained in most of the subsequent statistical analysis.[11]

---

indicating that the poorer the student the more negative his orientation to society and the more critical he is of education. Factor III was defined primarily by the three major scales reflecting family tensions—Family Problems, Family Tension, and Resentment of Family Life Style (since the last four short scales in Form II were not analyzed in this study, Resentment of Dependency has been left out). It is interesting to note that the only scale within the Mooney Problem Checklist which loads significantly on this family tension factor is the home problem scale. Factor V is comprised chiefly of the four main scales in Form I dealing with negative attitudes toward society; and Factor VII is defined by high loadings on Social Inadequacy, Self Inadequacy and Personal Adjustment from the CYS scales. Within the Mooney Problem Checklist, the only scales loading significantly on Factor VII are social problems, social-psychological problems, and problems in adjusting to college. The remaining two factors have no significant loadings on the CYS measures. These results are strikingly similar to those obtained for the high school population. In addition, comparisons between the Cooperative Youth scale instruments and the Mooney Problem Checklist show a high degree of consistency.

[11] Since there are fourteen scaled scores in Forms I and II, the most elegant statistical method would be multivariate analysis of variance, treating all fourteen scores simultaneously in the same complex design. At the time these analyses were

RELATIONSHIPS BETWEEN BACKGROUND FACTORS AND EXPRESSED ATTITUDES
AND PROBLEMS

The relationships between nine of the background variables, the fourteen scaled scores, and fifteen individual items from Forms I and II have been discussed in a general way as analyzed in the intercorrelational studies of the special sample of one thousand cases. These nine variables—age, number of siblings, total number in family, father's education, mother's education, father's occupation, mother's occupation, work to help support family, and number of rooms in the house—represent only a small part of the personal background information available on each student. None of the qualitative variables have been included in the intercorrelation analysis since they must be treated differently because of their nonmetric nature. Moreover, the intercorrelation analysis dealt with less than 10 per cent of the total sample, leading to only very general conclusions, rather than pin-pointing specifically the interaction of such background factors as community size, religious affiliation, and family structure.

Analyses of Variance

The statistical methods most appropriate to the study of such complex interactions among qualitatively different background factors are generally referred to as analysis of variance. Such background factors as race, sex, and community size can be varied systematically in one complex design to determine the relationships between such independent variables and scores on the attitude and personality scales.

Several dozen separate studies were designed and carried out employing analysis of variance methods. In each case certain restrictions were placed on the sample to insure clear meaning in the results. In one study, for example, only children from intact families were used. All cases were eliminated who had roomers or relatives outside the primary family living in the home. Students were included only if their chronological age matched their school grade (eliminating age variation within grades). And only white students were used. Such restrictions on the sample are often necessary to eliminate confounded factors that make interpretation of the results difficult or impossible. Having 13,000 cases proves of real value in controlling major variables that are usually badly confounded.

In addition to restrictions on the sample to insure clarity of results, more than one independent variable was generally included in a given design.

---

begun, computer facilities at our disposal were not of sufficiently high speed and high capacity to justify the great expense in time and money to carry out complete multivariate analyses. Consequently, concurrent analyses of variance were carried out simultaneously on all fourteen scales, treating each scale independently of the others.

In one of the major studies, for example, five background factors were varied systematically in order to make possible the analysis of complex interactions among these variables, as well as treatment of each one alone. The five variables were (a) grades (9, 10, 11, and 12); (b) sex; (c) number of siblings (0, 1, 2); (d) community size (small versus large); and (e) father's education (elementary, high school, and some college). This type of complex design can be referred to as a five-way analysis of variance with 144 cells in the design (four by two by three by two by three). Replication of cases within cells provides an appropriate error term for testing the statistical significance of any major effects, as well as building up the stability of results. In this particular example of a five-way analysis, 950 cases were employed.

Several dozen such analyses of variance designs were constructed, each on an independently drawn sample of cases where certain major variables were held constant or systematically varied as independent variables in the design. In every analysis the dependent variables or scores that were used consisted of all fourteen scaled scores plus occasional selected items that had been stored on the master IBM card (Card A). Altogether, over four hundred such complex analyses were carried out using an IBM 605 card-programmed electronic calculator.[12]

Since each of these analyses deals with a number of hypotheses bearing upon the relationship between background factors and scaled scores, each has been described separately in the preceding chapters, together with the significance of the obtained results. To illustrate the method, one analysis has been selected for detailed presentation in the next section.

A General Analysis of Sex, Parental Pattern, Number of Siblings, and Level of Father's Education

One of the major analyses of variance upon which many findings were based involved 1,440 cases selected to control four major background variables—sex of the student, parental pattern, number of siblings in the family, and level of father's education. Parental pattern consisted of three variations of special theoretical interest: (1) students with both parents present in the home; (2) students with only the mother present because of divorce, separation, or death of the father; and (3) students with mother and a stepfather present. The number of siblings varied systematically from none to nine in five categories. Level of father's education consisted of three categories: (1) elementary grades only; (2) at least some high school but not beyond;

---

[12] At the time these analyses were carried out, the IBM 650 computer was not yet installed within the University's Computation Center. The IBM 605 CPC proved quite satisfactory, however, for complex analysis of variance designs. Analyses on all of the dependent variables could be carried out simultaneously once the statistical program had been routinized.

and (3) at least some college level of study completed by the father. Only white students were used, age variation within school grade was controlled by eliminating students who were too young or too old within each of the four grades, and no cases were used in which any roomers or relatives outside the primary family were present in the home. Restrictions on the sample and the independent variables systematically studied are outlined in Table A-6.

TABLE A-6: *Independent Variables and the Selection of Cases for a Statistical Design Involving Sex, Parental Pattern, Number of Siblings, and Level of Father's Education*

RESTRICTIONS ON THE SAMPLE
1. No roomers or relatives living in the home
2. Age variation within school grade controlled
3. White students only

INDEPENDENT VARIABLES
1. Sex of the student
2. Number of siblings in the family: 0, 1, 2, 3, or 4, 5 to 9
3. Level of father's education: 0–8, 9–12, college
4. Parental pattern: true mother and father, mother alone, mother and stepfather

The use of all possible combinations of the four independent variables resulted in a four-way factorial design with ninety cells. A total of 1,440 cases was drawn from the sample of 12,892 cases to complete the design, care having been taken to preserve the orthogonality of the independent variables by maintaining strict proportionality across the cells.

TABLE A-7: *Complete Analysis of Variance for Four Background Variables and Their Interactions for Six Attitude Scale Scores in Form I*

| | | Mean Square Estimates (Variance) | | | | | |
Source of Variance	d.f.	Orientation to Society	Authoritarian Discipline	Criticism of Education	Criticism of Youth	Family Problems	Self Inadequacy
(4 main effects)							
Sex (X)	1	40.3‡	109.5‡	100.8‡	38.7‡	2.6	10.3
Parents (P)	2	0.4	28.1‡	4.1	11.5*	12.2	0.3
Number Siblings (S)..	4	10.4*	15.0‡	10.1*	5.0	23.2‡	6.1
Father's Education (F)	2	25.2‡	5.7	27.2‡	0.6	4.2	21.0‡
(6 first-order interactions)							
X by P	2	1.5	9.1	4.0	0.9	0.1	4.9
X by S	4	2.7	6.1	2.1	4.9	7.0	4.5
X by F	2	7.9	17.0†	2.4	7.9	7.4	0.7

* Significant at the .05 level
‡ Significant at the .001 level

TABLE A-7: *Complete Analysis of Variance for Four Background Variables and Their Interactions for Six Attitude Scale Scores in Form I—Continued*

Source of Variance	d.f.	Orientation to Society	Authoritarian Discipline	Criticism of Education	Criticism of Youth	Family Problems	Self Inadequacy
P by S	8	1.5	2.7	1.6	5.7	2.2	2.3
P by F	4	5.2	2.4	6.0	1.3	13.2°	3.9
S by F	8	5.2	7.5	4.3	5.5	2.5	4.2
(4 second-order interactions)							
X by P by S	8	1.8	1.4	2.3	2.5	4.2	4.9
X by P by F	4	3.3	4.4	0.9	1.9	11.9	4.8
X by S by F	8	2.8	2.0	6.2	2.1	6.7	2.2
P by S by F	16	4.3	3.6	2.8	1.8	3.2	3.9
(1 third-order interaction)							
X by P by S by F	16	2.5	4.1	3.7	3.3	4.0	1.9
Replication (error) ..	1,350	3.3	3.1	3.8	2.5	4.3	2.9

† Significant at the .01 level

The advantages of considering simultaneously all possible combinations of four major variables at once are obvious in Table A-7 where the complete analysis of variance for these four background variables and their interaction is summarized for the six attitude scales in Form I. A similar analysis for the eight scales in Form II is presented in Table A-8. Not only is it possible to say something about the significance of differences for each of the independent variables (main effects) considered alone, it is also possible to examine systematically the various interactions of these variables.

TABLE A-8: *Complete Analysis of Variance for Four Background Variables and Their Interactions for Eight Problem Scale Scores in Form II*

Source of Variance	d.f.	Tensions	Personal Social	LifeStyle	Conformity	Isolation	Financial	Dependency
(4 main effects)								
Sex (X)	1	26.1†	16.4°	2.1	0.2	0.5	0.3	1.3	8.3
Parents (P)	2	34.4‡	8.0	0.5	24.5†	1.1	0.7	9.8†	3.8
Number Siblings (S) ..	4	21.1‡	9.8°	12.1‡	46.1‡	9.2	4.3°	15.5‡	15.6‡
Father's Education (F)	2	5.4	2.1	16.9†	43.0‡	0.8	1.9	5.3	1.6
(6 first-order interactions)								
X by P	2	4.5	8.9	5.5	6.4	1.9	11.8†	1.7	1.0
X by S	4	9.6	2.5	0.9	7.0	3.3	2.1	3.5	5.0

° Significant at the .05 level
† Significant at the .01 level
‡ Significant at the .001 level

TABLE A-8: *Complete Analysis of Variance for Four Background Variables and Their Interactions for Eight Problem Scale Scores in Form II—Continued*

		Mean Square Estimates (Variance)							
Source of Variance	d.f.	Ten-sions	Per-sonal	Social	Life-Style	Con-formity	Isola-tion	Fi-nancial	Depend-ency
X by F	2	1.6	1.5	4.1	2.3	20.1†	6.0	2.0	1.8
P by S	8	3.6	5.3	3.9	11.1†	4.8	2.8	3.4	2.6
P by F	4	16.6‡	4.6	2.3	22.1†	1.4	1.7	3.1	8.7
S by F	8	2.8	1.9	1.3	3.4	1.0	1.1	1.5	2.1
(4 second-order interactions)									
X by P by S	8	1.9	3.4	2.3	4.9	1.6	0.8	0.5	2.0
X by P by F	4	1.9	1.5	0.9	0.4	2.6	2.8	2.2	1.5
X by S by F	8	6.6	1.8	1.7	5.1	3.0	2.8	0.6	1.0
P by S by F	16	1.9	6.9	2.8	6.2	1.4	1.8	2.5	3.0
(1 third-order interaction)									
X by P by S by F	16	3.1	3.8	3.1	1.6	1.6	2.0	2.2	3.3
Replication (error) ..	1,350	3.1	3.7	3.0	4.3	4.0	1.8	2.0	2.9

Taking the independent variables two at a time in all possible combinations yields six first-order interactions. When they are taken three at a time in all possible combinations, four second-order interactions can be extracted and examined for significance. Only one third-order interaction exists when all four variables are considered simultaneously. It is very difficult to make any sense out of such high order combinations unless one has rather compelling a priori hypotheses that require such complex interactions. The source of variance due to replication provides an independent estimate of variance due to individual differences within the ninety cells created by all possible combinations of the four main effects. The F-test was used for determining the statistical significance of each source of variance, using the replication component as the error term in the denominator of the F-ratio and the mean square for the particular source of variance in question as the numerator.

Because of the large number of comparisons made in such an analysis, some sources of variance will appear significant by chance alone. The following rules have been adopted generally for analysis and interpretation of results. When the F-ratio is significant only at the .05 level, no attention has been paid to the source of variance unless it is one of the main effects arising from consideration of single variables. Such sources of variance have been marked with an asterisk in Tables A-7 and A-8 to indicate a low order, slight trend that should be cautiously interpreted. An F-ratio which is sufficiently high to be significant at or beyond the .01 level indicates a source of variance that should be treated seriously. Such significant trends are marked with a single dagger. Those sources of variance which are significant at the .001 level or beyond are marked with a double dagger and should be interpreted as highly significant. Trends which are significant at the .001 level would appear by chance alone only one in a thousand times.

In reading Tables A-7 and A-8 one should keep in mind that many of the fourteen scaled scores are measuring similar traits as indicated in the earlier factor analyses. Consequently, when a source of variance proves highly significant for, say, Family Tension, it is also very likely to be significant for such scales as Resentment of Family Life Style, Family Problems, and Resentment of Dependency because of the intercorrelations among these variables.

Whenever a source of variance is significant, it means that the mean scores for the different categories of the variables in question differ significantly one from the other. The particular source of such significant differences can best be determined by inspection of the means to see what trend is evident. The numerous small graphs distributed throughout the preceding chapters illustrate these trends in specific instances where they are significant.

The most general sources of variance are the four main effects, each of which can be considered independently of the other. In some cases, however, higher order interactions such as Parental Pattern by Father's Education (P by F) for Family Tensions make it necessary to qualify statements concerning either variable when considered alone. A significant interaction between Parental Pattern and Father's Education would indicate that the relationship between level of true father's education and Family Tension is different for the three variations in parental pattern. This complex interaction is well illustrated by Figure 46 in Chapter IX where this interesting finding is discussed.

In this analysis of variance design much greater detail has been presented in Tables A-7 and A-8 than is necessary for an adequate understanding of the results. Such statistical detail illustrates the general approach that has been taken in all of the analysis of variance designs. First, the special population to be studied is carefully defined and a sample drawn from the total population of 12,892 cases with certain qualifications designed to eliminate extraneous or confounding variables. Next, the independent variables or factors which will be examined systematically are arranged in all of their possible combinations, and cases are drawn from the refined sample in order to fill out the cells of the design. Since the various independent factors must be proportionately represented in order to maintain orthogonality, many cases are eliminated randomly from further consideration. As many replications of the basic design as possible are drawn from the refined sample in order to provide the most precise test of mean differences, interactions and related trends among the independent variables in question. And finally, the statistical analysis itself is carried out simultaneously on all fourteen scaled scores, employing a priori rules as to the level of statistical significance necessary for a trend to deserve serious consideration. In each of the analysis of variance designs, the same general principles have been employed although the particular combination of background factors varies from one design to the next. Since it is impossible to include all background factors simultaneously within one design, the number included in any one analysis varies from one to five variables.

Quite frequently the same case will be employed in more than one design, but in combination with different cases in order to study different aspects of the relationships between background factors and scaled scores. Because of the general lack of independence from one analysis of variance design to the next, one should not weigh too heavily the fact that a given variable, such as sex or father's education, may yield somewhat similar results from one design to the next. While such consistency of results strengthens somewhat the validity of conclusions drawn from the analysis, the extent of such confirmation is rather indeterminant because of overlapping cases. In any event, none of the analyses presented can be considered a truly independent cross-validation of results obtained in any of the other analyses.

APPENDIX B: FORMS USED IN THE SURVEY

TEXAS COOPERATIVE YOUTH STUDY: 1956

Student Information Sheet

Name: ....   School: ....

Present
Address: ....   Grade: .... Sex: Male .... Female......................
              (Street or RFD)

....   Age: .... Height: .... Weight: ....
          (Town)

                                                 Check any Homemaking Courses you have taken or are taking now:

Check where you live: In country......................In town..................   None . . . . Hm. II . . . .

Place of birth: ....   7th and 8th . . . . Hm. III . . . .
       (Town or county)   (State)   Hm. I . . . . Hm. IV . . . .

Are you married? Yes............ No............   Home and Family Life . . . .

Check (∨) those which apply to you: Write in number of each of the following now living in your home:

Parents living together . . . .
       Mother . . . .   Half brothers . . . .

Parents separated . . . .
       Father . . . .   Stepsisters . . . .

Parents divorced . . . .
       Stepmother . . . .   Stepbrothers . . . .

Mother not living . . . .
       Stepfather . . . .   Grandmothers . . . .

Father not living . . . .
       Sisters . . . .   Grandfathers . . . .

Number older brothers . . . .
       Brothers . . . .   Other relatives . . . .

Number older sisters . . . .
       Half sisters . . . .   Others . . . .

Number younger brothers . . . .

Number younger sisters . . . .

What schooling did each of your parents have? (Check)

	Father	Mother		Father	Mother
No school	....	....	Business college	....	....
Grades 1–4	....	....	Had some college	....	....
Grades 5–8	....	....	Junior College graduate	....	....
Grades 9–11	....	....	4-year College graduate	....	....
Completed high school	....	....	Other: Father		
County Veterans' School	....	....	Mother		

What kind of work does your father do? (Example: Operates own farm; works on someone else's farm; is a carpenter; lawyer; rancher; etc.)

Kind of work: ....

Does your mother work outside the home? Yes............ No.... ...... Kind of work:..

Do you work after school at home? Yes............ No............ Hours per week?............ Kind of work:.....................................

Do you work outside the home part-time? Yes........ No............ Do you help support the family with money you earn part-time? Yes............ No............

Kind of work:..Hours per week:............

How many rooms in your home? (Including bathrooms) ....   What religious denomination do you prefer? ....
                                                              (Your answer to this is optional)

Do other persons share your bedroom? Yes .... No ....

                                                          ....

If so, with how many? ....   Do you ride a school bus? Yes .... No ....

Does your family own a car? Yes .... No ....   How long does it take to get to school? ....

Are you allowed to drive the car? Yes .... No ....

Texas Cooperative Youth Study: 1956

ATTITUDES TOWARD
PERSONAL AND FAMILY LIVING

DIRECTIONS

We are attempting to find out how you feel about yourself, your family, and your friends. Your answers will be treated with the strictest confidence, so please feel free to give honest replies.

You will mark your answers on a separate answer sheet. Make no marks on this booklet. You are to indicate the extent to which you agree with each statement. Read each statement and decide how **you** feel about it. Then mark your answer on the space provided on your answer sheet. Be sure to use the special I.B.M. pencil.

	1	2	3	4	5
If you **strongly agree,** blacken the space under 1	▌	∷	∷	∷	∷
If you **agree,** blacken the space under 2	∷	▌	∷	∷	∷
If you are **undecided or uncertain,** blacken the space under 3	∷	∷	▌	∷	∷
If you **disagree,** blacken the space under 4	∷	∷	∷	▌	∷
If you **strongly disagree,** blacken the space under 5	∷	∷	∷	∷	▌

There are no "right" or "wrong" answers, and there is no time limit. Work as rapidly as you can without being careless, and do not spend too much time on any one statement. PLEASE RESPOND TO EVERY ITEM. Thank you very much for your help.

1 – Strongly Agree
2 – Agree
3 – Undecided or Uncertain
4 – Disagree
5 – Strongly Disagree

1. I can always count on my family for help when I get in trouble or have a problem.

2. I dislike eating away from home for fear I'll do the wrong thing.

3. Most children should have more discipline than they get.

4. A child should never keep a secret from his parents.

5. The sole purpose of education should be to equip students to make a living.

6. I lack confidence in myself.

7. Too many boys and girls think they have to drink to be smart.

8. Clothes I like always seem to cost more than I can afford to pay.

9. I often have the feeling I will say something wrong.

10. I usually get fair treatment at home.

11. Girls ought to spend a lot of their time in high school learning about taking care of the home and family.

12. Children should feel it is their duty to care for their parents when their parents grow old.

13. The house and its furnishings have no effect on the relationships of the family.

14. People always get into trouble when they haven't anything to do.

15. It takes so long to make things that I don't like them when I finish them.

16. High school marriages can only lead to trouble.

17. A high school student should take the school courses which his parents decide would be best for him.

18. I find any discussion of sex embarrassing.

19. Children should be paid for work they do around the house.

20. A devoted mother has no time for her social life.

21. Parents should sacrifice everything for their children.

22. Most teachers are too rigid and narrow-minded.

23. Boys need some high school homemaking so they can learn to help manage a home.

24. Studying about health practices in class is a waste of time.

25. Too much freedom will make a child wild.

26. In our community young people don't have anything to do on dates that is fun.

27. I just never seem to get anything done.

28. Punishing a child is a father's job.

29. Relatives living in a home always make trouble for the family.

30. A wife shouldn't have to work to earn part of the family income.

31. I'm never satisfied unless I do a perfect job.

32. It's hardly fair to bring children into the world with the way things look for the future.

33. Whenever a girl marries, she should drop out of high school.

34. Most teachers lack understanding of the needs and interests of their students.

35. Students at our school are not cooperative and friendly.

36. Students can't be trusted to own and drive their own cars.

37. A person should insist on his own rights no matter what the cost.

GO ON TO THE NEXT PAGE

1 – Strongly Agree
2 – Agree
3 – Undecided or Uncertain
4 – Disagree
5 – Strongly Disagree

---

38. Members of my family feel hurt every time I want to go out with others instead of with them.

39. Going steady and being engaged are practically the same thing.

40. Some of my friends say that I am disagreeable and hard to get along with.

41. Every member of the family should have some say about how the family money is spent.

42. My family never gives me any privacy.

43. Silliness is one of the worst faults of most teen-agers.

44. We have enjoyable times together during meals in our home.

45. I see no reason for every boy and girl to understand the physical changes which occur during adolescence.

46. Planning ahead how to spend my money is a waste of time.

47. Parents should share in housekeeping, shopping, and everything it takes to run our home.

48. These days a person doesn't really know whom he can count on.

49. When you get right down to it no one is going to care much what is going to happen to you.

50. Too much affection will make a child a "softie."

51. Our house is too cluttered to be comfortable.

52. Generally speaking, football coaches contribute more to school life than do the teachers.

53. A parent has the right to read a high school student's letter without first asking permission.

54. One's reputation depends mostly on the people one goes with.

55. Strict discipline develops a fine strong character.

56. A mother should make it her business to know everything her children are thinking.

57. Children should not annoy parents with their unimportant problems.

58. There is too little concern in our family for religion.

59. A mother should shower her child with praise at all times.

60. Generally speaking, students cannot be expected to like their teachers.

61. Some children are just naturally bad.

62. It is not the duty of the parent to teach the child about sex.

63. We ought to worry about our own country and let the rest of the world take care of itself.

64. In spite of what some people say, the life for the average person is getting worse, not better.

65. I feel helpless around sick people because I don't know what to do for them.

66. There is no sense in keeping track of money spent.

67. In our house we have to be so careful of the furniture and everything that I get disgusted.

68. Most teen-agers have not yet learned to control their tempers.

69. Most teachers have special favorites instead of showing equal fairness and impartiality toward all.

70. I often feel as if I don't really belong anywhere.

71. Children should always be punished for being bad.

GO ON TO THE NEXT PAGE

1 – Strongly Agree
2 – Agree
3 – Undecided or Uncertain
4 – Disagree
5 – Strongly Disagree

72. People of different religions shouldn't get married.

73. The money I earn should be my own to spend anyway I want.

74. What is learned at school makes people want things they can't have.

75. I am free to talk about anything I want to in our family.

76. Playing too much with a child will spoil him.

77. Eating breakfast is more trouble than it is worth.

78. If a boy can't afford the cost of a date, he shouldn't ask a girl.

79. Children who always obey grow up to be the best adults.

80. If you don't watch yourself, people will take advantage of you.

81. Young children always make me nervous.

82. Students are not given enough freedom in selecting their own topics for themes and reports.

83. It is as important for girls to learn how to make clothes as how to buy them.

84. It is almost impossible for the average student to do all his assigned homework.

85. A girl who gets into trouble on a date has no one to blame but herself.

86. Most of the time, I am still tired when I get up in the morning.

87. Most of the time I'm so busy I can't get through a meal fast enough.

88. I don't like to bring anyone into my home because of the way it looks.

89. I worry about my family.

90. If children are to grow up and get somewhere in life, they must be continuously kept after.

91. Teenagers gossip too much about each other.

92. The main reason students cheat is because of the ridiculous assignments most teachers make.

93. Parents have a right to know how children spend their own money.

94. The illustrations, examples, and explanations given by most teachers are too dry or technical.

95. I dislike cooking.

96. Discussion of personal adjustment and family life should take place in classes having both boys and girls.

97. Children need some of the natural meanness taken out of them.

98. Our family never seems to plan anything ahead of time.

99. The kind of clothes you wear has no effect on your personality.

100. Having the opportunity to go to college is very important to me.

101. In our community, more youth disrespect public property today than ever before.

PLEASE STOP UNTIL TOLD TO GO ON

Texas Cooperative Youth Study: 1956

CONCERNS AND PROBLEMS IN PERSONAL AND FAMILY LIVING

DIRECTIONS

Here are some sentences that will give you an opportunity to express how you feel about certain personal and family concerns and problems. Your answers to these will be treated with the strictest confidence, so please be free to say exactly how you feel.

Some statements will not be true in your case or will not apply to you in any way. Others will be true, but will vary in how strongly you feel about them.

You will mark your answers on a separate answer sheet. Make no marks on this booklet. Read each statement and decide how **you** feel about it. Then mark your answer with a special I.B.M. pencil in the space provided on your answer sheet.

	1	2	3	4	5
If you feel the statement is either **false or does not apply to you,** blacken the space under 1	**I**	::	::	::	::
If you feel the statement is generally **true** but of **no concern** to you, blacken the space under 2	::	**I**	::	::	::
If you feel the statement is generally **true** but of **little concern** to you, blacken the space under 3	::	::	**I**	::	::
If you feel the statement is generally **true** but of **much concern** to you, blacken the space under 4	::	::	::	**I**	::
If you feel the statement is generally **true** and of **greatest concern** to you, blacken the space under 5	::	::	::	::	**I**

Some of these statements refer to your parents or to one of them. If you do not live with either of your parents, answer in terms of the person or persons you do live with and who serve in place of your parents.

There are no "right" or "wrong" answers, and there is no time limit. Work as rapidly as you can without being careless, and do not spend too much time on any one statement. PLEASE RESPOND TO EVERY ITEM. Thank you very much for your help.

DO NOT OPEN THIS BOOKLET UNTIL TOLD TO DO SO

1 – *False; or does not apply to me* in any way
2 – *True,* but of *no concern* to me
3 – *True,* but of *little concern* to me
4 – *True,* and of *much concern* to me
5 – *True,* and of *greatest concern* to me

---

151. I see boys and girls at school whom I'd like to meet but I never get a chance.

152. Mother is really the boss in our family.

153. Sometimes I feel that I have been very wicked.

154. My parents treat me as if I do not know right from wrong.

155. I'm often asked to drop out to let someone else have my place.

156. I am ashamed sometimes of the way my parents behave.

157. I'm teased a lot by other boys and girls.

158. I can't carry on a conversation in a group.

159. I always have to ask for money for things I want to do.

160. My mother is always nagging me to help around the house.

161. People gossip about me behind my back.

162. I can't seem to make other people understand I really like them.

163. Others always look better than I.

164. Housekeeping in our house is disorderly.

165. Sometimes I feel things are not real.

166. I don't have a chance to meet boys and girls my age except at school.

167. Some of my family members do not know good table manners.

168. I would like to get married as soon as possible.

169. Members of our family argue about buying things on credit.

170. Family problems are never talked over with me.

171. My parents rarely go to church.

172. I don't seem to live up to my religious teaching as well as others do.

173. I am often unable to look at people when I'm talking to them.

174. I like one of my parents much better than I like the other.

175. I can never save any money.

176. My parents never have time to help me.

177. I get mad and do things I shouldn't when I can't have my way.

178. I can never figure out what grownups want me to do.

179. I work hard but never get anything done.

180. I have trouble making friends easily.

181. Dad makes all the decisions at our house.

182. My parents usually disagree about things I am to be punished for.

183. I never feel I know what clothes make me look my best.

184. My parents won't let me drive a car even though I know how.

185. Arguments in my family always upset me.

186. Some people think I'm a prude because I don't like dirty jokes.

GO ON TO THE NEXT PAGE

1 – *False;* or *does not apply to me* in any way

2 – *True,* but of *no concern* to me

3 – *True,* but of *little concern* to me

4 – *True,* and of *much concern* to me

5 – *True,* and of *greatest concern* to me

---

187. I feel tired all the time.

188. My parents often pry into my private affairs.

189. I wonder if for my age I am normal in my physical development.

190. I want to be accepted by the gang but they won't have me.

191. I have trouble getting a job after school.

192. I think about sex a good deal of the time.

193. Mother won't let me help because she says I never do anything right.

194. My going steady presents real problems in petting.

195. I am never sure what I ought to wear to be dressed right for the occasion.

196. Everyone in my family seems to be against me.

197. I am always afraid in a crowd.

198. My parents are strict about my going out at night.

199. I'm afraid people will laugh at me because I'm not sure I know how to act.

200. My parents do not agree about religion.

201. My parents seem to change from day to day in the way they treat me.

202. Keeping our house in order is more important to mother than having fun in it.

203. It's hard for me to live up to the reputation of others in my family.

204. My parents quarrel and fight much of the time.

205. Others my age do not talk to me much.

206. I feel that I have often been punished when I didn't deserve it.

207. Often it seems that I hurt people's feelings without meaning to do so.

208. My parents always say their way is the best way when I try to tell them things I learn in school.

209. Sometimes I feel I just have to lower my standards to be popular.

210. My parents often object to the kind of boys and girls I go around with.

211. I often feel rather lonesome at home.

212. If you don't drink in our gang, they make you feel like a sissy.

213. If we didn't feel so crowded in our house, we'd be much happier.

214. Sometimes criticism gets me down.

215. I have to take care of the younger children in our family.

216. My parents never take part in school affairs.

217. I never get to go to parties or on dates.

218. I never seem to be able to get anywhere on time.

219. I'm never chosen by teacher to do any special task.

220. Our family seems to have more problems than others in our neighborhood.

GO ON TO THE NEXT PAGE

1 – *False;* or *does not apply to me* in any way

2 – *True,* but of *no concern* to me

3 – *True,* but of *little concern* to me

4 – *True,* and of *much concern* to me

5 – *True,* and of *greatest concern* to me

---

221. Dad always seems too busy to pal around with me.

222. My parents don't like to have me bring friends home.

223. My parents never really trust me.

224. People sometimes tell me I am a snob.

225. Even when I am with people, I feel lonely most of the time.

226. I don't sleep well.

227. I don't feel sure how to act on dates.

228. My parents avoid discussing sex with me.

229. Our family always seems to be in debt.

230. I feel ill at ease at parties.

231. Others like me to help with their lessons but they never give me a date.

232. Being out with people who get drunk scares me.

233. I avoid meeting the parents of my dates.

234. I am prejudiced against some people.

235. I am never able to discuss personal problems confidentially with either of my parents.

236. My parents do without too many things just so I can have what others my age have.

237. I have to do most of the cooking and housekeeping at home.

238. I often feel uncomfortable when I'm around others my age.

239. Our family watches what it spends so closely it spoils all our fun.

240. Sometimes I tell dirty jokes when I would rather not.

PLEASE STOP UNTIL TOLD TO GO ON

Texas Cooperative Youth Study: 1956

INTERESTS IN
PERSONAL AND FAMILY LIVING

DIRECTIONS

This is a list of statements about personal and family living. You are to indicate the extent to which you are interested in each statement. Your answers will be treated with the strictest confidence, so please be free to say exactly how you feel.

You will mark your answers on a separate answer sheet. Make no marks on this booklet. Read each statement and decide how interested you are in it. Then mark your answer in the space provided in your answer sheet. Be sure to use the special I.B.M. pencil.

	1	2	3	4	5
If you are **strongly interested,** blacken the space under 1	▮	∷	∷	∷	∷
If you are **mildly interested,** blacken the space under 2	∷	▮	∷	∷	∷
If you are **not interested,** blacken the space under 3	∷	∷	▮	∷	∷

We are not using the spaces under 4 and 5 so you will never blacken those spaces. Always leave spaces 4 and 5 clean. There are no "right" or "wrong" answers, and there is no time limit. Work as rapidly as you can without being careless, and do not spend too much time on any one statement. PLEASE RESPOND TO EVERY STATEMENT. Thank you very much for your help.

DO NOT OPEN THIS BOOKLET UNTIL TOLD TO DO SO

1. How to get along with other people.

2. The effects of the place one lives on personality.

3. Learning to buy clothers for the whole family.

4. How to launder, press, and make simple repairs on clothes.

5. Preparing quick family meals.

6. How to appreciate and enjoy all family members.

7. How to apply for a job—manners, grooming, clothing.

8. Expressing one's self well.

9. Why children suck fingers, bite fingernails, stammer and show other signs of problems.

10. Information about divorce and its effects on the family.

11. Skills which give the ability to construct and make clothes fit.

12. What sort of house and furnishings we could have on our income.

13. How to take care of and entertain sick children.

14. Feeding small children and the rest of the family.

15. How shyness happens and how to overcome it.

16. Getting the most from our family money.

17. What to do to get rid of body odor.

18. How to get rid of pimples and have a clear complexion.

19. Planning nutritious meals.

20. What and how to buy on "lay away," "time payment," "installment plan."

21. What to look for when you buy furniture.

22. What is acceptable behavior on dates.

23. When it is cheaper to buy clothes and when it is best to make them.

24. What health problems a family is likely to face.

25. Controlling one's temper.

26. How to handle fears.

27. What is involved in setting up and maintaining a home.

28. Where to go and things to do which will cost little or no money.

29. What to look for when buying or building a house.

30. First aid in a disaster or an emergency.

31. More about children in order to be able to earn money baby sitting.

32. Gaining or losing weight and how to maintain normal weight.

33. Planning for marriage.

34. Information about community services available for families.

35. To learn how to handle disagreements in the family.

36. Well planned activities that everyone in the family can participate in.

37. Planning for use of one's leisure time.

38. Judging advertising intelligently and buying wisely from it.

39. Authoritative and correct information about sex.

40. What health and protective services are available for families.

41. Games, puzzles and story telling for young children.

42. Social Security and how it applies to us.

43. How to judge what is a good buy by reading labels on cans, clothes, and appliances.

44. Why one person's personality differs from another.

45. How to "do-it-yourself" or "build-it-yourself" to make home more comfortable, convenient, and in good repair.

46. How to organize work to save time and energy.

47. How to buy and take care of appliances for the home.

48. How to have a place of my own for clothes and my other belongings.

49. How to understand and deal with problems families usually have.

GO ON TO THE NEXT PAGE

50. Child care in emergency situations.

51. Selecting appropriate clothes which will best suit my build and personality.

52. How children grow and develop.

53. Understanding prenatal care and how children are born.

54. Learning democratic family practices.

55. Exploring job opportunities using homemaking training.

56. How children form acceptable habits.

57. How to prepare one's self for a part-time job.

58. Understanding my behavior and that of others.

59. To learn how the family can plan together, share work and responsibilities.

60. Knowing my share of the family clothing money.

61. What is to be considered in choosing a marriage partner.

62. Investing the money one saves.

63. What kinds of insurance a family needs.

64. Getting a meal ready to serve so that all food will be ready at the same time.

65. What to do when somebody in the family gets sick.

66. Making toys and play equipment for children.

67. How to glamorize "hand-me-downs" and "made-overs."

68. Cooking different foods to get variety in family meals.

69. Jealousy as a personality problem.

70. How to assemble clothing babies need.

71. How to select, prepare and serve food for various occasions.

72. How to order food in a restaurant.

73. How one gets a good credit rating.

74. How to tell younger children there is to be a new baby.

75. How to get little children to behave.

76. Rearranging dark and unattractive rooms to make them more usable.

77. How to meet people and feel at ease with them.

78. How to get along with and do things for elderly people.

79. How to plan a house to fit our family needs.

80. How to cut down the cost of clothes and yet keep them good looking.

81. Understanding people of other nations and other races.

82. Taking care of the mother and an infant.

83. All kinds of information on the etiquette of dating.

84. How to develop citizenship through home and family living.

85. How to beautify the house and its grounds.

86. Why little children behave as they do.

87. How to deal with special food problems of family members.

88. Buying foods which will give us the most for our money.

89. What personality characteristics make for popularity.

90. Advantages af renting or owning a home.

91. Each family member having a place for his things.

92. Danger of following food fads.

93. How to get the family members to eat what they ought to.

94. When it is important to seek help from a doctor.

95. Making the home safe from accidents.

96. Keeping mentally and physically fit.

97. Dangers from self-doctoring.

98. Planning for food buying.

APPENDIX C: SCHOOLS INCLUDED IN THE SAMPLE

REGION I (East Texas)

Community	N	School	City or Town	County
Small White	53	Pecan Gap H. S.	Pecan Gap	Delta
	56	Bronson H. S.	Bronson	Sabine
	42	Point H. S.	Point	Rains
	71	Pleasant Grove H. S.	Quinlan	Hunt
	89	Waller H. S.	Waller	Waller
	104	Queen City H. S.	Queen City	Cass
	90	Mineola H. S.	Mineola	Wood
	106	Daingerfield H. S.	Daingerfield	Morris
	56	Broaddus H. S.	Broaddus	San Augustine
	90	Maud H. S.	Maud	Bowie
	62	Quinlan H. S.	Quinlan	Hunt
	66	New Caney H. S.	New Caney	Montgomery
	57	Madisonville H. S.	Madisonville	Madison
	66	Talco H. S.	Talco	Titus
	69	Central H. S.	Sumner	Lamar
	58	Honey Grove H. S.	Honey Grove	Fannin
	89	Groveton H. S.	Groveton	Trinity
	105	Emory H. S.	Emory	Rains
	25	Strong H. S.	Center	Shelby
	36	Campbell H. S.	Campbell	Hunt
subtotal	1,390			
Small Negro	66	Rhoades H. S.	Daingerfield	Morris
	35	Madisonville (Marian Anderson) H. S.	Madisonville	Madison
	43	McFarland H. S.	Mineola	Wood
	27	Albert Lee H. S.	Midway	Madison
	45	Centerville H. S.	Centerville	Leon
	53	Ralph J. Bunch H. S.	Brookshire	Waller
	95	Cheatham H. S.	Clarksville	Red River
subtotal	364			

Community	N	School	City or Town	County
Medium White	95	Henderson H. S.	Henderson	Rusk
	99	Paris H. S.	Paris	Lamar
	81	Gladewater H. S.	Gladewater	Gregg
subtotal	275			
Medium Negro	80	E. J. Campbell H. S.	Nacogdoches	Nacogdoches
subtotal	80			

Total for Region I—2,109 cases

REGION II (Coastal Texas)

Community	N	School	City or Town	County
Small White	75	Angleton J.H. & H.S.	Angleton	Brazoria
	110	Hardin H. S.	Hardin	Liberty
	101	Sugarland H. S.	Sugarland	Fort Bend
	90	Needville H. S.	Needville	Fort Bend
	91	Edna H. S.	Edna	Jackson
subtotal	467			
Small Negro	32	Herman H. S.	Van Vleck	Matagorda
	61	Charlie Brown H. S.	West Columbia	Brazoria
subtotal	93			
Medium White	83	El Campo H. S.	El Campo	Wharton
	80	Cleveland H. S.	Cleveland	Liberty
subtotal	163			
Medium Negro	114	A. W. Jackson H. S.	Rosenberg	Fort Bend
subtotal	114			
Metropolitan White (Urbanized)	115	Lovenberg J. H. & Ball H. S.	Galveston	Galveston
	99	Southmore J. H. & Pasadena H. S.	Pasadena	Harris
	100	Horace Mann J. H. & Robt. E. Lee H.S.	Baytown	Harris
	115	Luther Burbank J. H. & Milby H. S.	Houston	Harris

Community	N	School	City or Town	County
	88	Mary Brantly Smiley J. H. & H. S.	Houston	Harris
	110	Galena Park J. H. & H. S.	Galena Park	Harris
	117	Dow J. H. & John H. Reagan H. S.	Houston	Harris
	88	Amelia J. H. & South Park H. S.	Beaumont	Jefferson
	111	Woodrow Wilson J. H. & Thomas Jefferson H. S.	Port Arthur	Jefferson
	101	Wynn Seale J. H. & W. B. Ray H. S.	Corpus Christi	Nueces
subtotal	1,044			
Metropolitan	70	Central H. S.	Galveston	Galveston
Negro	200	G. W. Carver J. H. & H. S.	Houston	Harris
(Urbanized)	71	Charleton-Pollard H. S.	Beaumont	Jefferson
	65	Solomon Coles H. S.	Corpus Christi	Nueces
subtotal	406			
Metropolitan	56	Friendswood H. S.	Galveston	Galveston
White (Non-	80	Dickinson H. S.	Galveston	Galveston
Urbanized)	65	Crosby J. H. & H. S.	Crosby	Harris
	98	LaPorte H. S.	LaPorte	Harris
	68	Fannett H. S.	Beaumont	Jefferson
	61	Hampshire-New Holland H. S.	Hampshire	Jefferson
	71	Port Neches H. S.	Port Neches	Jefferson
	113	Nederland H. S.	Nederland	Jefferson
subtotal	612			
Metropolitan Negro (Non- Urbanized)	76	Lincoln H. S.	LaMarque	Galveston
subtotal	76			

Total for Region II—2,975 cases

REGION III (South Texas)

Community	N	School	City or Town	County
Small White	63	Cotulla H. S.	Cotulla	LaSalle
	51	Lytle H. S.	Lytle	Atascosa
	102	Dilley J. H. & H. S.	Dilley	Frio
subtotal	216			
Metropolitan White (Urbanized)	62	Harlingen H. S.	Harlingen	Cameron
	56	McAllen H. S.	McAllen	Hidalgo
subtotal	118			
Metropolitan White (Non-Urbanized)	33	LaFeria H. S.	LaFeria	Cameron
	64	Rio Hondo J. H. & H. S.	Rio Hondo	Cameron
	26	Edcouch-Elsa H. S.	Edcouch	Hidalgo
subtotal	123			

Total for Region III—457 cases

REGION IV (Central Texas)

Community	N	School	City or Town	County
Small White	28	Kosse H. S.	Kosse	Limestone
	115	Bremond H. S.	Bremond	Robertson
	83	Rosebud H. S.	Rosebud	Falls
	149	Llano H. S.	Llano	Llano
	78	Celina H. S.	Celina	Collin
	96	Kaufman H. S.	Kaufman	Kaufman
	83	Burnet H. S.	Burnet	Burnet
	64	Prosper H. S.	Prosper	Collin
	51	Garwood H. S.	Garwood	Colorado
	46	Sheridan H. S.	Sheridan	Colorado
	83	Troy H. S.	Troy	Bell
	79	Milano H. S.	Milano	Milam
	93	Holland H. S.	Holland	Bell
	90	Hearne H. S.	Hearne	Robertson
	121	Bowie J. H. & H. S.	Bowie	Montague
	80	Dawson H. S.	Dawson	Navarro
	53	Salado H. S.	Salado	Bell
	56	Fayetteville H. S.	Fayetteville	Fayette

Community	N	School	City or Town	County
	71	Karnes City H. S.	Karnes City	Karnes
	102	Luling H. S.	Luling	Caldwell
	68	Hubbard H. S.	Hubbard	Hill
	79	Schertz-Cibolo H.S.	Schertz	Guadalupe
	53	Wallis H. S.	Wallis	Austin
	100	Teague H. S.	Teague	Freestone
	87	Elgin J. H. & H. S.	Elgin	Bastrop
subtotal	2,008			
Small Negro	63	Elgin (Booker T. Washington) H. S.	Elgin	Bastrop
	49	Fairview H. S.	Giddings	Lee
	63	Randolph H. S.	LaGrange	Fayette
	47	Smithville H. S.	Smithville	Bastrop
subtotal	222			
Medium White	104	Denton J. H. & H. S.	Denton	Denton
	80	Brady J. H. & H. S.	Brady	McCulloch
	89	Belton J. H. & H. S.	Belton	Bell
	103	Sherman J.H. & H.S.	Sherman	Grayson
	73	Lockhart H. S.	Lockhart	Caldwell
	112	Stephenville H. S.	Stephenville	Erath
	91	Yoakum J.H. & H.S.	Yoakum	DeWitt
subtotal	652			
Medium Negro	68	Lincoln H. S.	College Station	Brazos
subtotal	68			
Metropolitan White (Urbanized)	106	Alamo Heights H. S.	San Antonio	Bexar
	192	Edison J. H. & San Antonio Tech H.S.	San Antonio	Bexar
	126	Burbank J. H. & G. W. Brackenridge H. S.	San Antonio	Bexar
	99	Harlandale H. S.	San Antonio	Bexar
	217	Edgewood H. S.	San Antonio	Bexar
	102	Alex W. Spence J. H. & Sunset H. S.	Dallas	Dallas

Community	N	School	City or Town	County
	109	J. L. Long J. H. & Woodrow Wilson H. S.	Dallas	Dallas
	100	Thos. J. Rusk J. H. & Forest Ave. H. S.	Dallas	Dallas
	78	University H. S.	Waco	McLennan
	67	Fulmore J. H. & Stephen F. Austin H. S.	Austin	Travis
	55	Zundelowitz J. H. & Wichita H. S.	Wichita Falls	Wichita
subtotal	1,251			
Metropolitan Negro (Urbanized)	64	Booker T. Washington H. S.	Dallas	Dallas
	94	O. J. Moore J. H. & H. S.	Waco	McLennan
	48	Anderson H. S.	Austin	Travis
	65	Booker T. Washington H. S.	Wichita Falls	Wichita
subtotal	271			
Metropolitan White (Non-Urbanized)	107	Richardson H. S.	Richardson	Dallas
	80	Seagoville H. S.	Seagoville	Dallas
	78	McGregor H. S.	McGregor	McLennan
	104	Moody H. S.	Moody	McLennan
	79	Midway H. S.	Waco (Rt. 8)	McLennan
	60	Euless H. S.	Hurst	Tarrant
	92	Birdville J. H. & H. S.	Fort Worth	Tarrant
	67	Pflugerville H. S.	Pflugerville	Travis
subtotal	667			

Total for Region IV—5,139 cases

REGION V (West Texas)

Community	N	School	City or Town	County
Small White	54	New Home H. S.	Tahoka	Lynn
	93	Fort Stockton H. S.	Fort Stockton	Pecos
	44	Blackwell H. S.	Blackwell	Nolan
	86	Matador J. H. & H. S.	Matador	Motley
	82	Samnorwood J. H. & H. S.	Samnorwood	Collingsworth
	44	Roaring Springs H. S.	Roaring Springs	Motley
	55	Cotton Center H. S.	Cotton Center	Hale
	86	Shamrock J. H. & H. S.	Shamrock	Wheeler
	52	Center Point H. S.	Center Point	Kerr
	64	Tahoka H. S.	Tahoka	Lynn
	79	Rankin H. S.	Rankin	Upton
	83	Rule H. S.	Rule	Haskell
	78	Lockney H. S.	Lockney	Floyd
	118	Sudan H. S.	Sudan	Lamb
	79	Plains H. S.	Plains	Yoakum
	21	Millersview H. S.	Millersview	Concho
subtotal	1,118			
Small Negro	11	Dunbar J. H. & H. S.	Shamrock	Wheeler
subtotal	11			
Medium White	90	Pampa J. H. & H. S.	Pampa	Grey
	100	Dumas J. H. & H. S.	Dumas	Moore
	93	Dalhart J. H. & H. S.	Dalhart	Dallam
	76	Sweetwater J. H. & H. S.	Sweetwater	Nolan
subtotal	359			
Metropolitan White (Urbanized)	104	El Paso H. S.	El Paso	El Paso
	102	Monterey H. S.	Lubbock	Lubbock
	24	R. W. Matthews J. H.	Lubbock	Lubbock
	94	Stephen F. Austin J.H. & Amarillo H.S.	Amarillo	Potter
	98	Lakeview H. S.	San Angelo	Tom Green
subtotal	422			

Community	N	School	City or Town	County
Metropolitan	76	Dunbar J. H. & H. S.	Lubbock	Lubbock
Negro	66	Carver H. S.	Amarillo	Potter
(Urbanized)				
subtotal	142			
Metropolitan	79	Slaton H. S.	Slaton	Lubbock
White (Non-	62	Idalou H. S.	Idalou	Lubbock
Urbanized)	19	Christoval H. S.	Christoval	Tom Green
subtotal	160			

Total for Region V—2,212 cases

Grand Total—12,892 cases

Small White

	Region I	1,390
	Region II	467
	Region III	216
	Region IV	2,008
	Region V	1,118
subtotal		5,199 cases

Small Negro

	Region I	364
	Region II	93
	Region IV	222
	Region V	11
subtotal		690 cases

Medium White

	Region I	275
	Region II	163
	Region IV	652
	Region V	359
subtotal		1,449 cases

Medium Negro

	Region I	80
	Region II	114
	Region IV	68
subtotal		262 cases

Metropolitan White (Urbanized)	Region II	1,044
	Region III	118
	Region IV	1,251
	Region V	422
subtotal		2,835 cases
Metropolitan Negro (Urbanized)	Region II	406
	Region IV	271
	Region V	142
subtotal		819 cases
Metropolitan White (Non-Urbanized)	Region II	612
	Region III	123
	Region IV	667
	Region V	160
subtotal		1,562 cases
Metropolitan Negro (Non-Urbanized)	Region II	76
subtotal		76 cases
grand total		12,892 cases

APPENDIX D

SUGGESTIONS FOR USE OF RESEARCH INSTRUMENTS

WITH HIGH SCHOOL YOUTH

TEXAS COOPERATIVE YOUTH STUDY

I. Explanation of the study for use with high school youth

(The explanation below is entirely suggestive. You should
say this in your own way, informally, and with whatever
variations occur to you. These are only reminders of what
points seem to warrant coverage in your introduction of the
Texas Cooperative Youth Study to high school participants.)

The Texas Cooperative Youth Study, which is being participated in by some
10,000 high school students in the state, is asking you to help us in learning
more about the needs, interests, and problems of young people in their personal
and family living.

Colleges and universities are cooperating in Texas through their Departments
of Home Economics. Others working on the study include the Home and Family Life
Education Division, Texas Education Agency and the Hogg Foundation for Mental
Hygiene, The University of Texas. We are from _____
                                              (Name of your own college)

This is not a test in any way. It is a set of forms designed to help you
tell us something of your attitudes, your problems and your interests in your
own and in your family living. Your answers, added to those of some 9,999 others,
will make it possible to plan your high school courses so that you may gain more
from them and to improve what your school offers in home and family education.
At the same time, we hope you will learn something of yourselves as you work out
your answers.

Your individual answers to the statements in these forms will never be revealed.
Your answer sheets, along with all the others in the state, will be processed by
an International Business Machine -- a sort of simplified mechanical brain -- after
they are sent to the college I represent. Your answers will appear only as a number among many other numbers. Final analysis of your answers will be made at The
University of Texas.

Your school will be given credit for the help you are giving. You will be
making a contribution to all other youth of your state by your efforts today and
to youth throughout the nation. We deeply appreciate your cooperation and your
thoughtful and honest answers.

Within two years, even if you are out of school, you may come back to your
high school and see the results of the work you and the students in approximately
144 other Texas communities are doing this spring.

Before you begin, we, of the Texas Cooperative Youth Study, want to thank you
sincerely for your careful effort and for the time you are giving this important
study.

II. Suggestions for administration of instruments

The research instruments of the Texas Cooperative Youth Study have already been filled in by over 2000 youth and adults in a series of test runs. From these experiences, several suggestions have come which will be of value to those administering the instruments in the study centers throughout the state.

1. Size of groups

Groups used in pre-testing the research instruments ranged from assemblies of two hundred youth to a classroom of twenty students. The maximum size for most satisfactory results would seem not to exceed seventy-five. If, however, a larger group is all that is available because of local school requirements, sufficient assistants should be used to answer queries from the youth.

2. Number of aides

One aide to every twenty youth has proven advisable when students are filling out the instruments of the Texas Cooperative Youth Study. Aides may be senior or graduate students from the college accompanying the college faculty member in charge of data collection. They may be the homemaking teacher, the high school counselor, and other teachers on the high school faculty. If the homemaking teacher is administering the instruments, she may use either other teachers or senior homemaking students who have been previously trained.

3. Forms to be administered

Each student in the study center who is participating in the research will work with the following forms:

  a. Student Information Sheet

  b. Attitudes Toward Personal and Family Living, CYS-Part I, answered on the front side of a double-faced IBM Answer Sheet

  c. Concerns and Problems in Personal and Family Living, CYS-Part II, answered on the reverse side of the double-faced IBM-Answer Sheet -- the front side having been used for CYS-Part I

  d. Interests in Personal and Family Living, CYS-Part III A, answered on the single-faced IBM Answer Sheet

4. I.B.M. pencils

The Student Information Sheet is the only instrument which does not require an I.B.M. (electrographic) pencil for answer.

I.B.M. pencils must be used on the front and back side of the double-faced I.B.M. Answer Sheet which accompanies CYS-Part I and CYS-Part II.

I.B.M. pencils must be used on the single faced I.B.M. Answer Sheet which accompanies CYS-Part III A.

ANSWER SHEETS CANNOT BE PROCESSED WHICH HAVE NOT BEEN FILLED IN
WITH I. B. M. PENCILS!!!

5. Supplies for each study center

   a. Enough copies of the <u>Student Information</u> Sheet, CYS-Part I,
      CYS-Part II, and the accompanying double-faced I.B.M. Answer
      Sheet; CYS-Part III A and the accompanying single-faced I. B.M.
      Answer Sheet; and an I. B. M. pencil for each participant, with
      each participant also furnished a paper clip to clip his Answer
      Sheets and Information Sheet together before turning them in.

   b. The <u>Student Information</u> Sheet and corresponding I. B. M. Answer
      Sheets (CYS-Parts I and II, and CYS-Part III A) for each student
      should be clipped together by the student or administrator when
      finished. These will be returned to the college from which they
      have come, to be processed or to be shipped to the Collating
      Center, Department of Home Economics, The University of Texas,
      Austin, 12, Texas.

   c. Printed instruments, <u>Attitudes Toward Personal and Family Living,</u>
      CYS-Part I; <u>Concerns and Problems in Personal and Family Living,</u>
      CYS-Part II; and <u>Interests in Personal and Family Living</u>, CYS-Part
      III A, will be collected after each use so that they can be re-used
      at the next study center. Each new center will need new <u>Student
      Information Sheets,</u> and new I. B. M. Answer Sheets -- one double
      and one single faced -- for each student participating.

   d. I.B.M. Pencils will be carefully collected at the close of each
      work session with youth and will be used over again at each new
      study center. Since these I.B.M. pencils are relatively expensive,
      aides should be sure of their return at the end of each session.

6. Familiarity with forms

   A training session is necessary with the person designated by the college
   or university as administrator of the research instruments at the study
   centers and with those who will assist her as aides. Each person working
   with the high school youth participating in the study should be familiar
   with each instrument, its content, and with possible questions which may
   be asked by students. Each should have practice in filling in the I.B.M.
   Answer Sheets in order to be of assistance to youth.

   <u>A word of caution is necessary.</u> No set of instruments can be included
   in the analysis of the study data unless each instrument of the set has
   been completely answered. Youth should be reminded:

   a. <u>Incomplete instruments are of no value at all to the study and will
      have to be discarded.</u>

   b. Students' complete names must be placed on:

      (1) The Student Information Sheet

      (2) The front side of the double-faced I.B.M. Answer Sheet

      (3) The front side of the single-faced I.B.M. Answer Sheet

Names will be used for matching purposes only. This is necessary to be able to clip together at the end of the sessions <u>all three</u> sheets from each student for shipment to the college or university.

Please ASSURE all students who are participants in this study that <u>no single set of instruments from any one youth will be analyzed,</u> but that <u>all instruments from each youth must be kept together</u> until a number has been assigned at the Collating Center at The University of Texas or at the college. Moreover, <u>no examination or use of any of these instruments will be made by the faculty of the local school.</u> They will be analyzed together with thousands of others by the use of the I.B.M. Machines at the colleges or university.

7. Time arrangement with the local school for administering the instruments

Three different time arrangements have been used in the pre-testing of the research instruments and are suggestive for consideration:

a. One session of not less than two hours with possibility for a little more time for slower workers

b. Two sessions of one hour each on successive days if class periods are of one hour duration with extra time possible for slower workers. Classes chosen for use should be those guaranteeing a good cross-section of high school youth, boys and girls, on each grade level -- 9th, 10th, 11th, and 12th. English classes have been used successfully. Home room periods are a possibility if the Home Room meets the requirement for a cross-section of youth and is arranged by grade levels.

c. Three forty-five minute sessions if the class periods of the school are of forty-five minute duration. Again, classes chosen should be representative as to sexes, as to abilities, and as to grade levels.

8. Suggested time schedule by length of periods available

<u>One Session</u>

When one session of two hours is utilized, the time plan would run:

a. A brief explanation of the study

b. A brief period for distribution of the battery of instruments: the Student Information Sheet; CYS-Part I and CYS-Part II with the double-faced I.B.M. Answer Sheet; CYS-Part III A with the single-faced I.B.M. Answer Sheet; and the I.B.M. pencil. A quick check should be made to see that each youth has a full battery of instruments, the two Answer Sheets, and the I.B.M. pencil.

c. The youth should then be requested to fill out the <u>Student Information Sheet.</u> When he has finished, he should be requested to fill in his name, grade, etc., on the front of each of the I.B.M. Answer Sheets, and to await further instructions before he begins work on CYS-Part I.

d. The administrator of the instruments should read aloud the instructions on the face of CYS-Part I; remind the youth to enter his name, school, grade, etc., on the I.B.M. Answer Sheets, and to use the front side of the double-faced I.B.M. Answer Sheet, Number 1 - 101, to record reactions to statements

from Number 1 - 101 in CYS-Part I, <u>Attitudes</u> <u>Toward</u> <u>Personal</u> <u>and</u> <u>Family</u> <u>Living.</u>
They should be requested to await further instructions when they finish.

e. When all but the exceptionally slow students have completed CYS-Part I, the
    administrator should read the instructions aloud on the face of CYS-Part II,
    remind the youth to turn over their double-faced I.B.M. Answer Sheets, and
    record their answers beginning with Number 151 and filling in proper columns
    through Number 240 -- these numbers correspond to the numbers of statements on
    CYS-Part II, <u>Concerns</u> <u>and</u> <u>Problems</u> <u>in</u> <u>Personal</u> <u>and</u> <u>Family</u> <u>Living.</u>

f. Since CYS-Part III A is a simpler form, youth may be advised to read carefully
    the instructions on the face of the instrument, fill in their names, grades,
    etc., on the I.B.M. Answer Sheet, and record answers on the single-faced I.B.M.
    Answer Sheet, from Number 1 - 98, corresponding to the numbers on the state-
    ments in CYS-Part III A, <u>Interests</u> <u>in</u> <u>Personal</u> <u>and</u> <u>Family</u> <u>Living.</u>

g. When finished, each student should be asked to clip together his own <u>Student</u>
    <u>Information</u> <u>Sheet</u> and the two I.B.M. Answer Sheets, making sure his name is on
    all three. All materials, including the I.B.M. pencil, should be turned in at
    a designated place. When they have finished, students should be allowed to
    leave the room in any way suggested by the high school principal.

h. When all are through, the administrator and her aides should check clipped
    Student Information Sheet, and two I.B.M. Answer Sheets, to see that the full
    set for each student is accounted for, These should be boxed separately from
    the research instruments, themselves, for return to the college or to the
    Collating Center at The University of Texas.

Two Sessions

When two sessions of one hour each are utilized, the time plan would run:

<u>Period 1:</u>

a. A brief explanation of the study

b. A brief period for distribution of the Student Information Sheet and CYS-Part
    III A, with the single-faced I.B.M. Answer Sheet, and the I.B.M. pencil.

c. The youth should then be requested to fill out the <u>Student</u> <u>Information</u> <u>Sheet.</u>
    When he has finished, he should be requested to fill in his name, school,
    grade, etc., on his I.B.M. Answer Sheet, waiting for further instructions.

d. The administrator of the instruments should read aloud the instructions on the
    face of CYS-Part III A; remind the youth to enter his name, school, grade, etc.,
    on the I.B.M. Answer Sheet; and to record answers on the I.B.M. Answer Sheet
    from Number 1 - 98, corresponding to the numbers on the statements in CYS-Part
    III A, <u>Interests</u> <u>in</u> <u>Personal</u> <u>and</u> <u>Family</u> <u>Living.</u>

e. Students should be asked to clip together their <u>Student</u> <u>Information</u> <u>Sheet</u> and
    their accompanying I.B.M. Answer Sheet; and to return these with the printed
    CYS-Part III A and the I.B.M. pencil to the administrator.

Period 2:

a. A brief reminder of the appreciation of everyone for the work being done to
   make the youth study successful

b. A brief period for distribution of the instruments, CYS-Part I, CYS-Part II,
   the double-faced I.B.M. Answer Sheet, and the I.B.M. pencil.

c. The youth should be requested to fill in his name, school, grade, etc., on the
   front side of the double-faced I.B.M. Answer Sheet and to await further instructions.

d. The administrator of the instruments should then read aloud the instructions
   on the face of CYS-Part I; remind the youth to enter his name, school, grade,
   etc., at the top of the front side of the double-faced I.B.M. Answer Sheet;
   and to record his reactions to statements from No. 1 - 101 in CYS-Part I,
   Attitudes Toward Personal and Family Living, in the proper columns by the corresponding numbers 1 through 101 on the front of the double-faced I.B.M. Answer
   Sheet.

e. When he has finished, he should read carefully the instructions on the face of
   CYS-Part II, Concerns and Problems in Personal and Family Living. He should be
   encouraged to ask assistance from the aides if he does not completely understand the instructions. He should then proceed immediately to record his reactions to the statements (Numbers 151 through 240) in the proper columns by
   the corresponding numbers on the reverse side of his double-faced I.B.M.
   Answer Sheet.

f. Students should be asked to check their I.B.M. Answer Sheet to see if their
   name, school, grade, etc., is properly entered; if each statement has been
   answered.

g. Students should be asked to return their completed I.B.M. Answer Sheet, the
   printed forms CYS-Part I and CYS-Part II, and the I.B.M. pencil to a designated
   place. After completing the instruments, students should be allowed to leave
   the room in any way designated by the high school principal.

h. The administrator and her aides should match and clip together the Student
   Information Sheet, the double-faced I.B.M. Answer Sheet, and the single-faced
   I.B.M. Answer Sheet for each youth. These sets should then be boxed to return
   to the college or to the Central Collating Center at The University of Texas.
   The printed forms and the I.B.M. pencils should be retained for use at the
   next study center.

Three Sessions

When three sessions of forty-five minutes each are utilized, the time plan would
run:

Period 1:

a. A brief explanation of the study

b. A brief period for distribution of the Student Information Sheet and CYS-Part
   III A, with the single-faced I.B.M. Answer Sheet, and the I.B.M. pencil.

   c. The youth should be requested to fill out the <u>Student Information Sheet.</u> When he has finished, he should be asked to fill in his name, school, grade, etc., on the I.B.M. Answer Sheet and await further instructions.

   d. The administrator of the instruments should read aloud the instructions on the face of CYS-Part III A; remind the youth to enter his name, school, grade, etc., on the I.B.M. Answer Sheet. He should then proceed to record answers on the I.B.M. Answer Sheet from Number 1 - 98, corresponding to the numbers on the statements in CYS-Part III A, <u>Interests in Personal and Family Living.</u>

   e. Each student should be asked to clip his <u>Student Information Sheet</u> and his accompanying I.B.M. Answer Sheet together; and to return these with the printed instrument, CYS-Part III A, and the I.B.M. pencil at the place designated by the administrator.

<u>Period II</u>

   a. A brief reminder of the appreciation of everyone for the work being done to make the youth study successful

   b. A brief period for distribution of the instrument, CYS-Part I, <u>Attitudes Toward Personal and Family Living</u>, the double-faced I.B.M. Answer Sheet, and the I.B.M. pencil.

   c. The youth should be requested to fill in his name, school, grade, etc., on the front side of the double-faced I.B.M. Answer Sheet and to await further instructions.

   d. The administrator of the instruments should then read aloud the instructions on the face of CYS-Part I; remind the youth to enter his name, school, grade, etc., on the front side of the double-faced I.B.M. Answer Sheet; then he should record his reactions to statements from No. 1 - 101 in CYS-Part I, <u>Attitudes Toward Personal and Family Living</u>, in the proper columns by the corresponding numbers 1 - 101 on the front of the double-faced I.B.M. Answer Sheet.

   e. Students should be asked to return their completed I.B.M. Answer Sheet, their printed instruments, CYS-Part I, and their I.B.M. pencils.

<u>Period III</u>

   a. A brief reminder of the appreciation of everyone for the work being done to make the youth study successful

   b. A brief period for distribution of CYS-Part II, <u>Concerns and Problems in Personal and Family Living</u> , and the <u>proper</u> double-faced <u>I.B.M. Answer Sheet</u> of each youth who had filled in answers on the face for CYS-Part I the day before.

   c. The administrator should then read aloud the instructions on the face of CYS-Part II, <u>Concerns and Problems in Personal and Family Living</u>, and ask the youth to check to be sure he has his <u>own</u> double-faced I.B.M. Answer Sheet. He should begin immediately to record his reactions to the statements, Numbers 151 - 240, in the proper columns by the corresponding numbers on the <u>reverse</u> side of his double-faced I.B.M. Answer Sheet.

d. Students should be asked to return their completed I.B.M. Answer Sheet, the printed form CYS-Part II, and the I.B.M. pencil to a designated place.

e. Following this final session, the administrator and her aides should match and clip together, the Student Information Sheet, the double-faced I.B.M. Answer Sheet, and the single-faced I.B.M. Answer Sheet for each youth who has participated in the study. These should be boxed for return to the college or for shipment to the Collating Center at The University of Texas.

g. The printed forms and the I.B.M. pencils can be used at the next study center of the college.

III. Disposition of finished instruments

1. A number of colleges and universities may undertake preliminary processing of instruments gathered in their centers. Where this is true, completed Student Information Sheets, with their accompanying I.B.M. Answer Sheets, will go direct to the college or university. Special instructions will be furnished by the Collating Center at The University of Texas to assure uniformity in processing.

2. Where colleges or universities are not in a position to complete preliminary processing, the Student Information Sheets and accompanying I.B.M. Answer Sheets will be shipped immediately to the Collating Center as soon as they are completed for each school in the sample for which the college has assumed responsibility.

Shipment should be by American Railway Express to:

> Collating Center
> Texas Cooperative Youth Study
> Department of Home Economics
> The University of Texas
> Austin, 12, Texas

APPENDIX E: CODING SHEET AND KEY FOR DATA ANALYSIS BY COMPUTING MACHINES

Texas Cooperative Youth Study: 1956

Coding Sheet A

IBM Col.	Variable	Code	IBM Col.	Variable	Code
1	Geog. Area		43	School Bus	
2	Community Type		44	I, 1 Orientation	
3, 4	School		45	I, 2 Discipline	
5	School Type		46	I, 3 Crit. Education	
6	School Size		47	I, 4 Crit. Youth	
7, 8, 9	Subject Ident.		48	I, 5 Family	
10	School Grade		49	I, 6 Self	
11	Sex		50	II, 1 Tensions	
12	Race		51	II, 2 Personal	
13	Age		52	II, 3 Social	
14	Guessed Height		53	II, 4 Life-Style	
15	Guessed Weight		54	II, 5 Conformity	
16	Community Size		55	II, 6 Isolation	
17	Residence		56	II, 7 Financial	
18	Birthplace		57	II, 8 Dependency	
19	Own Marital Status		58	CYS I, Item 12	
20	Homemaking		59	CYS I, Item 16	
21	Parents' Marital Status		60	CYS I, Item 21	
22	Older Brothers		61	CYS I, Item 29	
23	Older Sisters		62	CYS I, Item 30	
24	Younger Brothers		63	CYS I, Item 33	
25	Younger Sisters		64	CYS I, Item 47	
26	Total Siblings		65	CYS I, Item 53	
27	Parents		66	CYS I, Item 58	
28	Grand Parents		67	CYS I, Item 62	
29	Family Structure		68	CYS I, Item 72	
30	Household Membership		69	CYS I, Item 85	
31	Total in Home		70	CYS I, Item 100	
32	Father's Education		71	CYS II, Item 168	
33	Mother's Education		72	CYS II, Item 192	
34	Father's Occupation		73		
35	Mother's Occupation		74		
36	Work at Home		75		
37	Work on Job		76		
38	Support Family		77		
39	Rooms in House		78		
40	Sleeping Quarters		79		
41	Family Car		80		
42	Religion				

Texas Cooperative Youth Study: 1956 (Revised July)
Coding Key for IBM Card A (Coding Sheet A) and for IBM Cards B and C
IBM Card A (Red)   IBM Card B (White)   IBM Card C (Blue)

Coding Key for Coding Sheet A (Red IBM Card)

IBM Col.

1   Geographical Areas (See Table 1)   Card Code:

Code	Variable	*In Column 1*
1	I	R = Card A (Red)
2	II	X = Card B (White)
3	III	O = Card C (Blue)
4	IV	
5	V	

2   Community Type

Code	Variable
0	Small
1	Medium
2	Urban: Galveston, Cameron, Bexar, El Paso
3	Urban: Harris, Hidalgo, Dallas, Lubbock
4	Urban: Jefferson, Webb, McLennan, Potter
5	Urban: Nueces, Tarrant, Tom Green
6	Urban: Travis
7	Urban: Wichita
8	All Non-Urbanized Metropolitan

3, 4   School Identification Number

Code

01–26   (See Supplement)
70–up   for schools not in sample

5   Type of School

Code	Variable
0	White
1	Negro
2	Integrated

6   Size of School (Enrollment)

Code	Variable	Code	Variable
0	1– 50	5	401– 500
1	51–100	6	501– 700
2	101–200	7	701–1,000
3	201–300	8	1,001–1,500
4	301–400	9	over 1,500

7, 8, 9   Identification Number for Student 001–99

Code last three digits of number stamped on IBM answer sheet.

IBM Col.

10   *School Grade*

Code	Variable	Code	Variable
0	9th	3	12th
1	10th	X	Unknown
2	11th		

11   *Sex*

Code	Variable
0	Male
1	Female
X	Unknown

12   *Race*

Code	Variable	Code	Variable
0	White	2	Other
1	Negro	X	Unknown

13   *Age* (In years)

Code	Variable	Code	Variable
0	13 and under	5	18
1	14	6	19
2	15	7	20
3	16	8	21
4	17	X	Unknown

14   *Guessed Height* (In inches)

Code	Variable	Code	Variable
0	Less than 56	6	66–67
1	56–57	7	68–69
2	58–59	8	70–71
3	60–61	9	72–73
4	62–63	R	74 and greater
5	64–65	X	Unknown

15   *Guessed Weight* (In lbs.)

Code	Variable	Code	Variable
0	Less than 70	6	145–159
1	70– 84	7	160–174
2	85– 99	8	175–189
3	100–114	9	190–204
4	115–129	R	205 and greater
5	130–144	X	Unknown

16   *Size of Community* (1950 U. S. Census)
    (The school is in)

Code	Variable
0	Less than 1,000 population
1	1,000– 2,500

IBM Col.

2	2,501– 5,000
3	5,001– 10,000
4	10,001– 25,000
5	25,001– 50,000
6	50,001–100,000
7	over 100,000

17 *Where Student Lives* (Residence)

Code	*Variable*
0	In country
1	In town
X	Unknown

18 *Place of Birth* (See Table 1)

Code	*Variable*
0	Same county as present residence
1–5	For Texas Areas I–V (See Table 1)
6	Southern U. S. (La., Miss., Ala., Ga., Fla., S. C., N. C., Va., Ky., Tenn., Ark.)
7	Northeastern U. S. (Me., Vt., N. H., Mass., R. I., Conn., N. Y., Pa., Md., N. J., Del., W. Va.)
8	Midwestern U. S. (Ohio, Ind., Ill., Mich., Wisc., Minn., Ia., Mo., Okla., Kan., Neb., S. D., N. D.)
9	Western U. S. (N. M., Ariz., Colo., Utah, Wyo., Mont., Idaho, Wash., Ore., Calif., Nev.)
X	Unknown
R	Foreign

19 *Are you married?*

Code	*Variable*
0	No
1	Yes
X	Unknown

20 *Homemaking Courses*

Code	*Variable*
0	None
1	7th and 8th
2	Hm. I
3	Hm. II
4	Hm. III
5	Hm. IV
6	Home and Family Life
X	Unknown

IBM Col.

21   *Status of Parents, i.e.,* True Parents

      Code   *Variable*

       0   Parents living together

       1   Parents separated

       2   Parents divorced

       3   Mother not living

       4   Father not living

       5   Both not living

       X   Unknown

22   *Number of Older Brothers*

      Code   *Variable*

       0–9   Enter actual number using 9 to indicate 9 or more.

       X   Unknown

23   *Number of Older Sisters*

      Code   *Variable*

       0–9   Enter actual number using 9 to indicate 9 or more.

       X   Unknown

24   *Number of Younger Brothers*

      Code   *Variable*

       0–9   Enter actual number using 9 to indicate 9 or more.

       X   Unknown

25   *Number of Younger Sisters*

      Code   *Variable*

       0–9   Enter actual number using 9 to indicate 9 or more.

       X   Unknown

26   *Total Number of Siblings* (Include half and step children)

      Code   *Variable*

       0–9   Enter actual number using 9 to indicate 9 or more.

       X   Unknown

27   *Parents Living in House*

      Code   *Variable*

       0   Mother and Father

       1   Mother only

       2   Father only

       3   Stepmother and Stepfather

       4   Stepmother only

       5   Stepfather only

       6   Mother and Stepfather

       7   Father and Stepmother

       8   No parents or stepparents; living with guardians; living with spouse.

IBM Col.

	9	Orphanage or similar institution
	X	Unknown

28 *Grandparents Living in House*

Code	Variable
0	One Grandfather
1	One Grandmother
2	One of each
3	Two Grandfathers
4	Two Grandmothers
5	One Grandfather, two Grandmothers
6	Two Grandfathers, one Grandmother
7	Two of each
8	No Grandparents
X	Unknown

29 *Family Structure, i.e.,* step and/or half brothers or sisters, from the student's point of view.

Code	Variable
0	Biological parents and children, *i.e.,* no step or half children.
1	Family includes one or more step, but no half brothers or half sisters.
2	Family includes one or more half brothers or half sisters, but no stepbrothers or sisters.
3	Family includes one or more half brothers or half sisters, and one or more stepbrothers or sisters.
4	None of the above; orphanage; living with grandparents or some other person.
X	Unknown

30 *Household Membership*

Code	Variable
0	No roomers or relatives other than immediate family and grandparents.
1	One or more relatives other than grandparents.
2	One or more roomers unrelated to family.
3	One or more relatives other than grandparents, and one or more roomers unrelated to family.
X	Unknown

IBM Col.

31 *Total Number Living in House*

    Code   *Variable*

    1–9   Include sum total of all checked on face sheet plus one additional for respondent, enter actual number, using 9 to indicate 9 or more.

    X   Unknown

32 *Father's Education*

    Code   *Variable*

    0   No school

    1   Grades 1–4

    2   Grades 5–8

    3   Grades 9–11

    4   Completed high school

    5   Had some college

    6   Junior College graduate

    7   4-year College graduate

    R   Business College, County Veterans' School, other (the R code may be used in addition to any code from 0 through 7)

    X   Unknown

33 *Mother's Education*

    Codes 0–7, R, X, —same as for father's education

34 *Father's Occupation*

Code	*Variable*	
0	Farm Laborers	All non-owning, non-renting farm workers (except men who work on their own fathers' farms).
1	Unskilled Manual Workers	Garage laborers, sweepers, porters, janitors, street cleaners, construction laborers.
2	Farm Tenants	All farm tenants and sharecroppers.
3	Semi-Skilled Manual Workers	Truck drivers, machine operators, service station attendants, waiters, countermen.
4	Skilled Manual Workers	Carpenters, machinists, plumbers, masons, printers, barbers, cooks, include foreman.
5	Farm Owners and Managers	Any person who owns or manages a farm, ranch, grove.
6	White Collar	Clerks and kindred workers, salesmen, agents, semi-professional workers, technicians.

IBM Col.

	7	Small Business	Small retail dealers, contractors, proprietors of repair shops employing others; includes both owners and managers.
	8	Professional	Physicians, dentists, professors, teachers, ministers, engineers, lawyers.
	9	Large Business	Bankers, manufacturers, large department store owners, and managers, large farm and ranch owners.
	X	Unknown	
	R	Unemployed	

35 *Mother's Occupation*
    Codes 0–9 (Same as for father's occupation)
        R—Housewife

36 *Student's Work After School at Home*

	Code	Variable
	0	No (If yes, number of hours per week)
	1	1– 5 hours, or if no time indicated
	2	6–10 hours
	3	11–15 hours
	4	16–20 hours
	5	21–25 hours
	6	26–30 hours
	7	31–35 hours
	8	36–40 hours
	9	More than 40 hours
	X	Unknown

37 *Student's Work After School, Outside of the Home*

	Code	Variable
	0	No (If yes, number of hours per week. Use same scale as above)

38 *Do you help support the family with money you earn part-time?*

	Code	Variable
	0	Yes
	1	No
	X	Unknown

39 *How many rooms in your home?*

	Code	Variable
	1–9	Enter actual number of rooms (including bath) from face sheet, using 9 to indicate 9 or more rooms.
	X	Unknown

IBM Col.

40 *Do other persons share your bedroom?*

Code	Variable
0	No
1–9	If yes, enter actual number, not including respondent, using 9 to indicate 9 or more.
X	Unknown

41 *Does your family own a car?   Are you allowed to drive the car?*

Code	Variables	
0	Yes	Yes
1	Yes	No
2	No	No
3	No	Yes
4	Unknown	Yes
5	Unknown	No
6	Yes	Unknown
7	No	Unknown
X	Unknown	Unknown

42 *Religious Denomination*

Code	Variable
0	No preference stated
1	Baptist
2	Methodist
3	Presbyterian
4	Catholic
5	Episcopalian
6	Jewish
7	Christian (Disciples)
8	Lutheran
R	Other
X	Unknown

43 *Do you ride a school bus?   How long does it take to get to school?*

Code	Variable
0	1– 9 minutes
1	10– 19 minutes
2	20– 29 minutes
3	30– 39 minutes
4	40– 49 minutes
5	50– 59 minutes
6	60– 89 minutes
7	90–119 minutes
8	120–149 minutes

IBM Col.

9	150 minutes up	
X	Unknown	
R	Yes, to "Do you ride the school bus?" (The R code may be used in addition to any code from 0 through 9).	

44 *CYS I, Scale 1, Orientation to Society*

Code	Raw Score	Code	Raw Score
1	0–2	5	8
2	3–4	6	9–10
3	5	7	11–12
4	6–7	8	13–14
		9	15 and greater

45 *CYS I, Scale 2, Authoritarian Discipline*

Code	Raw Score	Code	Raw Score
1	0–1	5	7– 8
2	2–3	6	9
3	4	7	10
4	5–6	8	11–12
		9	13 and greater

46 *CYS I, Scale 3, Criticism of Education*

Code	Raw Score	Code	Raw Score
1	0–5	5	14–15
2	6–9	6	16–17
3	10–11	7	18
4	12–13	8	19
		9	20 and greater

47 *CYS I, Scale 4, Criticism of Youth*

Code	Raw Score	Code	Raw Score
1	0–1	5	5– 6
2	2	6	7
3	3	7	8– 9
4	4	8	10–11
		9	12 and greater

48 *CYS I, Scale 5, Family Problems*

Code	Raw Score	Code	Raw Score
1	0	5	4
2	1	6	5
3	2	7	6–7
4	3	8	8–9
		9	10 and greater

IBM Col.

49 *CYS I, Scale 6, Self Inadequacy*

Code	Raw Score	Code	Raw Score
1	0–2	5	8– 9
2	3–4	6	10
3	5–6	7	11–12
4	7	8	13–14
		9	15 and greater

50 *CYS II, Scale 1, Family Tensions*

Code	Raw Score	Code	Raw Score
1	0	5	7– 9
2	1	6	10–13
3	2–3	7	14–18
4	4–6	8	19–27
		9	28 and greater

51 *CYS II, Scale 2, Personal Adjustment*

Code	Raw Score	Code	Raw Score
1	0– 3	5	13–17
2	4– 6	6	18–21
3	7– 9	7	22–26
4	10–12	8	27–34
		9	35 and greater

52 *CYS II, Scale 3, Social Inadequacy*

Code	Raw Score	Code	Raw Score
2	0	6	7– 9
3	1	7	10–13
4	2–3	8	14–18
5	4–6	9	19 and greater

53 *CYS II, Scale 4, Resentment of Family Life Style*

Code	Raw Score	Code	Raw Score
1	0	5	4– 5
2	1	6	6– 7
3	2	7	8– 9
4	3	8	10–13
		9	14 and greater

54 *CYS II, Scale 5, Social Conformity*

Code	Raw Score	Code	Raw Score
3	0	6	4
4	1	7	5– 7
5	2–3	8	8–11
		9	12 and greater

IBM Col.

55   CYS II, Scale 6, Social Isolation

Code	Raw Score	Code	Raw Score
4	0	7	4– 6
5	1–2	8	7–11
6	3	9	12 and greater

56   CYS II, Scale 7, Financial Troubles

Code	Raw Score	Code	Raw Score
3	0	6	5– 7
4	1–2	7	8–10
5	3–4	8	11–13
		9	14 and greater

57   CYS II, Scale 8, Resentment of Dependency

Code	Raw Score	Code	Raw Score
3	0	6	5– 7
4	1–2	7	8–11
5	3–4	8	12–16
		9	17 and greater

58–72 From CYS I, items 12, 16, 21, 29, 30, 33, 47, 53, 58, 62, 72, 85, 100, and from CYS II, items 168 and 192 are coded in columns 58 through 72, respectively.

Code	Variable
1	If the space under 1 is blackened
2	If the space under 2 is blackened
3	If the space under 3 is blackened
4	If the space under 4 is blackened
5	If the space under 5 is blackened

73–80 These 8 columns are blank.

Coding Key for Coding Card B (White IBM Card)

IBM Col.

1–13 Copy onto the single faced IBM answer sheet the code in columns 1–13 from coding sheet A.

14–20 These 7 columns are blank.

21–80 CYS III, Items (Statements) 1–60 consecutively.

Code	Variable
1	If the space under 1 is blackened
2	If the space under 2 is blackened
3	If the space under 3 is blackened
4	If the space under 4 is blackened
5	If the space under 5 is blackened
X	If no space is blackened or if there is a double answer

Coding Key for Coding Card C (Blue IBM Card)

IBM Col.

1–13 Repeat the code in columns 1–13 from coding sheet A.

14–20 These 7 columns are blank.

21–58 CYS III, Items (Statements) 61 through 98 consecutively.

Code	Variable
1	If the space under 1 is blackened
2	If the space under 2 is blackened
3	If the space under 3 is blackened
4	Etc., as above

59–80 The following items from CYS I, Items 8, 11, 13, 15, 23, 24, 26, 45, 46, 51, 65, 66, 67, 74, 77, 83, 87, 88, 95, 96, 99; and from CYS II, Item 172, are coded in columns 59–80, respectively. The coding system is as follows:

Code	Variable
1	If the space under 1 is blackened
2	If the space under 2 is blackened
3	If the space under 3 is blackened
4	Etc., as above

Geographical Areas (For IBM col. 1 and 18)

Area		Counties		
I	Anderson	Hardin	Montgomery	San Jacinto
	Angelina	Harrison	Morris	Shelby
	Bowie	Henderson	Nacogdoches	Smith
	Camp	Hopkins	Newton	Titus
	Cass	Houston	Panola	Trinity
	Cherokee	Hunt	Polk	Tyler
	Delta	Jasper	Rains	Upshur
	Fannin	Lamar	Red River	Van Zandt
	Franklin	Leon	Rusk	Walker
	Gregg	Madison	Sabine	Waller
	Grimes	Marion	San Augustine	Wood
II	Aransas	Fort Bend	Jefferson	Refugio
	Bee	Galveston	Liberty	San Patricio
	Brazoria	Goliad	Matagorda	Victoria
	Calhoun	Harris	Nueces	Wharton
	Chambers	Jackson	Orange	
III	Atascosa	Hidalgo	Live Oak	Willacy
	Brooks	Jim Hogg	Maverick	Zapata
	Cameron	Jim Wells	McMullen	Zavala
	Dimmit	Kenedy	Medina	
	Duval	Kleberg	Starr	
	Frio	La Salle	Webb	
IV	Archer	Comanche	Hood	Parker
	Austin	Cooke	Jack	Robertson
	Bastrop	Coryell	Johnson	Rockwall
	Baylor	Dallas	Karnes	San Saba
	Bell	Denton	Kaufman	Shackelford
	Bexar	De Witt	Kendall	Somervell
	Blanco	Eastland	Lampasas	Stephens
	Bosque	Ellis	Lavaca	Tarrant
	Brazos	Erath	Lee	Throckmorton
	Brown	Falls	Limestone	Travis
	Burleson	Fayette	Llano	Washington
	Burnet	Freestone	Mason	Wichita
	Caldwell	Gillespie	McCulloch	Wilbarger
	Callahan	Gonzales	McLennan	Williamson
	Clay	Grayson	Milam	Wilson

Geographical Areas (For IBM col. 1 and 18)—*Continued*

Area | Counties

Coleman	Guadalupe	Mills	Wise
Collin	Hamilton	Montague	Young
Colorado	Hays	Navarro	
Comal	Hill	Palo Pinto	

V

Andrews	Ector	Kent	Randall
Armstrong	Edwards	Kerr	Reagan
Bailey	El Paso	Kimble	Real
Bandera	Fisher	King	Reeves
Borden	Floyd	Kinney	Roberts
Brewster	Foard	Knox	Runnels
Briscoe	Gaines	Lamb	Taylor
Carson	Garza	Lipscomb	Terrell
Castro	Glasscock	Loving	Terry
Childress	Gray	Lubbock	Tom Green
Cochran	Hale	Lynn	Schleicher
Coke	Hall	Martin	Scurry
Collingsworth	Hansford	Menard	Sherman
Concho	Hardeman	Midland	Sterling
Cottle	Hartley	Mitchell	Stonewall
Crane	Haskell	Moore	Sutton
Crockett	Hemphill	Motley	Swisher
Crosby	Hockley	Nolan	Upton
Culberson	Howard	Ocheltree	Uvalde
Dallam	Hudspeth	Oldham	Val Verde
Dawson	Hutchinson	Parmer	Ward
Deaf Smith	Irion	Pecos	Wheeler
Dickens	Jeff Davis	Potter	Winkler
Donley	Jones	Presidio	Yoakum

BIBLIOGRAPHY
and INDEX

BIBLIOGRAPHY

Allport, Gordon W. *Personality and the Social Encounter.* Boston: The Beacon Press, 1960.

American Council of Education. *The Education of Women: Information and Research Notes.* Washington, D. C.: The Commission on the Education of Women of the American Council of Education, 1959.

Anderson, J. E. "Prediction of Adjustment over Time," in *Nobles County Every Child Survey, 1949–1950.* [Minneapolis]: University of Minnesota, Institute of Child Development and Welfare, [1949]. A printed study instrument.

Bainbridge, John. *The Super-Americans.* New York: Doubleday and Company, Inc., 1961.

Baldwin, A. L., Joan Kalhorn, and Fay H. Breese. "The Appraisal of Parental Behavior," in *Psychological Monographs,* Vol. 63 (1949), No. 4 (Whole No. 299), pp. 1–85.

Bernert, Eleanor H. "Demographic Trends," in *The Family and Social Change.* Volume 1 of *The Nation's Children.* New York: Columbia University Press, 1960.

Bettelheim, Bruno. "Growing Up Female," in *Harper's Magazine,* CCXXV (October, 1962), 120–128.

Bossard, John H. S., and Eleanor Stoker Boll. *The Large Family System.* Philadelphia: University of Pennsylvania Press, 1956.

Brim, Orville G., Jr., David C. Glass, David E. Lavin, and Norman Goodman. *Personality and Decision Processes.* Stanford, California: Stanford University Press, 1962.

Bronfenbrenner, Urie. "The Changing American Child: A Speculative Analysis," in *The Journal of Social Issues,* Vol. 17 (1961), pp. 6–18.

Brown, W. F. "Motivational Orientations and Scholastic Achievement." Unpublished Ph.D. dissertation, The University of Texas, 1956.

Bunting, Mary. "One Woman, Two Lives," in *Time,* LXXVIII (November 3, 1961), 68–73.

Burchinal, Lee G. "Adolescent Role Deprivation and High School Age Marriage," in *Marriage and Family Living,* XXI (November, 1959), 378–384.

——. "Research on Young Marriage: Implications for Family Life Education," in *The Family Life Coordinator,* Vol. 9 (September–December, 1960), pp. 6–24.

Burgess, Ernest R., and Harvey J. Locke. *The Family: From Institution to Companionship.* New York: American Book Company, 1945.

Burnett, Joe, *et al.* "Education in Society." Section 1 of "Dewey and Creative Education," in *Saturday Review,* November 21, 1959, pp. 19–20.

Cattell, R. B. *Junior Personality Quiz.* Urbana, Illinois: Institute of Personality and Ability Testing, 1953.

Centers, Richard. *The Psychology of Social Classes.* Princeton, New Jersey: Princeton University Press, 1949.

Cloward, Richard A., and Lloyd E. Ohlin. *Delinquency and Opportunity.* Glencoe, Illinois: The Free Press, 1960.

College Research Committee, The. *Improving Mental Health.* Prairie View, Texas: Prairie View A. and M. College, 1957.

Conant, James B. *The American High School Today.* New York: McGraw-Hill Book Company, Inc., 1959.

—. *Slums and Suburbs.* New York: McGraw-Hill Book Company, Inc., 1961.

Davis, Kingsley. "The Early Marriage Trend," in *What's New,* No. 207 (Fall, 1958). Published in Chicago by Abbott Laboratories.

DuBois, P. H., Jane Loevinger, and Goldine C. Gleser. *The Construction of Homogeneous Keys for a Biographical Inventory.* Research Bulletin 52–18. Lackland AFB, Texas: USAF Air Training Command, Human Resources Research Center, 1952.

Duhl, Leonard J. (ed.). *The Urban Condition.* New York: Basic Books, Inc., 1963.

Erickson, Erik H. "Identity and the Life Cycle: Selected Papers," in *Psychological Issues,* Vol. I, Monograph 1. New York: International University Press, Inc., 1959.

Fairchild, Henry Pratt (ed.). *Dictionary of Sociology.* New York: Philosophical Library, Inc., 1944.

"Findings of General Federation of Women's Clubs Home Life Survey," in *The Journal of Home Economics,* LIV (June, 1962), 435–436.

Freedman, Ronald, Pascal K. Whelpton, and Arthur A. Campbell. *Family Planning Sterility and Population Growth.* New York: McGraw-Hill Book Company, Inc., 1959.

Fruchter, B. *Introduction to Factor Analysis.* Princeton, New Jersey: D. Van Nostrand Company, Inc., 1954.

Gladwin, Thomas. "Strategies in Delinquency Prevention," in *The Urban Condition,* ed. by Leonard J. Duhl. New York: Basic Books, Inc., 1963.

Glick, Paul C., and Hugh Carter. "Marriage Patterns and Educational Level," in *American Sociological Review,* XXIII (June, 1958), 294–300.

Goldsen, Rose K., Morris Rosenberg, Robin M. Williams, Jr., and Edward A. Suchman. *What College Students Think.* New York: D. Van Nostrand Company, Inc., 1960.

Goodman, Paul. *Growing Up Absurd*. London: Victor Gollancz, Ltd., 1961.

Groves, Ernest R., and Harry Estill Moore. *An Introduction to Sociology*. New York: Longmans, Green & Co., Inc., 1940.

Guilford, J. *Fundamental Statistics in Psychology and Education* (2nd edition). New York: McGraw-Hill Book Company, Inc., 1950.

Harrington, Michael. *The Other America*. New York: The Macmillan Company, 1963.

Hathaway, Starke R., and J. Charnley McKinley. *Minnesota Multiphasic Personality Inventory*. New York: The Psychological Corporation, 1951.

Havighurst, Robert J. "Adolescence," in *Human Development and Education*. New York: Longmans, Green & Co., Inc., 1953. Part 3, chapters 9 to 15.

Helton, William B., and Ruby Morris. "A Study of Honors Received and Rank in Class of White High School Graduates, Dallas, Texas, June, 1961." Unpublished. Department of Research and Guidance, Dallas Independent School District.

Interdepartmental Committee on Children and Youth. "Families Are Larger," in *Children in a Changing World*. Washington, D. C.: White House Conference on Children and Youth, 1960.

Kaiser, H. F. "Computer Program for Varimax Rotation in Factor Analysis," in *Educational and Psychological Measurement*, Vol. 19 (1959), pp. 413–420.

Keeler, Rhea I. "Early Marriage Trend," in *The Delta Kappa Gamma Bulletin*, Vol. 28 (Spring, 1962), pp. 42–45.

Maier, Norman R. F. *Principles of Human Relations*. New York: John Wiley & Sons, Inc., 1952.

Marks, J. C. "The Attitudes of the Mothers of Male Schizophrenics toward Child Behavior," in *Journal of Abnormal and Social Psychology*, Vol. 48 (1953), pp. 185–189.

Martinson, Floyd M. "Ego Deficiency as a Factor in Marriage: A Male Sample," in *Marriage and Family Living*, XXI (February, 1959), 48–52.

Mobilization for Youth, Inc. *A Proposal for the Prevention and Control of Delinquency by Expanding Opportunities*. New York: Mobilization for Youth, Inc., 1961.

Moss, J. Joel, and Ruby Gingles. "The Relationship of Personality to the Incidence of Early Marriage," in *Marriage and Family Living*, XXI (November, 1959), 373–377.

Mullahy, Patrick (ed.). *The Contributions of Harry Stack Sullivan*. New York: Hermitage House, Inc., 1952.

National Committee on Children and Youth in Urban Areas. *Social Dynamite: The Report of the Conference on Unemployed Out-of-School Youth in Urban Areas.* Washington, D. C.: National Committee on Children and Youth, 1961.

New York City Board of Education. *Demonstration Guidance Project: Junior High School 43, Manhattan, and George Washington High School.* New York: New York City Board of Education, n.d.

Parsons, Talcott. "Certain Primary Sources and Patterns of Aggression in the Social Structure of the Western World," in *Psychiatry*, X (May, 1947), 167–181.

—, and Robert F. Bales. *Family, Socialization and Interaction Process.* Glencoe, Illinois: The Free Press, 1955.

Plant, James S. *The Envelope.* New York: The Commonwealth Fund, 1950.

—. *Personality and the Cultural Pattern.* New York: The Commonwealth Fund, 1937.

Rainwater, Lee, Richard P. Coleman, and Gerald Handel. *Workingman's Wife.* New York: Oceana Publications, Inc., 1959.

Ryan, Edward J. "Personal Identity in an Urban Slum," in *The Urban Condition,* ed. by Leonard J. Duhl. New York: Basic Books, Inc., 1963.

Salisbury, Harrison E. "The Shook-Up Generation," in *The New York Times,* March 24–30, 1958. Reprint.

—. *The Shook-Up Generation.* New York: Harper & Brothers, 1958.

Saul, Leon J. *The Hostile Mind.* New York: Random House, Inc., 1956.

Schaefer, E. S., and R. Q. Bell. "Patterns of Attitudes toward Child Rearing and the Family," in *Journal of Abnormal and Social Psychology,* Vol. 54 (1957), pp. 391–395.

Sears, Robert R., Eleanor E. Maccoby, and Harry Levin. *Patterns of Child Rearing.* Evanston, Illinois: Row, Peterson & Company, 1957.

Seligman, Daniel, and Lawrence A. Mayer, "The Future Population 'Mix'," in *Fortune,* LIX (February, 1959), 94–97.

Sexton, Patricia Cayo. "Speaking for the Working-Class Wife," in *Harper's Magazine,* CCXXV (October, 1962), 129–133.

Sroles, Leo. "Social Integration and Certain Corollaries: An Exploratory Study," in *American Sociological Review,* XXI (December, 1956), 709–716.

Statistical Abstract of the United States, 1956. Washington, D.C.: U.S. Government Printing Office, 1956.

Suchman, E. A., R. M. Williams, Jr., and Rose K. Goldsen. "Student to Soldier." Unpublished report of a study of the impact of impending military service and the present international crisis upon college student's attitudes and behavior. Social Science Research Center, Cornell University, Ithaca, New York, 1952.

Sutherland, Robert L., Julian L. Woodward, and Milton A. Maxwell. *Introductory Sociology* (6th edition). Chicago: J. B. Lippincott Company, 1961.

Texas Almanac. Dallas: A. H. Belo Corporation, 1955, 1958–1959.

Texas Education Agency. *Texas Youth Participation for the White House Conference on Children and Youth.* Austin: multilithed by the Texas Education Agency, 1959. Report of the Standing Committee on Youth Participation, The Governor's Committee, September and October, 1959.

—. *A Working Guide for Developing Homemaking Education Curriculum in Local Communities.* Austin: Division of Home and Family Education, Texas Education Agency, 1957.

Thurston, L. L. *Multiple-Factor Analysis.* Chicago: University of Chicago Press, 1947.

United States Department of Health, Education and Welfare. "Marriages: Detailed Statistics for Reporting Areas, 1956," in *Vital Statistics—Special Reports: National Summaries,* Vol. 48 (October, 1958), No. 16.

United States Department of Labor. *Manpower Challenge of the 1960s.* Washington, D.C.: U.S. Government Printing Office, 1960.

—. *1958 Handbook on Women Workers.* Washington, D.C.: U.S. Government Printing Office, 1958.

—. *Spotlight on Women in the United States, 1956–1957.* Washington, D.C.: U.S. Government Printing Office, 1957.

Wherry, R. J., and B. J. Winer. "A Method for Factoring Large Numbers of Items," in *Psychometrika,* Vol. 18 (1953), pp. 161–179.

Williams, Robin M., Jr., *American Society: A Sociological Interpretation* (2nd edition). New York: Alfred A. Knopf, Inc., 1960.

Witmer, Helen L., and Ruth Kotinsky (eds.). *New Perspectives for Research on Juvenile Delinquency.* Washington, D.C.: Children's Bureau Publications, No. 356, 1956.

INDEX

age. SEE grade-level differences; grandparents

Aid to Dependent Children: 257

Aldine, Texas: 204 n.

Amarillo, Texas: 80

Anderson, John: scales of, 14, 16

Arbuckle, Anne: 44 n.

attitudes. SEE "Attitudes toward Personal and Family Living" (Form I); youth, attitudes of

"Attitudes toward Personal and Family Living" (Form I): source and function of, 15–16, 26–32; revision of, 18, 44; item classification of, 19, 20; scales for, 20–21; scale scores for, 23–24; item correlation of, 25; analysis of, 25 n., 26–32, 52–54, 55; item-scale analysis of, 26–32; final version of, 26–32, 44; scales of, reproduced, 27–32 (tables); administered to teachers, 31 n., 51; facsimile of, 305–308. SEE ALSO Authoritarian Discipline scale; Criticism of Education scale; Criticism of Youth scale; Family Problems scale; Orientation to Society scale; Self Inadequacy scale

Austin, Texas: 47, 52, 79–80, 114

Authoritarian Discipline scale: items selected for, 27–28

—, youth's responses to: mentioned, 3; and parents' education, 63–64, 223, 258; by geographic region, 81, 82–83; and community size, 86, 157–158; and socioeconomic group, 105; by sex membership, 105–106; and education in homemaking, 105–106; by grade level, 108–109; by Negro youth, 116, 119; by religious affiliation, 132, 134, 136, 149, 152, 157–158, 160; and parental arrangement, 165, 166–167; and size of family, 196–197; and ordinal position in family, 207; by married students, 221, 223; and working mothers, 268. SEE ALSO "Attitudes toward Personal and Family Living" (Form I)

Babcock, Gladys: 19 n., 21 n., 44 n.

Baldwin, A. L.: 27

Bales, Robert F.: on mother's role, 231; mentioned, 192

Baptist Church: membership of, 129; nature of, 130, 134; compared to Catholic Church, 156

Baptist youth, responses of: analysis of, 131, 148, 152, 153, 160; on social orientation, 132 (table), 134, 149 (table), 157 (table), 158–159, 160; on education, 132 (table), 141 (fig.), 149 (table), 157 (table), 160; on self inadequacy, 133 (table), 134, 157 (table); on care of parents, 137 (fig.), 154; on parental sacrifices, 138 (fig.), 154; on parental invasion of privacy, 139 (table); on religion in family, 140 (fig.), 141; on interfaith marriage, 142–143, 154; on high school marriages, 144 (fig.), 154; on sex education, 145 (fig.); and father's education, 147 (fig.), 148, 158–159; on social isolation, 149 (table), 150 (table), 157; on authoritarian discipline, 149 (table), 157–158; on family conflict, 149 (table), 150, 151 (fig.), 153, 157 (table), 160–161; on social inadequacy, 149 (table),